Creativity, Communication and Cultural Value

Keith Negus is Professor of Musicology at Goldsmiths College, University of London. His books include *Producing Pop* (1992), *Popular Music in Theory* (1996) and *Popular Music Studies* (2002), the latter jointly edited with David Hesmondhalgh. He is joint co-ordinating editor of the journal *Popular Music*.

Michael Pickering is Reader in Culture and Communications at Loughborough University. He has also taught at the University of Sunderland and Massey University, New Zealand. His books include *Everyday Culture* (1987 – co-edited with Tony Green); *History, Experience and Cultural Studies* (1997); *Researching Communications: A Practical Guide to Methods in Media and Cultural Analysis (1999* – with David Deacon, Peter Golding and Graham Murdock); and *Stereotyping: The Politics of Representation* (2001).

Creativity, Communication and Cultural Value

Keith Negus and Michael Pickering

Los Angeles | London | New Delhi
Singapore | Washington DC

First published 2004
Reprinted 2012

SAGE Publications Ltd
1 Oliver's Yard
55 City Road
London EC1Y 1SP

SAGE Publications Inc.
2455 Teller Road
Thousand Oaks, California 91320

SAGE Publications India Pvt Ltd
B 1/I 1, Mohan Cooperative Industrial Area
Mathura Road
New Delhi 110 044

SAGE Publications Asia-Pacific Pte Ltd
3 Church Street
#10-04 Samsung Hub
Singapore 049483

British Library Cataloguing in Publication data

A catalogue record for this book is available
from the British Library

ISBN 978-0-7619-7075-0
ISBN 978-0-7619-7076-7 (pbk)

Library of Congress Control Number available

Typeset by C&M Digitals (P) Ltd., Chennai, India
Printed in Great Britain by the MPG Books Group

Contents

Preface

It is hard to avoid the term creativity. It is one of the most used and abused of terms – at one moment invoked to praise a specific technical skill, at another uttered in the most vague and casual manner. In any newspaper or magazine we pick up, we are able to read about the creative work of film directors, actresses, novelists, musicians, singers and all manner of celebrities. Now a staple byword of the discourse of advertising, we're told about creative promotions and campaigns, and about the personnel awarded for their creative contributions to the industry. The term is used by teachers in their encouragement of children to express themselves, expand and grow, and by management consultants seeking to stimulate lateral thinking at work with the aim of improving company profitability. Scientists are trained to follow set procedures and methods, but cannot properly explain how they have come up with a model or theorem in these terms and so resort to notions of creative inspiration. The term creativity is deployed in so many different contexts, and with reference to so many different activities, that we may well ask if it has not been drained of any valid meaning or any useful critical application.

It is because we feel that the term is still worth thinking with, despite sometimes appearing as another specious item of jargon, that we have written this book. One of our aims is to counter both fallacious and opportunistic uses of it. There are of course certain words which historically have acquired so much ideological baggage that they are no longer of any valid or acceptable use in contemporary society, but we don't feel that creativity is one of these. It certainly carries baggage. Indeed, it comes to us laden with a host of meanings, connotations and applications which are regularly imported into a range of discourses, institutions and settings. In one sense, this is indicative of its importance. Yet, while the value and significance of the term are routinely noted, its conceptual status is frequently taken as an unquestioned commonplace. It is often assumed to be self-evident that we know what creativity is, or at least we do when we meet it. This assumption needs challenging. The term has been used in a variety of ways to describe many diverse actions and activities. More often than not, it is used vaguely and imprecisely, and sometimes in quite contradictory ways. The result usually mystifies more than it clarifies. This is not only the case with its use in contemporary mundane discourse; it is often casually introduced into cultural analysis and cultural policy debates as an uncritically received idea, bringing with it all manner of implications. In this way creativity is a dominant category, but a residual concept.

In this book we hope to clear some of the accumulated debris surrounding the notion of creativity and work towards a more refined understanding of it as a concept. We want to encourage a reflexive approach to its conceptual use, whether this is in academic research, intellectual critique, cultural policy or everyday social practice. We start by tracing some of the varying meanings of notions of creativity as these have developed over time, indicating both continuities and transformations. In the course of the book as a whole, we highlight how the meaning of creativity is integrally tied to changing historical processes, technologies and social conditions, and conceptions of individual and society. It is precisely because of such connections that the attribution of 'creative' to a social activity or humanly produced artefact necessarily implies value judgements. Recognition of this is often evaded or denied, as if the worth is assumed to be self-evident, yet we cannot use the term creativity or creative without implying judgement and discrimination. So, following from this, it not only becomes necessary to ask questions about the criteria whereby something, someone or some action is valued as creative. We also need to consider the changing circumstances within which certain creative labels and attributions (and not others) become possible, and the consequences of this for the evaluative process itself. Throughout the following chapters we discuss how the term creativity is used in a descriptive way – but also, significantly, how creativity is used as a way of according cultural value.

Our aim is not to present a singular model of creativity, nor have we set ourselves the unnecessary, and ultimately futile reductive task of defining what creativity might be. Instead, our intentions are both broader and more modest, and we hope, more valuable for being so. We want to encourage a critical approach to the term and an awareness of the legacies that it carries with it. We want to ask what creativity means in conceptual and philosophical terms. So, for example, our opening chapter traces the etymology of the term within what has been a very influential Judaeo-Christian tradition of thought – from divine creation to human creation. But we also want to ask what people mean (and what experiences they refer to) when they talk about creativity. This is why our second chapter follows by immediately exploring how we might understand various creative experiences (some of which seem to defy rational explanation through language, as if words are not enough to capture what's at stake in this experience) and how these relate to human experience more broadly. Our argument is that creativity is a process which brings experience into meaning and significance, and helps it attain communicative value.

We've tried to understand the relation between expression, communication and experience by developing an approach which can conceive of creativity as both ordinary and exceptional. The creative act involves a lot of often unacknowledged hard graft. Much time and energy is put into acquiring and perfecting a skill until the moment is reached of being at one with the activity – when the creative act seems to take on a life of its own. This is the instant when the singer becomes the song, the playwright or actress becomes the character, the artist becomes the painting. It is this aspect which often inspires awe. It can certainly be magical. But there's no reason why it should be treated as mysterious or unfathomable.

In attempting to assert and retain the magical quality of many creative experiences, while also trying to avoid mystifying them, we're presenting a series of critical reflections on creativity, organised around a number of key themes. These themes are signalled in the chapter headings and we hope that the word chosen makes this clear in each particular case. An awareness of these themes is signally important, not only conceptually and theoretically – but also practically. Many creative artists are daily grappling with how certain types of creativity are recognised and rewarded by industries; how they play within or seek to challenge conventions and traditions; how they are constrained or overtly oppressed by divisions of class, gender or race; and how many musicians, painters, novelists are esteemed for their exceptionality – or the exceptionality of at least some of what they produce. The special character of certain creative acts and artworks ultimately leads to the notion of genius, a concept which informs the self-understanding and strategies of artists as much as it impacts upon the critical assessments of what artists do and have done.

In exploring these themes we distinguish between the different meanings of creativity, as they have developed historically and grown in the breadth of their application and reference. In doing this we're able to see the retention of a spiritual dimension within the term. The significance of this is often neglected in contemporary discussion, but for us it points to an abiding source of value in the popular conception of creativity, even as the semantic range of that conception has widened and become secularised. The continuance of this dimension of meaning within the term may run in conflict with other dimensions, but it remains indicative of what is at stake in its currency.

As the meaning of creativity has changed, and as various interests have contested this meaning, there has been a movement away from what have been labelled elitist conceptions of creative exclusivity towards a more inclusive consideration of creativity in its more pervasive forms. This shift has not eradicated the apparent dichotomy. There are two important reasons why swinging to the polar opposite of exclusive notions is unhelpful. First, it encourages an all-too-easy abandonment of the question of exceptionality. Second, the endurance of a spiritual dimension of creativity tends to be dismissed or overlooked when numerous everyday activities are endowed with creative significance.

Whether we call it spiritual or affective, or see it as a form of imaginative engagement when people are 'taken out of themselves' by an artwork or cultural product, doesn't matter too much. What matters is that this engagement is of great importance to them. It answers a felt need that is perhaps not otherwise satisfied. It remains relevant when people are quickened, lifted up or enchanted by what they see, hear or read in an artistic or cultural product. The experience of this may then be related to exceptionality simply because their feelings are not normally stimulated and engaged in this way, not made to seem so connected with what lies beyond them because of the mundane sway of convention and routine. Caricaturing this experience may be necessary when it becomes aesthetically precious, socially pretentious or takes the form of tiresome attention-seeking. But such instances should not diminish its value, actual or potential, in creativity's range of significance.

This aspect of creativity's value is closely related to a sense of what is new for people. While innovation may be strikingly apparent within a particular artistic field, how new is new, and how successful any innovation may be, are questions that can only be decided in specific cases, and sometimes only with hindsight. Likewise, what is new to particular people is always contingent on who they are and where they are located. For reasons such as this, the relative distinctions between innovation and novelty are shifting and fluid. They should be seen as existing on a continuum along which processes of discovery operate both ways, moving between novelty and innovation in a wide range of distances and shifts from one or the other. A similar approach could be adopted to the vexed questions of authenticity and contrivance, not to mention the various other categories of evaluation and judgement which are in habitual aesthetic use. Throughout this book we shall be arguing that it's the relations *between* categories that count, not the gulfs and apparent boundaries between them.

One of our central motifs is the idea that creativity involves the communication of experience, a dynamic which can take on various forms and characteristics and which certainly does not imply a sender/receiver or encoding/decoding model of communication. The act of creation involves grappling with the conventions, traditions, media and institutional conditions through which any experience can be given communicative form. The creative act also entails a will to communicate outwards from self to others, from particular to general, from local to universal. We're not suggesting that this is the only way of approaching creativity. However, for us, the value of approaching creativity in terms of the communication of experience is that it enables us to counter text-based and artist-centred approaches to creativity at the same time as challenging any assumption that creativity is solely about an act of appreciation or interpretation. It enables us to keep in mind creativity as a relational process – the communication is as much between artistic creator and viewer, reader or listener as it is with other artistic creators and creations that are encountered via the accumulated artefacts and forms of various traditions and generic conventions.

To end our opening passage on a more personal note, this book started life as a series of conversations in the pubs of Leicestershire, sometime in the middle of the 1990s. There were no institutional imperatives driving our initial discussions – perversely, it might seem, we were winding down at the end of a working day. What animated our talk was an interest in and frustration with much that we'd been reading about the terms creative and creativity. It was some time before these dialogues suggested a book, and only comparatively recently that the book took on any coherent form or structure. It has been written in the spaces (or, probably more accurately, the cracks) between other projects, and between the day-to-day demands of academic jobs and family life. Writing the book has occasionally been a frustrating experience, as we've searched for a way to clarify our first muddled thoughts on an issue or to argue our case with greater coherence. At the same time, it has benefited from being co-written, as we've honed each other's prose and pooled our knowledge. We're very aware that this book is neither a definitive nor a conclusive final say on the subject – and we wouldn't wish it to be taken as such. Our hope is that what we've written will provoke and encourage further thinking, dialogue and critical debate about an activity and process central to our humanity. We dedicate the book to our children – Lucy, Joseph and Oscar – who have continually shown, in their imaginative encounters with the peculiarities of the world, the mark of their own creative responses and impulses.

1

Creation

A tangled web of meanings and associations has grown up around the word creativity. These threads link together conceptions of the elevated and the mundane, the exceptional and the ordinary. They are a legacy of the term's etymological development which are usually ignored, but are highly significant. They are important elements in the range of characteristics that have been attached to the term creativity.

It has often only been either the elevated and exceptional, or the everyday and ordinary, which have been highlighted. One confers on the term a rarefied and occasionally mystical air, the other can make the word seem commonplace and even banal. Rarely have the links between both these senses of the term creativity been retained and explored.

We seek to recover the power inherent in the term for bringing the elevated and the mundane into conjunction, and for illuminating how the exceptional and the ordinary feed off each other. In this chapter we begin exploring these connections and tensions by tracing the changing meanings of the term creativity within an influential western trajectory of thought. In doing this, we highlight the legacies that are carried into contemporary discussions and the false dichotomies and practical dynamics they produce.

From Creation to Creativity

Although most religions have some type of creation myth, the contemporary western concept of creativity can be traced back through a Judaeo-Christian tradition of thought to ideas about the divine creation of the physical and human world (Boorstin, 1992; Williams, 1976). The strength of this tradition made the emergence of its secularised meanings a slow and protracted process. The term changed only gradually from its earlier, exclusively cosmological reference, as in divine creation, bringing the world itself and the creatures within it into being, with the ancillary term creature deriving from the same etymological stem. Expansion of the sense of the term began in the sixteenth century, particularly in relation to processes of making by people. Its modern meanings emerge from this new humanist emphasis, the earliest tendency to which can be traced in Renaissance theory. Nevertheless, the prior cosmological reference remained powerful enough for human artistic creation to be at times unfavourably compared with nature as the external manifestation of divine creation, or for the word to be used pejoratively to indicate falseness and contrivance.

Consequently, the transfer of the attribution of creative power from God to Man, with a characteristically male monopoly of reference to transgender human energies and abilities, was both hesitant, because of the obvious danger of blasphemy, and intermixed, as in the idea of the revelatory powers of art, disclosing to human wonder the hand of the Almighty, or of art as an allegory of divine inspiration. The span of this long transfer of meaning is suggested by Donne's conception of poetry as 'counterfeit Creation' and, two hundred years later, Shelley's stress, in his *Defence of Poetry*, on the capacity of poetry to 'create anew the universe after it has been annihilated in our minds by the recurrence of impressions blunted by reiteration'. By the late nineteenth century, Shakespeare's 'poetic creativity' could be explicitly named as such, given an expressivist gloss and described as 'spontaneous flow' (Ward, 1875, Vol. 1: 506), for these aspects of the term had by then become established and distinctively modern. They would not have been available to Shakespeare himself, who used the earlier form of 'creation' to denote something false, as in that 'dagger of the mind' proceeding 'from the heat-oppressed brain' in *Macbeth*, or in the twinned questions posed in *The Comedy of Errors*: 'Are you a God? Would you create me new?' Such confinement of use was necessary because the modern sense of the word only began to gain in significance from the later seventeenth century onwards.

This specifically modern significance came about through its consciously validating association with art. By the time of the Romantics, the term's positive human value was assured, though strong threads of its earliest meanings were retained, with artistic activity carrying with it associations of something magical or metaphysical, and with creativity exclusively manifest in the poet as, in some guises, a sort of messenger from God or, in others, an intensely perceptive spirit able to elevate our seeing to a superior plane of reality. For example, the German Romantic poet and novelist, Novalis, valued artistic creation for being 'as much an end in itself as the divine creation of the universe, and one as original and as grounded on itself as the other: because the two are one, and God reveals himself in the poet as he gives himself corporeal form in the visible universe' (cited in Taylor, 1985: 230). This is a view which easily slides into pantheism, as a metaphysical reconciliation of God, world and human beings, but it is through ideas of poetic and artistic inspiration that the older meanings of the word 'creative' have proved resilient, even as the terms 'creation' and 'creativity' have themselves been more radically changed. The earliest example (1728) of an explicit connection of imaginative human creation with a noumenal source, in the mythological personification of an artistically inspiring goddess, mingles earlier and later senses together in one rolling phrase: 'companion of the Muse, Creative Power, Imagination' (Williams, 1976: 73). The reference to imagination is a specifically modern emphasis, while its companion connects back to the idea of some otherworldly assistance in the creative process.

The idea of a transcendent muse has for a long time seemed decidedly dated, with all the resonance of a mannered literary conceit, yet the conception of divine inspiration in the act of writing poetry remained a remarkably strong, even if less than central, element in modernism. The characteristic effect has been to play down the act of writing itself, as a deliberately learned and practised craft. This is a point to which we shall return but, as an example, it can be detected in Yeats's description of the act of poetic creation – 'I made it out of a mouthful of air' – as if his own shaping mind had been absent from the activity of composition. A poem for Yeats was 'self-begotten'. It would be wrong to suppose that this way of accounting for the act of poetic creation is merely an enchanting legacy of the Celtic Twilight. Throughout the twentieth century, when the term 'creativity' became established as denoting the faculty to which the verb 'create' relates as a process, these earlier associations continued to be invoked as a very active and more than residual sense of the term. In his essay 'The Painter of Modern Life', Baudelaire wrote of the way in which, for the 'true artist', the 'ideal execution' becomes 'unconscious' and 'flowing' (1972: 407–8). Similarly, John Lennon distinguished between the songs that he composed simply because a new album had to be produced, and the 'real music...the music of the spheres, the music that surpasses understanding...I'm just a channel...I transcribe it like a medium' (Waters, 1988). The composer, John Taverner, uses the same metaphor, and refers to 'auditory visions' when he feels that music is being dictated to him (Barber, 1999).

These descriptions of creative inspiration derive from the conception of it that grew to prominence during the Romantic period. This accommodated both the notion of being spoken through, used as a mouthpiece of the muse, and an emphasis on individual imagination and feeling, for it was through such faculties that authentic self-expression was felt to flow. More significantly, it was through imagination and feeling that the artist connected with the impulse of Nature, with the spirit, as Wordsworth felt it, that is deeply interfused in all living things and impels all objects of our thought. Allowing this impulse, this hidden current of life, to speak through us came to define the human act of creation for Romantic thinkers, with the artist become an emissary of the divine. The creative artist looked inward for a sense of providential order, harmony and moral significance, and strived to be in tune with Nature in order to experience life to its fullest and most complete. The connection backwards was with the sense of creation involving some metaphysical force, as in the divine ordination of the world and all in existence within it. But this force was now located within the individual human being, becoming the object of personal spiritual search for those seeking the wellspring of truth and beauty.

This organicist notion of creativity has had a powerful influence over the whole modern period, including among those who broke with Romanticism or developed aesthetic values counter to its central tenets. It distinguishes the artist as someone whose 'inner' voice emerges from self-exploration, and whose expressive power derives from imaginative depth. Artistic creativity has become synonymous with this sense of exploration and expressive power. As a form of radical subjectivism, it neglects other modes of creativity, such as the creativity sparked by dialogue and collaboration, or the creativity inherent in popular cultural traditions. Its influence over the development of the trend towards subject-centredness in modern culture, along with the accompanying ideal of authenticity, should not be underestimated.

The Romantic poet's spiritual communion with Nature co-existed of course with physical energies and carnal pleasures, with ritual worship at the shrine of the sexual body. In a line that runs from Rousseau to 1960s counterculture, sensuality was valorised as a source of spiritual fulfilment, so reinforcing the puritanical distrust of artists as morally suspect, if not already damned. The greatest influence of the Romantic conception of artistic creativity has nevertheless been through its strong sense of expression as conjuring something forth, giving form to what is inchoate, and bringing an inner voice or vision into being. When this happens, expression involves a much fuller realisation of human potential, and so produces a defining moment in our lives. Our individual lives are shaped and fulfilled by such moments, in what is taken as a realisation of the particular originality lying within us.

Changing ideas about creativity have thus become integrally wrapped up in the modern sense of individuality. This is perhaps why the term creativity is invariably used in the singular, for the highest form of creative practice is generally assumed to be realised in the individual artist, rather than in any openly manifest form of collective production. Throughout the modern period, art has been regarded as the consummate expression of individual selfhood, shaping and bringing into shape a distinctive sense of the world and of the artist within it. In its particular manifestations, this is what critics understand and praise as the achievement of artistic vision. Such achievement illustrates how, in its modern, secularised conception, creativity retains key links with notions of spirituality and spiritual life that are far from being merely residual. Art in this non-mimetic formulation becomes a locus of spirituality that is alternative to formal religion yet cognate with it. Indeed, in some versions it becomes a substitute for religion in recompense for loss of faith or materialist values which are thereby disavowed.

From the Romantics onwards, loss of religious faith or antipathy to the values of industrial capitalism could generate a need for escape from the realities of material life. The sense of artistic creativity offered a spiritual alternative to what was seen as an aesthetically debased, socially hostile, money-grubbing world where goodness, love and beauty were fleeting. So, for example, William Morris wrote of young men of his generation having grown up during a period of dull bourgeois philistinism and so being 'forced to turn back on ourselves', for 'only in ourselves and the world of art and literature was there any hope' (Thompson, 1977: 14). Art and literature remained a continuing source of refuge from the mundane realities of the street, the factory and the counting house. It is the opposition between them that underlies the pathos of Yeats's lines of retrospective self-assessment:

Players and painted stage took all my love,
And not those things that they were emblems of.

The tension between mystical ideal and mundane life – or put another way, between poetic representation and prosaic reality – is central to modern conceptions of art and creativity. Indeed, it is the contrast between the metaphysical and the material, the elevated and the profane, which make the concept of creativity both fascinating and frustrating.

We want to argue that an informed understanding of this can be reached by attempting to reintegrate both the exceptional and pervasive meanings of the term. Three sets of issues accompany this attempt. Each of them follow, in different ways, from the inherited meanings and associations of the term which derive from its historical development.

First, any effort to articulate the experience of the creative process pushes us to the edge of what words can say. It inevitably involves having to bridge the gap between the sensational experience of creating – whether a song, poem or painting – and the necessity of translating an understanding of that experience into language that can be communicated to others. The endurance of this gap is perhaps unavoidable, since those acts of creativity in which someone is immersed and at one with the act itself are quite distinct from subsequent, relatively self-conscious efforts to describe what the creative process involves. This is why we often look to metaphorical forms of expression in referring to the phenomenological experience of creating and it is why certain creative experiences are rendered in a pseudo-religious or non-rational manner. Yet because creativity is always achieved within quite specific social, historical and political circumstances, we should at least be cautious about making or accepting any grand generalisations about this or any aspect of the creative process.

A second issue concerns the opposition between that which is felt to be merely produced and that which is experienced as truly inspired, which in turn informs the valuation of the creative product itself. For example, some novels, films and popular songs have enjoyed considerable critical and commercial success that has subsequently proved ephemeral, whilst others, often less recognised initially, have endured and become 'classics'. The novels of Zola, the recordings of Robert Johnson, and the soundtracks to 1970s blaxploitation movies are cases in point, where their methods of production have retrospectively been re-assessed as more creative and inspired than had been recognised in contemporary judgements of the time, or where an earlier local recognition of their creative character has subsequently become more universally acknowledged. Regardless of the processes through which these shifts occur, the reasons for its occurrence and the evaluative principles applied are what generally go uninspected. The emphasis has been far more on certain kinds of art which possess a transcendental quality, any reference to which is generally the point at which analysis begins to evaporate.

This kind of distinction has at times been confounded with another of a much longer lineage, being manifest, for example, in the different aesthetic appreciation of poetry in Plato and Aristotle. The retention of an opposition between the claim that art represents a 'superior reality' and the denigration of it as 'mere romance' or 'inferior' fiction (pulp, trash or whatever) is, as Raymond Williams pointed out, a logical development of the theory of art as imitation, which can be traced back to its appearance in the ancient Greek classics (Williams, 1961: 27). The disparagement of artistic or literary work as social or historical observation is, by contrast, specifically modern, and from the nineteenth century was tied up with the development of positivism in the social sciences and of objectivism as a major aim of historiography. These negative evaluations run in counterpoint to the expressivist conception of creativity, as a sort of shadow inheritance. A sceptical regard of the use of literary sources still applies in professional historical practice, despite the insightful explanatory uses to which they have been put, and the recent attention paid, in meta-historical commentary to the use of rhetorical devices, tropes and narrative emplotments in actual historical writing.

A third and related point, following from the previous ones, is the way in which the idea of creative activity has retained an integral distinction between a type of inspired, 'real' or 'authentic' creativity and a more routine, self-conscious, manipulative and false sense of the term. This dichotomy is apparent on the one hand in the appeal to the spontaneity of creativity in reference to Shakespeare's work or in Lennon's reflections on his 'transcription' of 'real music', and on the other in its contrast with material produced as a result of the contractual obligations to deliver a new dramatic script or songs for the next album. It can be found, formulated in different ways, throughout the history of the concept and its gradual process of secularisation, or quasi-secularisation. This process led to the shift of emphasis onto human capacity, with its accompanying transfer of originality, of bringing into existence, from God to the human imagination.

Between Enlightenment and Romanticism

Though it was only realised in retrospect, the full accomplishment of this transfer of the capacity for creation marked a decisive break. Among its various repercussions, the relation between creativity and selfhood, and the rise of innovation as a distinct cultural value, are of enormous significance. They are both connected with the sense of originality, and with the realisation of a way of seeing, making or saying that is recognised as different from what has come before. Ideas about creativity have become integral to a modern sense of individuality and subjectivity, innovation and newness.

At the heart of these conceptions lies another dichotomy, one which becomes manifest in the conflict between imagination and reason. Romanticism's identification of the source of human creativity in the imagination was a reaction against the Enlightenment's championing of reason as the supreme human faculty. For the Romantics, the Enlightenment's claims for the sovereignty of reason raised the prospect of an instrumental secularity lacking in the moral or spiritual dimension necessary for personal fulfilment and cultural nourishment. Romanticism located this dimension in the creative imagination. The free, wakeful play of the imagination, it was felt, provided a life-enhancing presence in the process of being that would provide the appropriate balance to a secularised, utilitarian society, a force that would break the cold, clinical fetters of rationalism and instrumental approaches to knowledge.

The creative imagination became exalted as a human and aesthetic value precisely because the faculty of self-making and its perceived relation to self-produced cultures was felt to be inhibited, at the start of the modern period, by the newly established stance of intellectual disengagement, neutrality and calculation. It was because this stance was seen to lend vital support to scientific rationality and the means-end rationale of industrial capitalism that the creative imagination became revered as a way of realising a 'heightened, more vibrant quality of life' (Taylor, 1989: 372).

During the nineteenth century, the value assigned to the creative imagination in western societies gained in strength as a response to a crisis of faith and the gradual decline of religion as a significant source of meaning, insight and belief. Yet neither Nature as the external world nor the sense of 'nature within' have been able to offer a replacement of this source in the way the

Romantics believed. The Romantic argument has been that science has de-spiritualised Nature as the external world, robbing it of its mystery and magic, while industrial capitalism has tamed and now threatens to destroy it. While we can no longer be innocently attuned to Nature as a source of unquestionable moral good, an enduring spiritual need for art and art-making runs parallel to the desire for an integrated relationship to the natural world. It is partly because of this that ecological and environmental issues have become a rallying point of recent social movements. At the same time, Nature, construed in either sense, is no longer the locus of the creative imagination in the same way as it was for the Romantic movement.

The locus may have changed, but the value hasn't. The creative imagination continues to exert a strong pull against rationalistic modes of thought and action. It is commonly recognised that the twin traditions of the Enlightenment and Romanticism have guided us in quite contrary directions. What is not so commonly recognised is that their profound influence over the past two centuries lies also in attempts somehow to reconcile them, to draw on the powers of *both* disengaged reason and the creative imagination. So much of modern culture swings back and forth between them, but moving towards ways of resolving the tensions between them is also characteristically modern, even if the impetus towards such a reconciliation comes originally from Romanticism.

The Romantic vision of integration and wholeness conceived of spiritual and intellectual fulfilment as one. This has proved widely influential. So, for example, Marx's ideal of the all-round person embodied the central values of Romantic humanism. William Morris, likewise, fiercely opposed Victorian middle-class individualism while maintaining an intense interest in a free, full life in conscious pursuit of its broadest creative potential. The aspiration to full consciousness and all-roundness in life has remained in circulation ever since. It certainly informed Adorno's critique of the negative consequences of Enlightenment thought, and his polemics against the use of culture for propaganda and by the culture industry. It was his hope – briefly glimpsed perhaps in the work of Beethoven and Schoenberg – of a union of subject/object, individual/totality that informed his despair at the way such possibilities are impeded by modern forms of commercial culture. Today, people may feel sceptical of the Romantic ideals of a spiritualised nature and of self-completion through art, but because of loss of faith in both God and science, they continue to aspire to expressive wholeness, or to this in combination with deliberative rationality. Creativity would not have developed and maintained its largely positive connotations in the modern period without this continuing aspiration.

The aim of self-creation requires appropriate models, and chief among these is art. The link forged between artistic creation and self-discovery or self-making remains important as an alternative resource to religious faith, or to scientism and the 'iron cage' of reason. Ideas about creativity have become integral to the modern sense of individuality because the sense of being ourselves implies expressing ourselves, in speech and in action, and so arriving at what is distinctive and special about us, or what it is we strive towards. Since the days of Herder and Hegel and the European Romantics, the expressivist turn has fed directly into this modern conception of the individual, and the artist has been heroised as the agent *par excellence* of original self-creation: 'Artistic creation becomes the paradigm mode in which people can come to self-definition' (Taylor, 1991: 62).

Many writers and artists have come to revere this conception of self-definition through the long historical route in which the twin traditions of the Enlightenment and Romanticism have played themselves off in a cultural tango across time. The search for a model of mature self-identity has switched between both traditions, yet it is the artist, and artistic imagination, which remain paradigmatic, rather than the scientist and scientific rationality. Albert Einstein, perhaps the most iconic figure of modern western science, readily acknowledged this debt to artistic inspiration when he said that 'I'm enough of an artist to draw freely on my imagination, which I think is more important than knowledge. Knowledge is limited. Imagination encircles the world' (Viereck, 1929).

Imagination remains key to thinking about creativity because it is continually regarded as the source of challenge to rules and conventions, as a way of recombining different aspects of tradition and knowledge in their previous arrangements, and perhaps most importantly, as a means to move beyond existing horizons of experience. What has accompanied the modern value placed on imagination has been a decisive move to the dynamic sense of creating difference, in both art and self-development. This has shifted the model of both art and individuality from imitation (mimesis) to innovation (creation). The ascendancy of innovation as a cultural value is the second major consequence of the transfer of creation and originality from God to the human imagination, and it is to this that we now turn.

Between Novelty and Innovation

Imagination in creative practice has become the vital criterion of innovation. One way the significance of this criterion was established was through the distinction which grew up between innovation and novelty. This raises the question of where variation ends and innovation begins. There is no single yardstick for knowing this. Creativity is obviously associated with newness, but knowing what is significantly new may require guesswork as much as mature judgement.

Any recognition of innovation is also usually made in retrospect, in ways which are subject not only to vested interests and institutional values, but also, as those interests and values are contested, to further historical modifications of critical response. We can at least delineate various forms of newness which are valued in a range of different writings.

Along with its kin-word novelty, the term novel can convey a positive and serious meaning. It can refer to something fresh and unusual, such as a novel occurrence, proceeding, image or performance, but that which is *merely* novel is assumed to be qualitatively inferior to innovation. The association with whatever is regarded as trivial or trivialising is not a recent addition. It had already become strikingly clear by the late eighteenth century. A clear example occurs in William Cowper's poem *The Task*, where he referred to Pleasure as a 'reeling goddess … leaning on the arm of Novelty, her fickle, frail support' (Cowper, 1857: 296). This sort of devaluation has had a tremendous influence, outweighing more positive connotations. The negative equation of pleasure and novelty remained powerful long into the twentieth century, particularly with regard to popular culture and the notion of light entertainment. For instance, in the early twentieth century certain songs were referred to as novelty songs or numbers, usually delivering a short, comic narrative which a mid-century jazz historian described, in pejorative, put-down terms, as depending on 'some obvious contrivance for its appeal, such as a reorganised nursery rhyme or an infectious sort of gibberish' (Ulanov, 1952: 352).

The ascription of passing or relatively superficial value was not confined to items of cheap allure or ephemeral appeal. In both mass culture critique and critical theory, it became more broadly attached to mass cultural commodities. Their devaluation operated in antagonistic contrast to the works of 'high' culture, in part because of the associated opposition between short-term pleasure (trivial or kitsch value) and long-term durability (absolute worth). Within this aesthetic template, the products of 'mass' culture were seen to be at the mercy of short-term market cycles in which contemporary novelties presuppose others that will rapidly succeed them. This has in turn been linked with the particular character of consumer aesthetics in which novelty value achieves a fetishistic form.

If we expect to benefit from novelties it becomes conventional for us to assign them positive value. Commercialised forms of novelty generate conventional expectations of what consumer pleasures and satisfactions they will bring. The most important of these expectations is that of novelty itself. This consumerist expectation results from the short-lived cycles of successive rotation in the cultural economy. Satisfying this expectation requires expertise in the design and manufacture of cultural products with a sufficient degree of newness to ensure their reiterated turnover. Constant turnover in the production and consumption of goods is central to market success in capitalist societies, leading to waves of newness which are defined by the economic imperatives that are in operation. The imperative of built-in obsolescence – whether informing the manufacture of toothbrushes, training shoes, cameras or cars – has become vital according to the growth criteria by which modern economies are judged to function correctly. The ever-rolling mobility of pleasure, frustrated desire, obsolescence and new desire has been rationally incorporated into a commodity system maintained by the techniques of advertising, publicity and marketing.

This, in summary form, is the standard critical account of the production and consumption of cultural commodities. It relies on an idealised opposition between authentic and artificial forms of creativity, and assumes that the marketisation of culture generates only a spurious creativity which consists of manufacturing devices for keeping people continually in the process of coming back for more new things. These may be cars, confectionery, clothes, domestic gadgets or digital media: we're seduced by the promotion of their symbolic value for enhancing our lives. For much of the twentieth century, such things were even denied any recognition as culture, in both left- and right-wing variants of the same critical stance. The specifically Marxist line of analysis was that the value of novelty in new commodities was fetishistic in the same way as the commodity's disavowal of the labour and production process involved in their manufacture. This can be taken up and adapted in various ways, as, for instance, by focusing on the occlusion of social process in the fetishistic emphasis on novel appeal. The novelty in a new commodity can then be seen as disavowing the continuity of time and the consequences of this continuity – things become worn out, fashions feed off each other's demise, we ourselves grow old – because of the unceasing stress on its one-dimensional temporality. What was once so alluringly 'now' soon becomes dismissed as 'so last year'. Driving desire through successive cycles of newness denies us the scope for assimilating things into an established continuity of use, into established practice and longer-term structures of experience. Commodities compress time into market-governed schedules through the positive avowal of their predetermined redundancies. They are radically anti-tradition in the imperatives that govern them.

In some ways this argument remains useful. It does at least remind us of the broader dimensions of temporality which may be repressed in the fetishisation of novelty. But the polarised opposition between (durable) art and (ephemeral) commodified culture has proved unsustainable, for a whole range of different reasons. High culture and commodity culture were falsely set off against other, in what was a further legacy of the aesthetics of Romanticism. Such aesthetics posed art and the artist as existing asocially in an idealised bubble of isolation. While historically artistic production and the figure of the artist have been marginalised in capitalist societies, nevertheless, Romantic aesthetics and commodity culture developed out of the same dynamic of social and historical change, and both were cultural formations in the western capitalist order. Their coexistence has continued across the past two centuries. The Romantic sensibility fed into modern consumerism by encouraging and legitimising the myth of autonomous hedonism, while at the same time offering a philosophy of recreation – manifest in the search for self-expression and self-realisation – necessary for a dynamic consumerism. Hence the premium on ever-renewing novelty. Romanticism also provided a vision that has been taken over by consumer culture, promising to satisfy the need for passion, plenitude, creative dreaming and an integrated self.

So the stark differentiation between art and marketised culture is clearly ideological: 'Modern societies simultaneously need *exposure* – to broaden the market and the consumption of goods in order to increase the rate of profit – and *distinction* – which, in order to confront the massifying effects of exposure, recreates the signs that differentiate the hegemonic sectors' (García Canclini, 1995: 17, emphases in original). In practice, many people have moved – and increasingly move – between high culture and commodity culture and are not everywhere stratified into fixed positions of attachment and affiliation.

Critical opposition to a consumerist aesthetic, which has taken various political shades, assumes that consumerism is a promise which is as ever unfulfilled as it is endlessly repeated. While empirical evidence for this is often lacking, it is clear that consumerism can hardly bear the burdens of self-definition, appetite and longing which are placed upon it. Consumer spectacle and pleasure are one side of modern life. On its reverse are resentment, frustration and dissatisfaction with the limits of commodity culture, where the dreams of consumption collapse into disappointment because they cannot satisfy our more radical needs for new ways of being in the world. Since they do not, they shouldn't detract from the force of the opposition to cold calculation and a strict means-end approach to social organisation and arrangements. It is central to our argument that this opposition derives a good deal of its force from the alternative values vested in the idea of creativity, and in turn of creativity as an alternative source of innovation. These alternative values and the practices associated with them may be exploited in business and marketing, but they remain distinct from commercial logic and are not always and everywhere synonymous with consumer culture.

Such opposition may seem increasingly in danger of being absorbed by consumer culture but it retains sources of creative fantasy and dreaming outside of consumerism. Critical evaluation of experience, both inner experience and the experience of social encounters and relationships, as represented in ballad, novel, biography or film, is also clearly based on far more than market efficiency and personal satisfaction. Confining attention to such efficiency and satisfaction is the Benthamite position, leading directly to the view that 'push-pin is of equal value with poetry' (Bentham, 1962: 253). Evaluation is built on qualitative contrasts, and abandonment of such contrasts is a utilitarian option. To take this option would leave us only with calculative methods when faced with situations where calculation is not appropriate. It would leave us without a vocabulary for expressing and assigning differential values to things. Without such a vocabulary, our lives would be mechanical and shallow and our sense of agency seriously diminished.

The concept of agency brings us back to the question of self-discovery and self-making. If agency is vital for an adequate sense of selfhood, then to be a person is to be an agent who has an understanding of self *as* agent (Taylor, 1985: 103). Agency in this sense enables a move beyond the utilitarian scheduling of satisfactions, towards a critical evaluation of wants and desires in terms of their quality and worth. The capacity for strength of evaluation is therefore 'not just a condition of articulacy about preferences, but also about the quality of life, the kind of beings we are or want to be' (ibid.: 26). Such capacity is a condition of identity, and while there are numerous conditions involved in the formation of identity, many people continue to feel that who they are or want to be is bound up with what they value and where they find expressive quality that stirs them, in things they can speak of and things that seem to fly beyond the confines of what they can say, even as they feel them very strongly.

Such value and quality are not only found in established literary and artistic canons, since they are located in the whole range of cultural experience, in popular culture as much as in the 'classics'. In this respect, the premium put upon novelty is not necessarily at odds with exemplary past achievements. Bearing in mind the negative evaluations that are still placed on novelty, the continuance of a positive dimension for the term is what is especially interesting about the associative properties it has acquired. This dimension of its meaning continues to co-exist with the emphasis on short-lived, superficial features and their quality of inherent redundancy, but it now places an alternative emphasis on the newness in what is novel as a quality that is actively endorsed and identified with, even if we may feel an occasional need to support this with a qualifying adverb, as in 'truly novel'. This sort of evaluation is, of course, problematic. What is 'truly novel' is always easy to claim but difficult to establish, particularly when it exceeds anyone's specific cultural experience, as for instance of a narrative genre involving an appreciation of its finer variations and cumulative accretions of development. This is not available to those with little knowledge of, or with actual distaste for, what they see as its characteristic features. The same is true of other forms of art and cultural production. So, for instance, Roger Scruton, in responding to grunge rock and heavy metal, can only call such genres a 'negation of music, a dehumanising of the spirit of song' because of his use of aesthetic standards and criteria from the tradition of harmonic texture and tonality associated with western art music, and because of his failure to attend to what informed popular audiences experience and understand when they listen to such genres (2002: 131; and see Gracyk, 2002: 135–47).

Despite the difficulties of evaluation and judgement, cultural practices are continually being drawn on, updated and revised in everyday life. This is what happens when we borrow a figurative phrase we have heard and apply it in a different situation for comic or dramatic effect; when we tell a story about certain experiences in our lives, drawing on, yet subtly diverging from, the tacitly known rules and repertoires of storytelling; when we take an old song and use it in a new social context; or when we collaborate with others in organising and thinking up novel elements for a specific public performance, such as a commemorative event, or a local exhibition or pageant. What occurs in such cases is modification and variation, leading to degrees of newness in relation to what is established and already in social circulation. These adaptations operate within established cultural themes, codes and conventions, but are worked up to suit specific people or social groups and an immediate social purpose. As Ruth Finnegan has put it, they can represent 'an intensely personal creation, not just an automatic reflection' of the cultural resources which both mould and are moulded by them (1997a: 93). For certain cultural practices and artistic modes, then, 'it is only through the co-operative observance of agreed conventions and collaborative networks that individuals actively participate' (Finnegan, 1997b: 129).

The active participation in these revisions, and sometimes subtly realised qualities of newness, is quite different to the moment of innovation which is subsequently evaluated as a radical disruption of generic rules and expectations. Yet both require and entail the practice of creativity, and so pluralise its meaning and value. The different kinds of creative response to what is culturally novel and to the various discoveries that people make in the course of individual lives can be vitally important in growing up, in learning and in exploring the worlds of both natural and social reality. In taking these discoveries into account, we have to recognise the full range of creative practice and response, and the tensions of use, participation and understanding that run across it. These cover intensely personal creations, and hitherto unrealised conjugations of images, styles and idioms that affect a whole artistic or cultural field. They involve both modifications to what is commonplace and ordinary, and abrupt shifts from familiar form and settled convention, when a new quality of discovery opens up in what is now suddenly knowable rather than already, durably, known. Such contrasts give the idea of creativity its dynamic sense and force of meaning.

From Competence to Creative Experience

It is probably impossible to get away from contrasts between novelty and innovation in developing any understanding of both the phenomenology of creativity and its use as a descriptive term. Yet we should be wary of how they have been mapped onto a distinction between exclusive and inclusive approaches, which in turn have been harnessed to ongoing debates about elitism and populism. From an exclusive perspective, human creativity is firmly associated with originality while innovation requires unique, insightful and inspired musicians, artists, novelists and dramatists. In contrast, a more inclusive approach uses the term to refer to a task executed with considerable skill, a problem solved with imagination and panache, an act performed with grace, vivacity or élan, or even an interpretation of a particular artefact such as a song or film score which is judged to be particularly insightful, or at least ingenious. These widened applications of the term, where the reference is to whatever is positively commended, now seem to be potentially without limit. There is, nevertheless, a sharp descent in the conventional value of the term when it is used to designate such commercial practices as 'creative advertising copy' or 'creative accounting'. Although such designations are at times deliberately ironic, this expanded conception of creativity imbues the most banal of habitual working practices with an aura of artistic inspiration, human worth and social good, as with the commonplace use of creative to distinguish product designers from executives in the advertising industry. Whilst the expanded conception is, at least for some people, motivated by a democratic impulse against forms of elitism, it slips too easily into populist trivialisation, embracing and celebrating as creative all manner of routine discursive practices, postmodern ironic strategies, grounded appropriations, decodings and re-writings, and everyday symbolic resistance.

Such a divergence of meaning and value leads to various problems. Stress on the rarity of originality retains traces of an elitist approach to culture and social life, whereby certain gifted or mystically inspired individuals have creative abilities, and the rest do not, being able to do efficiently only that which they have been socialised into, or acquired through formal training. An exclusivist emphasis denies the possibility of a reflexive, critical or analytical perspective to a process whose wellsprings are held to lie at a psychically deeper level than the one at which rational thinking and analysis operates. The appeal is then to metaphysical, religious or unconscious sources of the creative faculties. Strong retentions of mystical or metaphysical explanations of creativity are found when, for example, singers, performers or dancers explain their creative acts as inspired by, and derived from, the experience of some divine or transcendental entity. Similar continuities apply when all manner of musical artists speak of not being in control of their own bodies or thought processes when composing, writing or improvising.

We can neither accept nor dismiss these as metaphorical conceits or misguided delusions. They are actually integral to the issue we're concerned with. Although we live in an apparently cynical and knowing postmodern age, we still have to engage with religious and metaphysical explanations of creative inspiration because of the ways in which they distil important spiritual and aesthetic concerns for many people. That is why we have emphasised the links with notions of spirituality and spiritual life which are retained in the modern, secularised conception of creativity. Our broader interest lies in establishing the relations between the ordinary and the exceptional, and clearly an approach which locates art on the border of numinous experience runs against this in associating creativity exclusively with radical innovation and an ethereal artistic inspiration as its source. That, in turn, is why we have dwelt at length on the difficulties associated with ideas about novelty as these vacillate between inclusive and exclusive senses of what is new or what is to be evaluated as new.

So while spiritual and aesthetic concerns are part of the continuing evaluative meanings associated with creativity, we need to place them within the general gamut of its significances without at the same time widening them to the extent that the term dissolves into banality. One way of doing this is to consider how anyone may become adept at an artistic or cultural practice in the first place. There is no one, fixed, or universally applicable route through which this process occurs but, as an example of a particular approach, we want to draw on and adapt the phenomenology of human learning provided by Hubert and Stuart Dreyfus (Dreyfus and Dreyfus, 1986; see also Dreyfus, 2001; Flyvbjerg, 2001). This was developed in a different tradition of enquiry to that which concerns us here, and their model fights shy of dealing substantively with creativity. It nevertheless seems to us suggestive in thinking about the human acquisition of skills, attributes and abilities in a manner appropriate to the aspects of creativity we're discussing. The outline we sketch takes us beyond the point of becoming competent where skills and capacities are raised to a level of practice that attains – or seems to attain – its own dynamic rhythm and movement. This is more or less the way many musicians, poets and writers talk of creative practice, in both the fine and popular arts, when they refer to being at one with what they do, forgetting the means by which their making or performing is accomplished and losing sense of where they are, temporally and spatially. It is then as if their skills and capacities are not consciously applied and the process of making or performing feels different and is perceived in a different way. This difference is sometimes caught in the contrast people make between doing something deliberately and doing the same thing naturally, as for instance with dancing or playing a musical instrument. Although what 'naturally' means here is problematic and in need of qualification, it is clearly distinct from what is felt to be contrived or laboured, a point succinctly made by the film actor and dancer, Gene Kelly: 'If it looks like working, you ain't working hard enough'. It is this distinction which seems to us to signal an important aspect of creativity that needs to be put back on the map of cultural studies and the sociology of art. What follows is intended as a few steps towards the objective of exploring the complex process through which creativity occurs without subsuming it wholesale into an argument about the ideological attribution of value.

To begin with, when people learn anything new, as children or adults, they start with certain basic rules and procedures. They have to recognise these and follow them in order to acquire the rudiments of any skill. As we have already seen in discussing modification and variation in cultural practice, established codes and conventions form the basis from which people shape cultural resources to new purposes. If they are to gain any advantage from them, they need to move beyond mechanical application by learning to adapt their initial skill in imitating a model so as to apply it in different ways in different contexts. These have themselves to be understood for their relevance and value to the process of adaptation. With the skills they have acquired, people develop the competence to delve further into existing domains and solve certain problems that may then arise. They learn by examples or by experiments. Their competence is always partly gauged by the dexterity with which they are able to do this.

While the attainment of competence is a necessary step in the development of any form of cultural or artistic practice, any understanding or assessment of who is competent and what this competence involves must inevitably entail some form of value judgement. As Pierre Bourdieu has argued, a 'love of art' is acquired as a result of a very specific type of education and training. We cannot abstract competence from the social context within which it is judged, and more specifically we cannot detach competence as an acquired practical skill from competence to judge and appreciate the consequences of those skills. As Bourdieu has suggested, anyone's competence in art appreciation is measured by the degree to which they have become proficient in 'the interpretative schemes which are the prerequisite for the appropriation of art capital or, in other words, the prerequisite for the deciphering of works of art offered to a given society at a given moment' (1993: 220–1). For Bourdieu, a competent understanding of art is integrally connected to the cultural resources and opportunities which are available to people, and therefore to existing economic and social inequalities, and to structures and relations of power and authority.

These are important qualifications and the disparities they involve are certainly not confined to the possession of cultural capital. For example, so-called naïve artists may have acquired certain craft skills which they use with dexterity and flair, but they 'do not learn the conventional vocabulary of motives and explanations for their work' (Becker, 1984: 266). Their explanations are often highly idiosyncratic and for this reason they may be dismissed as eccentric or cranky. This dismissal is usually made on the basis of a level of competence conventional within the art world and not that of their own immediate social circle or their own perceptions and values. In some ways, though, applying Bourdieu's explanation of competence to the attainment of creative proficiency in art and cultural production may reduce skills and abilities to social class, upbringing and education.

Creative competence and skill is acquired from more than formal education. Competence operates with a grasp of what is objectively possible, but in becoming proficient there is an ascent of experience and understanding from analytical rationality to an unencumbered command of action happening in tune with situation and context. In writing, dancing or making music, acting, sculpting or painting, the difference is between thinking what to do and no longer distinguishing between thinking and doing. It is about bridging the ideological divide between rationality and intuition, for what is happening now is a rational grasp of what is intuitively right and an intuitive grasp of what is rationally possible. It is effort becoming effortless. Analytical rationality cannot grasp such performance, yet we all know it when we see it, whether this is on a football pitch or a concert stage. The performer plays like an angel.

This colloquialism is an appropriate expression for what is involved in the appreciation of such performance, even if it is somewhat hackneyed. It shows how people use a metaphorical expression with connections to religious mythology and spirituality in order to indicate their feeling of delight in excellence, but they use a cliché in order to maintain its links with ordinariness. So we need to stress that it doesn't belong in a privileged aesthetic realm. Our examples deliberately bring high and low culture together in disqualification of the divide between them, while consciously playing on the word 'play' in doing this. For it is this unselfconscious absorption in the play that is important, enabling us to use a cliché to rejuvenate a cliché. The simultaneous loss and realisation of self in play occurs in every cultural form and entails a move beyond the rational accomplishment of competence.

This move beyond competence in the creative process cannot be explained entirely by reference to the structures and gradations of social difference. If this was the case then all artistic and cultural production would be causally linked to people's relative position in the social structure and to what this position makes objectively possible. Certainly class or other social differences may be ideologically inscribed in aesthetic judgements about creativity and innovation, but this is different to the realisation of creative practice, at whatever gradation this occurs. Creativity is not simply the functional correlation of competence and social class. The danger remains that of subsuming all questions not only of aesthetic significance and value, but also of cultural production and performance, into their sociological explanation.

The path we're tracing is from learning how to act in already structured situations to knowing how to respond to situations which are relatively unstructured. This requires a synthesis of abstract knowledge and concrete know-how. It involves a shift from exercising deliberative rationality contextually and adaptively, to embodied involvement in performance where we move on the turning wing with what is being done. There is in this movement an implicit rejection of the false divide between rationality and intuition, for they have come to act in concert with each other, in a mutually enhancing absorption and understanding.

This is different to analytical rationality. Such rationality has its own values, but these are not absolute. In the embrace of human experience they are applicable to some practices, but not to all. Failing to recognise this leads to a foreshortened view in the social analysis of art and culture, and at times even to a justification of this failure in the interests of demystification. We share in those interests, and not least because in referring to the intuitive grasp of skills and conventions in creative practice, we are not at all invoking some mystical spirit that guides anyone towards the goal of artistic originality. Nonetheless, we do want to find a way of encompassing what people tangibly experience as creative proficiency, as talent in sure touch with its own actions and its self-absorbed flow.

This is clearly related to the sense of being taken over by the process of acting creatively. In one way we can regard the retention of metaphysical traces in many people's conception of creativity as resulting from the difficulty they have in explaining it, but in quite another way this aspect of their conception remains a positive value to which they consciously adhere. Many poets, musicians, painters and writers have spoken of the experience of being so caught up in the making of their art that they seem to be taken over, as if the strokes of the brush or pen are occurring of their own accord. When interviewed and asked to reflect on how he wrote drama scripts, Dennis Potter spoke of the skills involved, his awareness of how these skills were different to other forms of writing, and the sense of both shaping and being shaped by the writing – the sensation which comes when effort becomes effortless:

It doesn't feel like writing an essay. It doesn't feel like making an argument. It doesn't feel like having a purpose. It feels like something you knew but didn't know you knew. It feels like dreaming. Sometimes you get that sense of *déjà vu*, then you say, 'I've been here,' or, 'surely you've said that before.' That slightly creepy, prickly feeling that there's a script. Or a memory will come plunging at you through an old piece of music, however banal, or through a smell or a shape. The way a room is patterned will remind you of another room, one you haven't thought about in thirty or forty years.

Writing is like that. I never have a plot. I don't have a schema. I want to know what's happening. I want to know why. But I don't do it *because* I want to know why. I'm doing it, and *then* I want to know why…

When you're doing it, it's a bit like a dream, but a troubled dream – the kind of dream you want to wake from, although not a nightmare. But the intensity of the experience is such that you are almost receiving what you're writing. Of course, you're shaping it at the same time, and then you add to it also. It's an odd thing, knowing that a scene has got to come to an end, or that you've got to make a turn. You don't know what it's going to be, just that you *must* – then it's done. It's being on a trip. It's being subject to it as well as controlling it. (Potter, 1993: 26–8)

At times like these the phenomenological experience of creating – writing, improvising or composing music, painting, dancing – seems unconnected or slightly removed from the initial motivation to write, paint, compose or dance. This aspect of the sensory experience is what is then valued in our aesthetic involvement with music, painting, poetry and drama, regardless of the medium through which it is conveyed. It is not a mystical spirit that is valued. Instead, it is the intense magnification of ability and skill which characterises these moments of creative experience. This is what Potter is grappling with and seeking to elucidate in the above quote – it is the hard achieved skill and ability which allows for this dreamlike or mysterious sense of being at one with and receiving artistic ideas. This aspect of the creative act is not so mysterious as it seems – although it is certainly magical.

It may *seem* as if these moments belie all the antecedent effort and toil laying the ground for what will arise from it, and we are left simply awe-struck. This not only occurs to the creative artist, but also to those of us listening, watching or reading. When we attend to certain recordings, paintings or works of literary fiction we are sometimes overwhelmed with their achievement, and faced with this difficulty of explanation. It may then seem to us that these moments are the outgrowth of some process that defies explanation, that simply goes beyond what can be said, in even the most felicitous choice of words. We face again the problem of moving to the edge of what words can say in relation to what is experientially felt.

The interplay between representation and experience is of critical importance for creative practice. Thinking about creativity in the way we're proposing shifts the balance from a theoretical emphasis on meaning derived from the study of language as a system to utterance, communication as a social process. Once this shift has been made there still arises the danger of idealisation. The history of philosophical aesthetics is strewn with examples of those who have succumbed to this danger, whether it lies in seeing meaning as the unified product of a work, in conceiving of appreciation outside of its contexts, or in regarding value as immanent in the text, sound or object.

To oppose such idealisation by denying the concept of creativity or explaining it solely in terms of its sociological co-ordinates is to disregard the anthropological reality of people remaking culture, and the phenomenological experience which accompanies this. The creative uses of discourse, sounds, images, physical form and motion – the improvisatory play of cultural practice and its exploratory pursuit of contingent possibilities – are an implicit challenge to any form of determinism.

2

Experience

Thinking about creativity entails understanding an experience – or range of experiences – as much as engaging with the changing meanings of a concept. The creative *experience* is something which is intensely felt. It often seems to defy language as if words are incapable of fully capturing the sensation involved, or of explaining what went into the making of a particular artistic form. While we must keep this in mind, it remains the case that the creative experience requires a will to expression, and to communication with others. This is evident in numerous narratives and anecdotes through which artists and inventors have sought to provide an account of what their creative efforts have involved and been driven by.

In devoting a chapter to experience, we wish to emphasise these two issues: expression and communication. In doing this we don't mean to present experience as something which comes prior to or which simply follows artistic expression and communication. Instead, we argue that our experience of the world is shaped and given significance by the act of creation, and that our understanding of the world is realised through the process of communication. People do not – as artists, writers, musicians – have some pre-formed condition which they then seek to express in an art form and communicate to others. The contours and characteristics of experience are given form, meaning and value through the process of expression and communication.

If this sounds rather abstract we can take a couple of simple examples. A songwriter may decide to write a sad song, regardless of how they're feeling at that moment. A painter may wish to convey a sense of anger at the atrocities of war. We may hear the song or see the painting and interpret it as an example of someone condensing their experience into song form or pictorial representation and then relaying it to us. But the act of expressing whatever sadness or anger we may recognise and relate to is realised in the act of making the song and painting. It doesn't exist in some pure or prior state which words, music or paint then approximate in some way or other. And while different media may impart certain features and characteristics to what is communicated, they do not in themselves account for the significance of what is communicated.

What we are suggesting is that experience is not realised, is not given meaning and significance, until it has achieved its communicative form. Achieving this form in ways which reach others and resonate within their own experience completes the creative process. It doesn't matter if this is one person sitting in the same room, or on the end of a telephone, or whether it's a stadium full of rock fans cheering at what they hear, or an art gallery full of people meandering among the objects set out for them to see. The creative experience is *recognised*. Conceiving the experience of creativity in this way means that we cannot confine creativity to the artist or cultural producer alone. Creativity entails a communicative experience which is cross-relational. It is an intersubjective and interactive dialogue bringing its participants together in the activity of interpretation, exchange and understanding.

Suppose you draw a picture alone in your room, or make a soufflé, or write a song. Is this still creative? Only potentially. As creativity is a social process, entailing a dynamic of according value and receiving recognition, we can say that it is never realised as a creative act until it is achieved within some social encounter. A poet or composer may conceive their art in isolation, and not reveal what they have produced in their notebook or music-copy to others. They may not even feel free or secure enough to do this if they live in autocratic political regimes, or under conditions of oppression such as racism. For many artists this lone activity is in any case usually an integral part of the creative process. But without communication the creative process is never complete.

Whatever its level of achievement, the creative effort in communicating our experience is a general human phenomenon, and not the exclusive preserve of an artificially separated realm of art. Of course, we can recognise the significance of 'the arts' because of the different ways in which, as Raymond Williams described it, 'they command very powerful means of this sharing' of experience. But Williams then immediately added that 'again, in most arts, these means are developments from general communication' (1961: 24). This is the balance we wish to strike, and although Williams concentrated on the 'high' literary tradition in his own work, it extends to popular culture and the popular arts as well.

In *Private Lives*, first staged in 1930, Noel Coward offered what has become an oft-quoted quip: 'Extraordinary how potent cheap music is'. The observation combines its tone of surprised praise with a louche sense of irony, but what it recognises, in its backhanded way, is that the expressive quality which is valued in popular music is the effective attainment of communicated experience – how it reaches and moves us. Such an attainment is a full conjunction of expression and the assimilation of this, achieving an inclusive relation between people that is of great value to them. To quote Williams again: 'The distinction of value, in actual works of art, is always, in the first instance, in the actual power to communicate' (ibid.: 34). Potent forms of such communication occur in popular culture – 'cheap music' – as well as in 'actual works of art'. They may also be realised in the intimate tale told in a letter, or in the felicity of a choice expression that seems to encapsulate a particular moment of experience. Distinctive value can even belong to the momentary complicity that goes with a wink.

We discuss creativity as the communication of experience because it involves a relational conception of what is achieved and valued. The communication of experience in art and culture always involves this passage from what is lived to what is grasped in telling it. Communicated experience is always refigured experience. It is through such refiguring that we gain in understanding and knowledge. Refiguring experience means moving from experience to narration and back to experience again, in a renewal of our grasp of it. Each aspect of this movement is important in giving meaning and significance to experience and helping us add to the stock of what we make of our lives and our relations with the world.

Creativity as the communication of experience is a relational conception in another sense, for it keeps in view a sense of the approach to creativity we are developing in this book as an act of conferral as well as a moment of inventiveness or sudden breakthrough. If such moments are not recognised and accepted, then creativity has little social resonance and worth. The communication of experience entails a relationship which brings together an addresser, addressee and the created expression of the experience that passes between them. These components may take on multiple forms which vary historically and geographically, but in their interactive working together they are vital for the realisation of communicated experience, and what Williams referred to as the actively shared basis of the communication.

In this chapter we place our emphasis on the communication of experience for three reasons. First, experience only acquires meaning and resonance once it has been creatively worked on, shared and exchanged. Second, cultural and artistic products are regularly valued for what they say to people about experience and for the creative quality with which they say it. Third, an emphasis on experience can help counter the tendencies to relegate artistic practices to the status of industrial manufacture, to equate aesthetic value and political worth, to advance authoritative readings of isolated texts, and to abstract the affective dimension of creativity into apparently objective sociological structures.

Creativity as Human Expression

In emphasising communicative experience, we reject the idea of an artwork or cultural product as the expression of certain feelings, ideas, or values which exist independently of the creative product and which simply result from the intention to communicate them. They only exist as realised in their expressive medium. Expression in this sense condenses experience into meaningful shape through the words, images and sounds given to it. In referring to expression we're not suggesting that a painter, writer or musician is engaged in directly relaying either a pre-given psychological state or some essential aspect of social experience. How we understand jealousy, for example, or how we're able to relate to what people may have suffered, physically or emotionally, is inseparable from the form in which it is communicated. It is within their art and practice that painters, writers and musicians give a voice to and convey a potent sense of such states and experiences as combinations of sounds, words and images. Poets or songwriters are not simply aware of the prior meaning of what they feel in their hearts and then merely find the words and rhythms to express this feeling. This is a Romantic fallacy. What is felt is mediated by the verse, lyrics, rhythm or beat as a form of creative expression. It is realised in sounds, words and gestures. Psychological states of experience like love or anger are given form by the language and music in which they achieve expression even though they don't consist entirely of this expression. The expression itself partly forms them, in dynamic interaction with known or intuitively sensed inter-emotional states or feelings.

So we don't have a fully formed, reflexively comprehended experience which we then reproduce in verbal, sonic or plastic form. What this experience means to us, and how we may value it, is usually only discovered in the form of utterance or figuration that is given to it. The expression not only forms the experience but also transforms it, making it into something whose meaning changes our understanding of it. Without its representation in words or sounds an experience often doesn't signify for us at all, for a feeling or an idea associated with it is made manifest through the combination of materials that characterise any particular cultural representation. It's because of this that poets, composers and musicians are often taken aback at what they create and often only retrospectively comprehend what they were attempting to express. For example, John Ashbery, an American poet, has said of his writing: 'If I did not write, I would have no idea of what I can write. I suppose that I write so as to find what I have to write' (Clark, 1997: 18). The French philosopher Merleau-Ponty put it this way – 'my own words take me by surprise and teach me what I think' (ibid.: 19). For some, the experience of surprise may provide the basis for an urge to create and express precisely what the experience signifies. The surrealist painter de Chirico couched his sense of exceeding the limits of any conscious artistic intent in terms of the strangeness of everything in the world:

I remember one vivid winter's day at Versailles. Silence and calm reigned supreme. Everything gazed at me with mysterious, questioning eyes. And then I realised that every corner of the palace, every column, every window possessed a spirit, an impenetrable soul. I looked around at the marble heroes, motionless in the lucid air, beneath the frozen rays of that winter sun which pours down on us *without love*, like perfect song. A bird was warbling in a window cage. At that moment I grew aware of the mystery which urges men to create certain strange forms. And the creation appeared more extraordinary than the creators. (cited in Harrison and Wood, 2001: 60–1, emphasis in original)

Such experience of surprise – even revelation in de Chirico's case – and of later recognition of the meaning and worth of a piece of work should not be confused with the misleading notion that intensity of feeling can result directly in an expressive quality. This is why we clarify our use of the term 'expression'. We use it quite consciously and literally in its root-sense to refer to the process whereby meanings are ex-pressed or pressed out of experience, so that when an experience is realised *as* experience, the creative expression of it constitutes its communicative meaning. For us, this is an important emphasis because so often today, in cultural studies and the sociology of art, the term is eschewed, as if it has been irremediably corrupted by its Romantic associations. These include the notion that expression conveys an essentialised self or the unchanging spirit of a people, as for example in the notion of a poet's inner soul, or the idealisation of collective identity in the category of the 'folk'. The term doesn't necessarily have to trail these associations in its wake.

We use the term expression to designate the particular style or manner which emerges as a defining aspect of creating or performing, whether this is writing, painting, dancing or playing a musical instrument. More loosely, it can be used to refer to someone's way of speaking or some distinctive colloquialism. It may be related to what is characteristic of particular individuals but, unfortunate associations aside, it does emerge as well as an aspect of collective identity. So, for instance, in the historically located formation of a subculture certain social groups 'develop distinct patterns of life, and give *expressive form* to their social and material life-experience' (Clarke et al., 1977: 10, emphasis in original). Alternative terms such as construction or production may seem preferable in the appropriate contexts, serving to remind us of the mediated and socially achieved nature of cultural making, but they can easily flatten out the practices involved in such making, so that they seem hardly different to general production or other forms of industrial manufacture. They also reduce or negate the sense of agency involved in cultural making, either on the part of particular individuals or of social groupings attempting more self-consciously communal or collective expressive strategies, as for instance in the Harlem Renaissance of the 1920s, or the late 1970s/early 1980s Rock Against Racism campaign. Expression retains a sense of agency and so, among other things, can remind us of the sheer effort and struggle that may be entailed in attempting to realise a creative idea or project.

Using a medium for the expression of experience draws the medium into the creation of meaning, whether this involves painting, photography, drama or song. It always involves a conversion of what is used, for whether it is wood or marble, sound, gesture or bodily movement that are taken up, they are turned into something quite different. As these different materials and forms are worked with, so the experience that is drawn on also changes. Its expressive meaning comes to reside in this transformation, or at least initially, since how its meaning is negotiated and understood is a pluralised process without any final or absolute point of rest. Change is intrinsic to creative human expression. A particular event or occasion may provide the generating impulse for working up a particular idea or feeling in a chosen medium, but this is quite distinct from what is creatively worked up. Cumulatively as well, a range of prior experiences are assimilated into acts of expression in ways which transform both what is past and what is done with past experience. Our continually developing sense of self is always informed by the ways in which we have, over time, given expressive form to experience.

Expression is of course not confined to any particular medium. Elsewhere we shall refer to various forms and media of cultural expression but, for clarity's sake, we want to confine our discussion of the relation between experience and expressive form to the multiple ways in which we communicate with words, drawing on our available vocabulary, and at any particular time on our degree of verbal dexterity, as the means for doing this. Although the ascendancy of the visual image in photography, film, television and video has been judged by some to have altered the overall balance of relations between cultural technologies of communication, language remains foremost among them. It is, after all, the first which every child has to learn to use effectively, even though they may initially orient themselves in terms of pre-linguistic sounds in the womb and environment, and then to various images prior to any regular and relatively effective use of words. The prominence of language as an expressive medium is manifest in its frequent use as a metaphor for other media, as for instance when reference is made to the language of music, film or fashion.

In emphasising how much we need to learn in order to use language effectively and creatively in the communication of experience, we need equally to emphasise its character as a common, vernacular inheritance. Walt Whitman remarked that language 'is not an abstract construction of the learned, or of dictionary makers'. Rather, it arises 'out of the work, needs, ties, joys, affections, tastes, of long generations of humanity, and has its bases broad and low, close to the ground' (Whitman, 1982: 1166). This means that, when we talk of ourselves personally, we do so within the terms of a communal resource, broad and based close to the ground, but at the same time capable of being used to reach new heights of expressive power.

Whitman's own poetry provides distinctive examples of this capability even as it is rooted in the rhythms and cadences of common speech.

Expression is always a question of restrictions and possibilities. These together define what is culturally and historically particular about the uses of language. It is this which is adapted in the expression of experience, and which always bears the imprint of time and place. The manner or style of this particularity is what constitutes our capacity for being historical, for being historically conscious of ourselves. Such consciousness doesn't exist in an intrinsically self-defining form, as our sense of it arises out of its contrast with other times, other scribes. It is this sense of difference which enables us to think historically and have a history.

Referring the communication of experience to language and the uses of language involves thinking of human creativity as against the grain of modern individualism. We may think and act for ourselves as individuals, but the conditions for this are unavoidably set within linguistic and semiotic frameworks. As we accept this, how do we explain the emergence of new and different forms of expressive power without falling back on the individualist ethos? One way of explaining it is in terms of the expressive power of language as such. This is different to the use of language to describe things, such as a tree or a dog, for it refers to words and sentences used in relation to what is not materially tangible, such as a state of mind or feeling. In achieving expressive form we use language not for the direct description of an object but figuratively, as a way of manifesting an abstract idea or affective state. Such things cannot be directly seen in the same way as we see a tree or a dog, but that doesn't make them any the less manifest. This perhaps becomes more obvious with other symbolic forms not reliant on spoken or written language, such as dance and music, or non-representational paintings which dispense with naturalistic depiction of any kind. But expression is just as much a dimension of natural language, as for instance when Whitman wrote, in a famous line: 'I am large, I contain multitudes'. This is not a literal description. It is an example of expressive language giving form to felt experience.

In this line, Whitman rejected the notion of individualist uniqueness while giving individual expression to a feeling of social expansiveness that was at one with his whole approach to writing poetry. The line also illustrates the interconnectedness of descriptive and expressive language, for the way we interpret 'large' in this expressive use of it depends on the contrast we make when we use it with reference to, say, the described object 'mountain' (as indeed our word for that object in the physical landscape may be set off against its foothills). These two modes of language use not only serve different functions but derive their power from the sense of contrast or comparison between them. It's also because of this that combining descriptive and expressive uses of language at one and the same time can increase the power and impact of the communicated experience. This may, for instance, be realised when there is a shift from the description of an experience to an expressive use of language which takes an imaginative leap and requires a similar leap of imaginative sympathy to be appropriately understood. In other words, what it may mean to us cannot be grasped unless it is interpreted expressively. We may feel that Whitman was giving utterance to his own capacity for being historical, for having historical consciousness and finding a form for the contemporary promise of collective participation and achievement – his democratic vistas. But the power of his statement lies in its appeal to our imagination. We can only feel this power if we accept that what is being said bears no correlation with physical self-definition, where the sign 'large' designates body weight and corporeal bulk. As an expressive statement, it makes sense only within the terms set up by the expressive statement itself, for it is this which gives form to the feeling and makes it manifest. In poetry, as in other arts, the creative imagination thrives on our abilities to deal in expressive meaning, and interpret it as a way of communicating experience.

At this point we confront a dynamic which analytical rationality cannot grasp, and yet can easily dismiss as subjectivism or a merely subjective communication of experience. This dismissal soon fades when we understand the need to relate the quality of what is ex-pressed, what is pressed *out* of experience, to the value of an imaginative dimension in the modern semantic range of creativity. Among other reasons, people attend to and value such art forms as dance, music, poetry and sculpture because they express a way of seeing or feeling, make new connections between things in the world, and refigure our relations with them. There are various sources of appeal in this. Such art forms may remind people that these expressive relations remain possible within a fragmented world, that such a vision of integrated wholeness ('I am large, I contain multitudes') is still worth clinging to in societies that are divided within and between themselves. Or it may be that people require language to be more than just literal description, more than just a way of classifying objects, ordering rational ideas and controlling the world, since this requires strict definitions and transparent meanings and allows no place for ambivalence of sense, word-play and the figurative expression of feeling.

There is nothing necessarily elevated about this. We use expressive forms all the time in everyday life. Whatever our activities or interactions, we use these forms to make sense of experience. This occurs in the world of practical concerns, actions and knowledge. It is these which give experience its significance when refigured in expressive forms. Meanings are realised through their communication in language, and in making manifest what we feel or think we create the reflexive basis for changing our feelings and thoughts because of the constitutive character of expressive speech. It is this character which 'turns our attention toward the creative dimension of expression', for it is this which 'makes possible its own content' (Taylor, 1995: 107).

Creative expression seems most effective when it is seamlessly continuous with its content. When this succeeds, the creator becomes absorbed in working with an intuitive grasp of what can be done within the available possibilities. As expressive form and content are interwoven, the sense is then of being at one with the activity. The dancer becomes the dance.

In William Benzon's (2001) exploration of the brain and creativity, he cites numerous examples of musicians, composers and conductors who feel a sense of being at one with the music they are creating or making – how this often entails a sense of removal from the everyday world, of leaving the ordinary self, and experiencing a transformed sense of time and space. In the previous chapter, we outlined the structure of movement this involves in its development from a level of competence in a practice. Moving beyond this level entails the realisation of proficiency and an unselfconscious virtuosity of performance in what is being done. It is this which unifies the uses of the creative imagination and makes possible the felt sense of removal and transformation which many artists have experienced.

Our understanding of creativity in this sense finds its parallel in how we approach experience as ordinary in its continuous flow through the mundane habits and routine acts of our lives, and yet also extraordinary in its culminating stages and landmark events. Creativity is central to this process in producing a state of consciousness which is active, open and alert to feeling, perception and thought. We don't mean by this anything that is rare, ineffable or the propensity of only a few privileged individuals. What we are referring to is a mood of mental and sensual arousal in which we acquire a sharpened sense of our experience or of the expressive form already given to an experience by someone else, in whatever medium this may be set. Such arousal of intellect and feeling is something which commonly occurs throughout our lives and everyone at times finds themselves in these moments when it seems that what's vital to experience is distilled into a specific form, action or moment.

John Dewey described these events as moments of fulfilment. While of variable duration, they punctuate the common stream of experience and mark out *an* experience as something singular, distinctive and complete. They are the outcome of a temporal process and mark out a new beginning in the ongoing course of events whilst directly embodying the quality of the particular situation which impels them. It is such experiences that make life 'a thing of histories, each with its own plot, its own inception and movement towards its close, each having its own particular rhythmic movement; each with its own unrepeated quality pervading it throughout' (Dewey, 1980: 35–6). Art, for Dewey, represents the communicated expression of this 'heightened vitality' of experience (ibid.: 19). The distinctive quality of *an* experience is not necessarily about happiness, pleasure or solace. It can just as readily be about what divides us, what hurts us, or what terrifies us. But Dewey's primary focus is not so much the thematic content or the various consequences of *an* experience. It is directed towards the movement and connection which progressively integrates the different stages of experience into a tense, dramatic unity. 'The existence of this unity is constituted by a single *quality* that pervades the entire experience in spite of the variation of its constituent parts' (ibid.: 37).

It is this quality which makes a poem or painting seem singular and complete within itself, as for instance in Thomas Hardy's *Faintheart in a Railway Train* (describing an experience of regret at a lost opportunity for love) or Chagall's *The Birthday* (depicting an experience of joy in a found reciprocity of love). Yet as the creative effort in communicating our experience is a general human phenomenon and not exclusive to art, this quality is generated in the course of our ordinary lives as well. A rupture in a friendship following a quarrel or a catastrophe finally averted by a hair's breadth are examples cited by Dewey producing this intensification of attention and feeling, when what happens seems subsequently to be etched into our memory as an exceptional episode or event. Most of our experience is not like this. We may be distracted by routine demands, or our energies may be dissipated by the pressures of time. Our self-confidence may wane or our morale sink. We may succumb to excessive caution or hesitancy in the face of risk. Often, we may simply follow stock practice and procedure. These are obstacles to experience becoming a point of illumination in our lives. As Dewey puts it:

> Things happen, but they are neither definitely included nor decisively excluded; we drift. We yield according to external pressure, or evade and compromise. There are beginnings and cessations, but no genuine initiations and concludings. One thing replaces another, but does not absorb it and carry it on. There is experience, but so slack and discursive that it is not *an* experience. (ibid.: 40)

The more exceptional form of experience we're discussing may attain its quality as a result of an encounter with the unforeseen and strange. When life is steady and habitual, our experience doesn't become focused as *an* experience. The moment when this does happen is 'when the material experienced runs its course to fulfilment' (Dewey, 1980: 35). Things become different.

An experience emerges from a welter of relatively unassociated experiences, bringing them together around a new point whose significance reflects backwards and forwards in time, yet within such experiences we're not directly concerned with 'the connection of one incident with what went before and what comes after'. We're not attentively selecting and rejecting 'what shall be organised into the developing experience' (ibid.: 40). We're absorbed into the moment of the experience, even as it arises out of what is commonplace, so we see a commonplace situation or setting in a different light or derive from it a hitherto unrealised understanding. In his novel *Atonement*, Ian McEwan writes of his character Cecilia standing by a swimming pool and seeing the scene there for a moment as if it was fixed, carved out of time, producing in her the feeling that 'all outcomes, on all scales – from the tiniest to the most colossal – were already in place':

> Whatever happened in the future, however superficially strange or shocking, would also have an unsurprising, familiar quality, inviting her to say, but only to herself, Oh yes, of course. That. I should have known. (McEwan, 2002: 53)

This sense of *an* experience illuminates the rest of the narrative, providing an intimation of subsequent developments which, in retrospect, Cecilia could, should or might have predicted. Her feeling of things 'already in place' represents a condensation of preceding experience with various potential implications for the future, and for how she matures as a person. So what distinguishes *an* experience of this kind from the amorphous drift of experience is the individual character it acquires as a moment of completion and fulfilment, and as a memory whose significance is magnified by the passage of time. It's this which gives *an* experience its character of genuine initiation or consummation in what we do or know.

In terms of the expressive quality of communicated experience, creativity requires the capacity to reach others and achieve a resonance within their lives. This capacity is realised when a specific experience becomes clarified and intensified in a way that moves it to completion, gives it a more general significance, and makes it a source of illumination for others. It's then that it comes to resonate in their lives just as *an* experience gains its sense of being an exceptional moment in the flow of time. Yet it is only exceptional in relation to that flow. The exceptional moment is never an isolated moment. The unique feeling of *an* experience is implicated in intersubjective communication with others, and integral to our everyday associations and relations. Even when such moments seem fixed and carved out of time, they are only understood in relation to process, movement and change.

Experience and the Life-Story

One of the most common forms for accomplishing the creative realisation of *an* experience is storytelling. It is storytelling which makes life a thing of histories, which gives meaning and value to events and episodes in our lives. As much as any other form of expression, storytelling makes art continuous with everyday life. Stories as human narratives are not exclusive to classical myths, epic verse or the canonical works of high culture. Nor are they the preserve of novelists, songwriters, poets and playwrights. They belong to us all. Historically and by definition, we are creatures of stories because we are storytelling creatures.

We turn experience into stories all the time in our everyday life, and these stories range in their importance according to how significant they become for us in the present, in memories and in the re-evaluations we make of them in successive periods of our lives. The actions and experiences of other people are made intelligible by the stories told of them or by them. Our own actions and experiences are rendered meaningful by the narratives in which they are placed and as these communicate with other people. 'It is because we all live out narratives in our lives and because we understand our own lives in terms of the narratives that we live out that the form of narrative is appropriate for understanding the actions of others.' Narrative is thus central to understanding human action: 'I can only answer the question "What am I to do?" if I can answer the prior question "Of what story or stories do I find myself a part"' (MacIntyre, 1985: 212, 216). Indeed, the importance of narrative is such that it has been claimed as perhaps the most fundamental form for making sense of experience, for narratives 'not only give meaningful form to experiences we have lived through' but also 'provide us a forward glance, helping us to anticipate situations even before we encounter them, allowing us to envision alternative futures' (Flyvbjerg, 2001: 137). Richard Rorty has claimed that narrative, and storytelling, are central to how we acquire knowledge of ourselves and other people and cultures in the modern world. He argues that 'the novel, the movie, and the TV programme have, gradually but steadily, replaced the sermon and the treatise as the principle vehicles of moral change and progress' (1989: xvi).

Communicating experience through the stories we make of it allows us to share our experience with others and so help to make sense of it. Refiguring our lives in narrative form does not occur spontaneously but is shaped by social location, historical circumstances and interaction with parents, siblings, friends and strangers. In communicating through stories we draw on shared linguistic and cultural resources and shape them to our will. It is in this shaping of experience to form that creativity often achieves its value for us, whether as producers or perceivers of its results.

Sometimes putting events, episodes or relationships into narrative form enables us to see and understand them differently. We may respond to existing social conditions and circumstances through the distance which stories afford. It is then through such stories that we're able to loosen their hold on us, so enabling us to move on and away from what has previously tied us down.

The formation of individual narratives is closely related to the ideal of self-determination in modern societies whereby it is believed that the primary responsibility for our own self-development lies with us and not with anyone else. This common ideal has been reinforced by the growth of a critically reflexive approach to our biographical past and the spread of an ethically loaded notion that we actively construct our own life-narratives. The sense that we are creators of our identities is manifest in the expressive form we give to them.

Narrative is the way in which we make sense of memories and prognoses, chance and coincidence, limits and possibilities. In life we frequently occupy the position of a storyteller in the midst of the story we are living. Striving to bring together the teller, the telling and the told for ourselves and for others is then the problem of identity, articulating our experience of reality as both acting on us, and being acted on by us, in a reciprocal relation. In communicating experience we creatively transform it, bringing into synthesis what would otherwise remain diffuse and dispersed, and in that synthesis posing a new set of possibilities. In the various forms and genres we utilise, we recreate the past and so transform it into something different, whether this is based on childhood experience or remembered events such as a car crash, a political demonstration or a celebrity's public humiliation. Creativity works with the materials given to it by experience in order to make something more meaningful, compelling or 'true' than experience itself as, for instance, may be the case with a love poem, a gospel song or a Greek tragedy. The creative realisation of experience in this sense seems to make it more real.

As this occurs, the creative realisation of experience may sometimes involve an intense, even anguished struggle against inherited meanings and forms. Trying to say something in an innovative way, or move beyond common-sense meanings and conventional storylines, can be an arduous and not necessarily fruitful quest. It may seem that that the past weighs down heavily on the effort to achieve a new way of expressing our experience or, in the face of stock codes and outworn conventions, articulating a more faithful narration of it in a changed present. This is, for instance, why James Joyce felt that it was imperative to escape from the nets of nationality, language and religion which bore down on him as components of his education and heritage. His escape from these nets involved a self-chosen exile, an intransigent absence from his homeland which he maintained in order 'to give force to his artistic vocation...to sustain the strictest opposition to what was familiar' (Said, 1984: 168). There his achievement as a novelist was in forging innovative fictional modes for encompassing ordinary experience in everyday life, so de-familiarising it and showing us how extraordinary it is. His novel *Ulysses* bears marvellous witness to this. Exile abroad also creatively freed him from the illusion of authorial omniscience and the need to provide his readers with an apparently secure and transparent position in relation to the narrative text. His writing became inherently multifaceted, playful, ambiguous, even – in *Finnegan's Wake* – cacophonous in its break with the sense of any necessary relay between literary representation and a reality outside language and discourse.

Later generations of Irish writers have, in different ways, felt the same need to break with the national ethos, to subvert expectation and escape restriction. In the late 1930s, Patrick Kavanagh moved to Dublin from the border county of Monaghan. He was installed in the self-styled literary metropolis of Dublin as 'the authentic peasant' by those he later denounced as 'rascals pretending to have an interest in poetry'. Kavanagh defied this rustic inscription since he found it deeply patronising – stereotypically stage-Irish, offering only a self-limiting passivity. The configuration of Irish national literature which he confronted was at that time set in the shadow of the late Celtic Twilight, with its hugely rhetorical investment in a false pastoral, a view of Ireland invented by Yeats, Lady Gregory and Synge, and subsequently lauded for supposedly distilling 'the Irish quality'. Put that together with 'peasant quality' and you have a measure of the difficulties facing Kavanagh in his effort to write honestly about his own experience. His view was caustic. The so-called Irish literary movement was for him 'a thoroughly English-bred lie', while the Irishness it advanced was little other than 'anti-art' (Kavanagh, 1964: 9, 12, 15, 22–3).

Each generation faces new kinds of restriction and reduction of who they are or might be. These stand in need of challenge and disruption. The successors of Kavanagh in this regard include those contemporary women poets in Ireland who seek in their work to subvert the incarnation of land and nation in such clichéd, ornamental figures as Cathleen ni Houlihan or Dark Rosaleen: passive, controlled images that instruct and obstruct the expression of women's experience. For Eavan Boland, for instance, the national ethos has to be resisted and circumvented where the permissions it issues as to what poetry can be about deny that articulation of female experience, in the lives of ordinary Irish women. Ideologically it turns 'the woman as subject into the image as object'. The transaction of the passive/feminine/national and the active/expressive/male Irish poet is for her the major form of these negative permissions and reductions, and it is this which has now been disestablished: 'I can't think of anything more disruptive than that Irish women within a generation should alter that arrangement and break the terms of that long-standing contract' (Bowland, 1995: 44–5; see also Ryan, 2002).

In grappling with experience creativity can be thwarted by the pain and misery of remembering what that experience involved. Certain experiences may be repressed because the trauma associated with them has become too much for our conscious selves to carry in their full recognition. Sexual abuse, rape, sadistic forms of humiliation or the wartime experience of violence and brutality all provide examples of experiences whose repression runs counter to an exhilarating narrative sense of Proustian recovery, when what emerges from involuntary memory produces a feeling of renewal, freshness and light. Resistance to communicating past experience may arise from reasons we cannot acknowledge, are not capable of acknowledging fully, even if we try, or are able to acknowledge all too well. From the account provided, it would seem that the 'child killer', Mary Bell, found it painful to tell her biographer, Gitta Sereny, of the hatred and abuse she suffered in her childhood, yet equally the families of the two younger boys she killed found the biography itself an intensely unwelcome intrusion from the past. As the mother of one of these boys said: 'I was actually losing the hate of Mary Bell until this, and now it's all just come back again. Fresh grief' (*The Observer*, 3 May 1998; and Sereny, 1999). In an interview with Anthony Clare from the radio series *In the Psychiatrist's Chair*, Claire Raynor refers to 'stirring up the mud at the bottom of the pond' (Clare, 1992: 217–40). The experience of someone attempting to poke about analytically in the mud of her childhood, when she was abused and rejected, caused her to break down uncontrollably. In this interview she insists that too much raking through the past can sometimes be very damaging, getting in the way of going on living.

Exactly the opposite may be true of those denied a legitimate outlet for their memories, particularly where these involve distress, suffering or trauma. This is a different kind of denial getting in the way of going on living. Dominick LaCapra makes this point about survivors of the Holocaust, suggesting that we can only begin to understand their experience by hearing their testimony, and trying to put ourselves in their place without undermining or appropriating their position as those who have endured the trauma (LaCapra, 1994). Memory and the creative reworking of memory in story, song, film or drama can be intensely personal, yet it requires a shared form of representation, and is mediated by the collective resources of language, sounds, images and per-formed action. Its meanings inhere in this mediation, enabling not only the communication of experience between self and other, but also between past and present.

This begs the broader question of whether creative artists also exploit painful experiences for the sake of their art. Any answer to this question must depend on case and context, for while some art may do this, it is equally clear that creativity, in painting, music or dance, can be therapeutic, can provide what Blake Morrison refers to as 'easement or appeasement' of whatever's been nagging away, causing pain, and troubling the mind. If creativity can be about confronting suffering, it's also about healing, about the power 'to reno-vate and repair us, and lift us up when fallen' (Morrison, 2001: 6–12). Morrison relates this power to the task of turning experience into *an* experi-ence, transforming in our expression of them those 'experiences which haunt us, preoccupy us, linger in the consciousness or surface as dreams'. He sug-gests that while they may be pre-verbal and 'almost always contain an element that can't be satisfactorily explained', trying 'to explain them, or reproduce them, or find other ways to express them, is what creativity is about' (ibid.: 7).

Despite the blockages, ruptures and severe twists of memory that can obstruct our remembering and retellings of the past, we live our lives through our attempts to make a coherent narrative out of them. We develop an understanding of ourselves by configuring our lives as a developing narrative. This informs our sense of who we are by providing 'a notion of how we have become and of where we are going' (Taylor, 1989: 47). Of course, in the stories we tell of our lives, or the attention we pay to the stories other people tell of their lives, we follow certain narrative conventions, certain ways of effectively aligning form and content in the communication of experience. Tacitly or otherwise, we identify general features in such storytelling, as for example the placing of events and episodes in temporal sequence and order, or the charting of an intelligible plot that comes to unite them. These are ways of organising experience, and attaining to some form of coherence across all that happens to us in our lives. In Ruth Finnegan's words, it is 'through storytelling that we experience – and recognise that experience'. In doing so, in their self-narratives, people 'play a creative role in formulating both their own identities and, by extension, the culture in which they are participants' (Finnegan, 1997a: 76–7).

Achieving Communicative Value

Expressive form and narrative are important in making meaning out of our experience because it is through them that we achieve communicative value. If this is a common linkage between art and everyday life, along with continual assessments about the character and extent of such achievement, then creativity cannot be spirited away to a realm which transcends that life. Raymond Williams was surely right in saying that 'there are, essentially, no "ordinary" activities, if by "ordinary" we mean the absence of creative interpretation and effort' (1961: 37). The range and scope of creative interpretation and effort is therefore considerable, but cannot be reduced to the same level as any banal everyday activity. That is why we're focusing on creativity in terms of the communication of experience and the achievement of communicative value.

Dewey's 'moments of fulfilment' are moments of creativity because it is in their articulation as expression and narrative that communicative value is achieved. Just as the stories we tell and the stories we listen to, in everyday life, are weighed and evaluated, so too is art in its organisation and communication of experience. What is attended to critically is the quality of the relationship between experience and communication. Creativity is judged in terms of its ability to communicate experience and its potential for this to be shared: art is the 'organisation of experience, especially in its effect on a spectator or an audience' (ibid.: 31). Williams suggested that for art to succeed it must 'convey an experience to others in such a form that the experience is actively re-created – not contemplated, not examined, not passively received, but by response to the means, actually lived through, by those to whom it is offered. At this stage, a number of art-works already fail' (ibid.: 34–5).

The virtue of thinking of creativity as the effectively achieved and actively received communication of experience is that it affirms a view of creativity as a socially inclusive rather than exclusive ability without evading the value question, and leads us away from a focus simply on the 'text itself'. The whole point of trying to understand creativity in terms of the quality of communicated experience and the forms in which such experience is re-created is that it refuses the reification of artistic or cultural work, whether this is a novel, a painting, a popular song or a film. Reification, in this sense, occurs when an artwork or performance is conceived in abstract isolation, as a text or practice removed from the social contexts of which it is or was a component part. Reification in cultural analysis relates to the outmoded, yet still prevalent, view that a cultural text or performance has only inherent meaning.

So for instance, in this view music, particularly that selectively identified and canonised as great, has an intrinsic autonomy that raises it above the social and political world. This autonomy guarantees its greatness. Reified aesthetics have been applied not only to art music but also to certain forms of popular music. For example, Carl Engel, in an organicist metaphor adopted without acknowledgement by Cecil Sharp, described what have become known as folk songs as akin to the 'wild flowers indigenous to a country, which thrive unaided by art' (Engel, 1866: 23; Sharp, 1907: 1). In England, during the later nineteenth and early twentieth centuries, this notion informed and supported the co-option of 'folk' music in the nationalist mission of its musical renaissance (see Hughes and Stradling, 2001). But the aesthetics of 'music in itself' have had a much broader influence, acting, for instance, as a central tenet of professional musicology's maintenance of boundaries and enclosures and providing appropriate collateral for a 'life and works' paradigm of intellectual scholarship which fails to connect musical composition and structure to 'ideology, or social space, or power, or to the formation of an individual (and by no means sovereign) ego' (Said, 1991: xii–xiii).

Our emphasis on achieving communicative value through experience is intended to connect music and other forms of art not only with these large-scale sociological issues, but also with the realisation of creative possibility in the phenomena of everyday life. A nice example of what this involves, bringing art and popular music together and confounding their artificial separation, is the way in which Mahler drew on his childhood experience of apparently unrelated sounds coming from different directions, as for instance in his Third Symphony. Natalie Bauer-Lechner recalled a trip to a country fair with the composer:

Not only were innumerable barrel-organs blaring out from merry-go-rounds, see-saws, shooting galleries and puppet shows, but a military band and a men's choral society had established themselves there as well. All these groups, in the same forest clearing, were creating an incredible musical pandemonium without paying the slightest attention to each other. Mahler exclaimed: 'You hear? That's polyphony, and that's where I get it from!' (Mitchell, 1975: 342)

If a specific experience being communicated is not part of a broader configuration of practices and human relations, its meanings or sentiments will not register. Its communicative possibilities will not be realised. What is communicated as interpreted experience enters into a series of encounters between old and new cultural forms and practices, traditional and emergent ways of seeing, listening, and thinking about the world, as in the case of Mahler. Williams referred to this process as the testing of new observations, comparisons and meanings in experience, occurring in any cultural formation in ways that are 'always both traditional and creative' and that involve 'both the most ordinary common meanings and the finest individual meanings' (Williams, 1989: 4). It is through the encounter of structures of feeling and configurations of experience, of creative effort and common understanding, that emergent and settled meanings meet. What is new is placed within the networks of relationship in which people find value in and through each other.

This insight is important because it is only in and through the continuities and changes that potential participation becomes possible. The evaluative or emotional response to experience we're focusing on operates in the space between general purposes and individual meanings, between coming together in experience and exploring experience for what it means for us in our own understanding and self-knowledge. It involves us in going beyond the local whilst also recognising the value of localised experience and practice as we try to relate the particular to the general, the abstract to the concrete, the unit to the universal. As J. Michael Dash has written in his introduction to the selected essays of Edouard Glissant: 'Universality paradoxically springs from regionalism. Thomas Hardy saw the world in Wessex, R.K. Narayan the world in Malgudi, García Márquez the world in Macondo. Edouard Glissant similarly locates in the Caribbean a process of global dimensions' (1989: xxxix). And, as Thomas Hardy himself wrote:

though the people in most of the novels (and in much of the shorter verse) are dwellers in a province bounded on the north by the Thames, on the south by the English Channel, on the east by a line running from Hayling Island to Windsor Forest, and on the west by the Cornish coast, they were meant to be typical and essentially those of any and every place where 'Thought's the slave of life, and life time's fool' – beings in whose hearts and minds that which is apparently local should be really universal. (Hardy, 1967: 46; and see *Henry IV*, V, iv, 81 for the quotation)

These negotiations between particular and universal, local and global, can also involve an open recognition of the contrasts between different cultural traditions and ideals and the impetus to move beyond them towards more open forms of social and cultural relationship. Social and cultural relations can never be fully settled or fixed; in our contemporary life, ever more mediated by electronic technologies and the mass media, they no longer belong to any particular place or time, in any irrevocable sense. They now have to be forged in the face of the widespread discontinuity, rupture and displacement that increasingly defines a common human experience for large numbers of people.

We make this point to argue that creativity arises not from a cultural context which exists in monolithic isolation, but from cultural borrowings and transactions. Mozart's exposure, on tours as a young child, to significant contemporary compositions in Germany, France, Italy and England, and his understanding and love of music frivolous, provocative and profound (prior to the high/popular split), meant that his aesthetic sensibility was formed from a sense of movement across cultural boundaries. Likewise, many years later, Duke Ellington's boundary-less musical journey, always pushing up against the social walls of racism, formed his self-conscious desire to be 'beyond category' (Hasse, 1995). More recently, Salman Rushdie has spoken of the creative fertility that can follow from movement between different cultures, as for instance with Anglo-Indian novelists: 'If literature is in part the business of finding new angles at which to enter reality, then once again our distance, our long geographical perspective, may provide us with such angles' (1991: 15). Similarly, the artistic creativity of various English and American, women emigré writers, who lived and worked in Paris in the early twentieth century, was predicated on their escape from England or North America and their search for a freedom that would enable them 'to explore their creative intuitions'. For despite 'its emphasis on propriety, etiquette, forms, and politeness, France offered the perfect background for such creativity' (Benstock, 1987, cited in Wolff, 1995: 11).

We need to see not only music and writing in these ways, but also culture more generally. Edward Said has observed that culture 'is never just a matter of ownership, of borrowing and lending with absolute debtors and creditors, but rather of appropriations, common experiences, and interdependencies of all kinds among different cultures' (1994: 261–2). The permeability of cultures, languages and aesthetic codes is a condition of their ongoing change and a source of creative movement and vitality, yet this is inevitably realised locally by particular people in variable conditions and through quite specific experiences. Interpreted experience as we encounter it in a novel, ballad, dance, drama, film or painting is always re-interpreted in relation to what we ourselves bring to it and what we attempt to take from it. We do not engage with it in some pristine or insular mode of apprehension, nor does our encounter with it result in some abstract act of transparent understanding. Our understanding of it is based on the degree to which we realise and exceed the finite illusion of the mutual separation of cultures and histories. This is where our imaginative grasp of the possibilities posed by other cultures, traditions and languages becomes a locus of creative extension of our own temporally and spatially specific cultural experience. It is the creation of an enduring relationship between the near and the far which becomes a key dynamic of cultural change and creative renewal.

Experience and the Aesthetic

Bringing what is proximate and distant into a creative encounter can only happen when the results of the encounter resonate productively within experience. This potent sense of resonance returns us to John Dewey, not simply because experience was the signature of his philosophy, but more importantly because in seeking to reconceive art as continuous with everyday experience, he mounted a radical challenge to Kantian aesthetics and its hierarchy of experiences, and this long before Bourdieu and from another direction. As Isobel Armstrong has observed, Dewey never split the aesthetic up between the producer or artist, the artwork, and consumers or audiences. 'Experience crosses the boundaries between maker, art object, and response and reconfigures them' (Armstrong, 2000: 162).

Dewey was critical of the conception of fine art as esoteric and requiring a highly cultivated disposition for its proper appreciation. This was because he insisted on the continuity of art with the social immediacy of aesthetic experience and its experienced value (see, for example, 1925: 389; 1980: 14, 292). As with Bourdieu, he opposed the appropriation of art by those claiming social exclusivity and a 'superior cultural status'. Art, for him, had nothing properly to do with status, never mind social ostentation and snobbery. He opposed the elevation of aesthetic individualism through 'the insignia of taste and certificate of modern capital', and sought to overcome the gulf between ordinary and aesthetic experience where it was based around false 'contemplative' theories of art. 'Art for art's sake' was for Dewey simply the obverse of utilitarianism and technological rationality (1925: 377; 1980: 9–10, 252–3). His concern was to realign 'the refined and intensified forms of experience that are works of art and the everyday events, doings, sufferings that are universally recognised to constitute experience' (1980: 3). The message he gave is clear: art should not be confined to the sequestered world of the art gallery, theatre or concert hall, and we should dispense altogether with what Nelson Goodman called 'the absurd and awkward myth of the insularity of aesthetic experience' (Goodman, 1968: 260).

Dewey's argument for a democratic art and aesthetic lay not only in these now familiar criticisms of officially accredited art and aestheticism but also in his conception of art and the aesthetic as constitutive of experience. This emerges from his refusal to set art and the aesthetic off from everyday life. Their spiritualised separation from everyday life, with upper-case Art becoming 'the beauty parlour of civilisation' (1980: 14), is a loss for both art and the everyday. Art becomes irrelevant to everyday life when cut off from its intimate social connection, while everyday life is considered primarily in instrumental terms as the realm from which labour can be extracted and utilised without reference to the need people have for an imaginative, affective and holistic engagement in what they do, day by day, when they work. Art becomes a place of refuge and escape; labour becomes alienated from its own sources of satisfaction and reward.

Art is important for everyday life because it can change our way of seeing, thinking and experiencing, and not just incidentally or peripherally. For Dewey, though, the main point at issue is this: 'the conditions that create the gulf which exists generally between producer and consumer in modern society operate to create also a chasm between ordinary and aesthetic experience', with so much of production 'a form of postponed living' and so much of consumption 'a form of superimposed enjoyment' (1980: 10, 27). These divides in modern life result in an asocially conceived aestheticism and the beauty parlour conception of art, along with a hierarchical division of artistic and cultural production. Dewey opposed this by emphasising the importance of ordinary experience in creating and receiving artworks and cultural products. What matters aesthetically is thus not the work of art or cultural product as objects which, once reified, become commodified and fetishised. What matters is how artistic creativity and cultural production relate to experience, what an art product does with and in experience, how experience becomes aesthetically funded and so resonant with expressive meaning. It is then that the 'rhythm of genuinely creative or appreciative experience is not broken by the shift between means and end, for means here are never "merely" means nor are ends superlatively and aloofly set off by themselves' (Geiger, 1974: 34–5). 'Art', as Dewey wrote, 'is the sole alternative to luck; and divorce from each other of the meaning and value of instrumentalities and ends is the essence of luck. The esoteric character of ['high'] culture and the supernatural quality of religion are both expressions of the divorce' (1925: 372).

Experience and what is made of it, the art object and how it is experienced, are concurrent and cut across the false dichotomies of mind and body, subject and object, feeling and thought, 'high' and 'low' art. 'Such distinctions create artificial boundaries and exclusions, made "in fear of what life may bring forth"' (1980: 22; and Armstrong, 2000: 164). Dewey's opposition to these artificial boundaries and exclusions was consonant with his critique of conventional genre demarcations and the entrenched divisions between different academic disciplines and critical practices. His emphasis instead was on continuity and holism. While at times this veered off into organicist tendencies and nostalgic indulgences, Dewey sought to think of art outside of its sanitised museum conception, its reified categories and its fixed genre compartmentalisation. His insistence on the inter-relatedness of various artistic components and their continuity with everyday life is important for countering the reduction of art to social determinants or the notion that authentic creativity operates as some pure, autonomous realm shorn clear away from everyday life, social institutions and market forces. To see creativity as a realm of freedom somehow removed from the rest of social and historical process is an illusion. Among other things, it may serve class snobbery and provide support for capital accumulation while leading to an attenuated, socially rarefied conception of creativity – the preserve of the isolated, privileged artist.

The artwork or cultural product is not simply a fixed object to be consumed or an essential attribute or quality regarded with a special attitude of contemplation and discrimination that is never applied in ordinary life. It is an event, situated in the flow of time and occurring in a broader context of culture and history than that associated with a museum, library or exhibition. It works with and in experience and encounter, drawing on and gaining expressive power from its social and cultural matrix. If you see art as belonging only in the gallery or concert hall, you understand it only in the abstract, and your connection with it is formalist. This is the same optic that Said derides in relation to 'textuality' as the object of literary theory. Once textuality is isolated 'from the circumstances, the events, the physical sense that made it possible and render it intelligible as the result of human work', then what is studied is only a 'mystical and disinfected subject matter'. Textuality is then the quality of an artform without context, 'the exact antithesis and displacement of what might be called history' (Said, 1983: 3–4). We are back in the museum, lost from any sense of what implicates culture in its worldly affiliations, what connects ordinary experience and the expressive configuration of its aesthetic dimension.

Writing in the early twentieth century against an orthodox separation of aesthetics and experience, Dewey made a major contribution to the development of a democratic conception of art. The significance of his philosophy of art is his attempt to emphasise the continuities between art and experience. This he does, most of all, by realigning art and the aesthetic dimension of experience, which is realised in those moments when 'the material experienced runs its course to fulfilment' and becomes an experience. The endeavour is the reverse of cultural populism since it seeks to revalue value in the terms of these continuities – how effectively they are managed, how coherently they are articulated, and how vitally they are achieved. Most of Dewey's examples and cases come from the fine arts and high culture – Rembrandt, Keats, Beethoven – but the main tenets of his argument apply just as well to popular culture and the popular arts, and central to these is the set of relations between art and experience. Rather than seeing popular forms as inferior because they are so much a part of everyday life, we need to see 'high' cultural aesthetics as deficient when their connections with the everyday are denied. What counts for any cultural product or performance is not how it is aesthetically ranked, but how it runs its course to fulfilment. Focusing on creativity as the communication of experience returns art to time, but a time of heightened vitality when an experience is completed because it absorbs the past and future into itself in a new and dynamic resolution. Through the expressive and narrative forms given to experiences of this kind, we realise the meanings of experiences we have lived through, and gain forward glances to new possibilities.

These are the moments of creativity in which our lives are illuminated backwards and forwards, but the illumination they bring is only realised in acts of communication. Our lives as a series of experiences are woven together and given significance through the ways they attain communicative value. This value lies in its connections of the ordinary and the exceptional. Artforms of whatever kind alter and enhance our ways of conceiving and communicating experience. They are not independent of the realm of everyday experience since they inform, question, intensify and clarify our response to what occurs in such experience. In this sense it is not possible to understand experience without reference to the category of the aesthetic. Here is where analytic rationality falls short, or hits its own limit, at which point it can only see art as wayward, subjectivist or esoteric. Any theory of experience falls short if it casts this category aside or gives it only minimal consideration as happens, for example, when experience is treated solely in terms of cognition.

The aesthetic dimension of experience is neither something separate from everyday life, nor some special, rarefied kind of experience. It is generally only tacit in ordinary experience, and one of the values we place on artistic and cultural products of all kinds is their capacity to help us make this dimension more palpable. Although this capacity may be realised anywhere across a broad range of specific forms, it means that creativity has achieved some form of communicative value. Intensifying, clarifying and shifting perception is part of what goes into *an* experience in the creative realisation of itself, regardless of the form in which it occurs. 'The action and its consequences must be joined in perception. This relationship is what gives meaning; to grasp it is the objective of all intelligence' (Dewey, 1980: 44). Perception in this sense is at one with the way experience advances, connects, and realises that aesthetic dimension which makes art continuous with everyday living, rather than separate from it as a special and refined object.

At the same time, we cannot collapse creativity into everyday life, as if they are indistinguishable. This is not part of our argument. Only certain of our everyday experiences involve creativity; only some of our everyday actions are creative. The tendency that has developed of dissolving creative practice into everyday life, even at its most banal, should be stoutly resisted. To say that all our everyday actions are in some way creative might have a certain polemical appeal, but that is all. What we're arguing for instead are the intrinsic connections *between* creative practice and everyday life, for it's important that we don't forget how the heightened moments of creativity are always linked to routine and the daily round, and how a particular artwork or cultural product may catch us within the midst of ordinary habitual life. So, for instance, a painting may remind us of the tragedies that can overtake us at any time in our lives; a song may catch us unawares as we go about some usual task and seem then to clutch at our hearts and cause our tears to flow. The painting may have arisen out of everyday experience in the past and been related to the artist's understanding of human pain, humiliation and conflict, but its consequence for us is how it helps define our own sense of these. Similarly, the song may connect with our experience of sadness and the value judgements we make about a sad song, but once we've been swept over by it in such an intense way, the song becomes almost synonymous with the moment and the feeling it seems to encapsulate. It is then through the continuities between a heightened sense of creativity and the apparent trivialities of everyday living that we may come to see what is extraordinary in ordinary life, and what is strange in its mundane familiarity.

Industry

Notions of creativity pervade the day-to-day working lives of practitioners involved in media and cultural production, from the talent scout watching a band in a smoky club to the producer considering a screenplay and the senior executive weighing up the acquisition of companies and new media investment opportunities. The annual reports of media and entertainment corporations frequently emphasise their abilities to provide a creative working environment, to recruit creative people, and to employ people with the ability to manage such personnel. Inevitably, these claims are disputed by those who complain about the very inability of such corporate institutions to facilitate the creative process, and who counter that the increasingly conglomerate corporate organisation of cultural production has very little to do with artistic creativity. It can exploit it, package it, and even impede its development, but large corporate institutions can't act as facilitators of the creative process. From such an angle, the phrase 'the creative industries' is an oxymoron.

As we have seen, such a position is informed by an argument which can be followed back to the Romantic response to the rise of industrial capitalism. It continues to endure in debates that cluster around the apparent dichotomy of commerce versus creativity whereby cultural production is characterised in terms of a conflict between the two: commerce (industry) is posed as perpetually in conflict with creativity (the artists, producers, directors, novelists). Here it is claimed that commerce corrupts creativity and leads to compromise, fake or fabricated cultural forms which adhere to the most vulgar of market-oriented formats and formulae. The polarised opposition of commerce and creativity, and the polemical claims which follow from it, are not just a theoretical preserve of sociologists and political economists. For example, a key figure in the advertising industry regards creative people as 'insecure, egotistical, stubborn, rebellious, poor timekeeping perfectionists who seek fame' (Fletcher, 1990). Implicit in such a clichéd definition is that quite contrary attributes are manifest by the so-called 'suits' of advertising, and by managers and executives in the cultural industries more generally. On the other side of the equation, the belief that acting creatively is at odds with being controlled industrially continues to inform the view that subcultures, fans and audiences more generally can creatively appropriate, resist, re-claim and hence transform the products that are disseminated by the commercial industry. This is a stark divide.

In contrast, commerce is sometimes viewed as the condition that inspires creativity – a view found amongst many writings on and from the world of big business. The commercial reward and the financial imperative inspires people to create great songs, films, books and art. From this perspective, the corporate routines, organisational habits and stylistic formulas are not so much constraints as necessary frameworks which focus people's thinking. James Ettema and Charles Whitney, for example, argue that the demands of television production routines and the necessary constraints in organisational politics do not 'so much compromise as energise the producer's creative activities' (1982: 8). At times a further claim is made: the commercial imperative means that things get done – without the financial contract as an incentive, no one would do anything. This is often linked to an assumption that creative artists are rather lazy and wouldn't stir themselves without the pressure of deadlines and contractual imperatives. Such a claim has been made of Mozart, Bing Crosby, and any number of rock musicians.

A third position proposes that commerce and creativity have become so mixed-up and inextricably bound together in the modern economy as to be indistinguishable. It is misleading to attempt to separate them, as if they are autonomous forces. Instead, contemporary cultural production entails fusions, blurrings and genre crossings – at the level of both texts and occupational worlds. This effectively dissolves the distinctions between commerce and creativity or advertising and art. So, for example, a novelist or scriptwriter may work as a copywriter in an advertising agency whilst attempting to get their books or scripts recognised and taken up. Acclaimed film directors make advertisements and pop videos, just as songwriters may have once written jingles or may now compose music for computer games. Salman Rushdie, Alan Parker and David Bowie all began their 'media careers' in advertising. Martin Amis can now write disparagingly about the ad world as a sunset home for literary talent, so adopting a similar tone of opposition to that of early twentieth-century novelists like Joseph Conrad, H.G. Wells, Sinclair Lewis and Christopher Isherwood, but one of his first jobs was as a trainee copywriter in the advertising agency, J. Walter Thompson (Amis, 2000: 34). When Fay Weldon's novel *The Bulgari Connection* was commissioned and printed by the Italian jewellery firm Bulgari, and featured the company prominently in the narrative, this was reported to have 'broken down one of the last barriers between art and commerce' by introducing 'product placement' into literature (Kennedy, 2001: 4).

The assumption that the boundaries of art and business are dissolving, and the stark dichotomy of commerce vs. creativity is no longer relevant, can be found in Simon Frith's and Howard Horne's celebration of the vibrant contribution of British art schools to popular music culture (Frith and Horne, 1987) and in Fredric Jameson's (1991) melancholic account of the capitalist cultures of postmodernity. Whether we accept both or either of these arguments in their entirety, they provide enough evidence to suggest that we must develop ways of understanding the unstable and changing interplay of what constitutes commerce and creativity at any one time.

We want to think about the various tensions that are generated during the juxtaposition and meeting of creativity and commerce by acknowledging these complexities. In doing so, we wish to retain a sense of two distinct dynamics that are nevertheless intertwined. Capitalist industry obviously has an impact on creative work and, indeed, on the very significance of what we now understand as creative. Creative practice can be subtly or overtly shaped by commercial agendas, uncritically accepted occupational roles, production routines and marketing routes. The very specific organisation of small and large companies can directly impact upon the creation of aesthetic beliefs and reputations as much as it can mould the production of specific artefacts and forms.

At the same time, the process is still relatively indeterminate. The businesses involved in cultural production don't possess any single set of criteria or uniform guidelines for harnessing creative practices to the requirements of their owners and shareholders. As in many industries which are dependent upon the production of new or novel items, formal managerial control is often less emphatic – if only for purely practical reasons during the development of new television programmes or popular music recordings. Following from this, we wish to think about a slightly more subtle and occasionally overlooked process, whereby these very businesses and industries have themselves been constituted from creative practices in the first place. If commercially driven industries undoubtedly mould creativity, we also have to realise that creativity has influenced, and continues to influence, industrial production. We might even say that the industries have been 'created'.

Our purpose in this chapter is to highlight how understandings of creativity are linked to, but not determined by (and, indeed, do not themselves determine) modern industry and commerce. We start by considering the use of the creative or culture industries as a descriptive category, highlighting how this fails to acknowledge a set of value judgements. The qualifying term 'creative' operates as more than a descriptive category when applied to industries. The use of the label creativity provides a means of according value, and establishing a cultural hierarchy. It provides a means of evaluation, a way of positioning people against one another. To designate specific practices as creative, or isolate particular businesses as culture industries, inevitably entails making value judgements which often go unexamined (some things are, by implication, not 'creative'). Such designation of either practices or businesses means that a very particular value is being conferred on them. This particular value is carried, often unnoticed, from the positive associations of the terms creativity and culture. In a banal conflation, aesthetic value and market value become tautologous.

Abandoning Adorno

The very notion of a 'culture industry' was introduced in the work of Theodor Adorno and Max Horkheimer. They wrote at a time when ideas about collective democracy had moved from being associated with emancipatory political movements and had become incorporated into the vocabularies used to comprehend the new electronic media of communication and aesthetic reproduction. They coined the term 'culture industry' to distance themselves from the idea that 'mass culture' could be equated with people's culture as 'something like a culture that arises spontaneously from the masses themselves' (Adorno, 1991: 85). This was a time when new cultural forms such as radio, television and cinema were being viewed as potentially liberating, and often seen as both of the people and for the people, encouraging democracy and continuing a process of greater public enlightenment, a possibility implied in some of Walter Benjamin's writings. Adorno and Horkheimer were suspicious of such apparently democratic possibilities of communicating to numerous people and vehemently critical of the impact of commerce on independent individual creative work. Their point was that this was deceptive. The rhetoric of public democracy was being used commercially to generate profits for private corporations, and also politically for the purposes of propaganda. Adorno and Horkheimer sought to challenge those who were celebrating the possibilities provided by these new media and cultural technologies.

Adorno and Horkheimer wrote their famous culture industry essay in a deliberately polemical and provocative manner. It is misleading to assume that their references to the 'assembly line' should be taken literally as if it was intended as a description of an entity that was out there, something to be empirically described or statistically verified. Despite his continual emphasis on rational standardisation, Adorno also noted that 'producing hit songs still remains at the handicraft stage' (1990: 306). In making this and other observations he suggested that the standardisation which occurs in cultural production is not simply the same as the 'standardisation of motor car and breakfast cereals' (1990: 306). The song composer, novelist or filmmaker was not physically located on a rationally organised factory assembly line. Instead, the pressure to adhere to formulas was induced by the need to compete for attention in a commercial market where standard patterns were more easily distributed, promoted and recognised. Adorno and Horkheimer were seeking to highlight a *process* they observed occurring – the fusion of art forms as a result of commodification and as a result of the commercial use of new technologies of mass communication. It was because of this that they emphasised the increasingly standardised character of cultural production, and the way in which the culture industry seeks to incorporate producer and consumer, artist and audience into the process.

We might also say that this argument was deliberately ironic in the way it sought to retain rather than resolve the contradictions involved. The last sentence from the culture industry essay tells us that the 'triumph of advertising in the culture industry is that consumers feel compelled to buy and use its products even though they see through them' (Adorno and Horkheimer, 1979: 167). As Jay Bernstein observes, a recurring theme in Adorno's writings is that of the public 'simultaneously seeing through and obeying ... not believing and believing at the same time' (Bernstein in Adorno, 1991: 11) – a point Adorno developed in his analysis of the astrology column of *The Los Angeles Times* (Adorno, 1994).

It is worth remembering that Adorno's approach was opposed to 'classificatory thinking' – the assumption that knowledge can be acquired by categorising things in the correct way. This is an assumption of one-dimensional analytical rationality, the limits of which we have already explored in discussing creativity, imagination and the dynamics of expressive meaning. The most basic point of Adorno's dialectical thinking, for all the frequent density of his prose, is that there is always something more – classification and definitions can never capture all the qualities of some thing if they don't allow for contradiction which is not due to 'an accidental error on the part of the thinker' (Jarvis, 1998: 170), but to tensions and antagonisms that arise as a result of human activity and being in the world.

This element of human creative tension and even the mystical human possibility that sometimes informs Adorno's more speculative reasoning has been lost in the subsequent pluralised notion of the culture/cultural industries which has been adopted by a number of writers wishing to establish an agenda for intervening institutionally in cultural production (see Garnham, 1990; Miège, 1989; UNESCO, 1982). What is particularly striking about such writing is the shift in emphasis which has occurred since the late 1970s. This is signalled by the movement from a notion of the culture industry (singular) as a critical concept, towards a concept of the cultural industries as a plural and descriptive concept. This has been accompanied by another shift from a concern with the plight of the creative artist to a concern with the character of a creative industry. Attention is redirected from how capitalism impacts upon creative work to how capitalism manages, organises and provides the conditions within which creativity can be realised. This reconstructs a notion of the many plural culture industries as an object of study enabling policy makers to intervene ideologically and economically. It is this focus which informs many later writings on the culture/cultural industries (Beck, 2003; Bennett, 1998; Hesmondhalgh, 2002).

A key issue here concerns the question of what artistic creation involves within an industrial setting. Bernard Miège is critical of what he claims is Adorno's emphasis on the individual creative artist, and the implication that an artist confronts the power of industry and capital (a common image and certainly one which can be detected in Adorno's writings). Miège is worried that this type of approach can all too easily imply that creativity entails the individual in an ideal state of free creation (the Romantic image). Garnham notes how this idea also fed into the guiding principles informing public intervention in the arts in Britain which have been mainly based on subsidies for individuals. Like other writers, Garnham argued against the assumption that great individuals are the source of cultural value.

These arguments are fair enough – it's something of a sociological commonplace to de-emphasise the individual creator and seek to emphasise, if not valorise, the social and collective. But this type of shift sets in play a movement away from the creativity of artists and towards the creativity of industries. One of the implications of such a sociological critique entails a non-ironic reversal: from creative artist to creative industries. The consequence is a move from Adorno's anxiety about the impact of capitalist industry *on* the creative act and artist (or the constitution of their mediated art within a capitalist system) to the designation of a vaguely defined category of capitalist industries *as* creative. By calling something a 'culture' industry or 'creative' industry, or even by saying that the culture industries are a key site for studying creativity, aesthetic value is being superimposed on market value. Angela McRobbie's (1998) research within the fashion trade has also shown how the epithets of creative or cultural applied to these industries conceal a less glamorous world of hard work, long hours, insecurity, temporary contracts, gender inequalities and discrimination.

There is a critical issue lurking within this shift in emphasis. It entails two deceptively simple questions: what is creative about the creative industries, and why should the cultural industries be a prime focus for any discussion of creativity? These questions clearly concern the contribution of those personnel who derive their livelihood from an involvement in the production of music, film, art works, theatre, poetry and novels, and who claim a particular mediating role in 'the creative process'. There can be little doubt that arts and entertainment corporations occupy a significant position between artist and audience and, as such, are a crucial site for studying and understanding the mediations and modifications that connect the intentions of artists with the interpretations of their listeners and viewers. Nonetheless, we cannot assume that this is necessarily any more creative than other business, or that these should be privileged as cultural industries – as if food, banking, tobacco, insurance and other industries are not creative and somehow less concerned with circulating meanings and influencing cultural practices.

Access, Intervention and Ascension

One way to begin exploring the contribution and consequences of these industries is to note, as numerous writers have, that a small number of major corporations (such as BMG, Sony, Disney, Universal, News International) account for the vast majority of income derived from the international sales and world wide circulation of commodified cultural artefacts and artistic forms. This does not necessarily mean that these companies *dominate* creative production in any simple sense. The major corporations do not account for most of the diverse range of creative forms being produced and circulated at any one time, certainly not in quantitative terms, and would prefer to sell two million copies of a Madonna album or a Titanic blockbuster movie than 25,000 copies of 80 different performers or films. In many parts of the world there are, quantitatively, far more locally produced films, musical recordings, books and television programmes being made, circulated and broadcast. It remains the case that such products do not usually generate the same amount of revenue as the products prioritised and promoted by the transnational corporations. Nor are these local producers able to exert the same kind of influence over viewing and listening habits, buying patterns and the professional judgements made by editors, talent scouts and marketing executives. The large corporations *are* involved in financing the production and distribution of the bulk of commercial cultural products that sell in large numbers and make the most money. These companies also occupy strategic geographical locations, wield influence and carry an infrastructure which enables them to collect this money, according to systems conducive to their own preferred regimes of remuneration and rights. That is to say, these companies exert a decisive influence over how contracts are drawn up, deals are done and how creativity is *economically* recognised and rewarded.

Yet these major companies are frequently less successful in influencing the cultural constitution of creativity and the complex ways that this *becomes* part of the economic process. As Raymond Williams once pointed out, whilst the term 'industry' has come to signify the 'institutions for production or trade', it can also be used to refer to 'the human quality of sustained application and effort' (1976: 137). This is industry as an effort of will, as a dynamic human quality rather than as a bureaucratised institution. Industry in the upper case is in this regard a reification of human energy, volition and work, whereas the actual capacity to produce is more strongly retained in the adjectival form, as for instance when people are praised for being 'industrious'. This distinction is useful in reminding us that many cultural forms and artefacts are moving across the world due to human cultural industry (hard work) and not as a result of any corporate institution. This may be construed as a pedantic point but we think it crucial, for it is usually neglected by those writers who present overtly mechanistic or deterministic models of industries and who forget that human industry is part of corporate industry.

Whilst many artists, novelists, musicians and actors might be internationally successful *because* of the investment, resources and promotional techniques utilised by the major entertainment corporations, there are many others who are internationally successful *despite* them. A simple and basic contrast might be between the well-organised and in many respects imperialist strategies and struggles through which the sounds, words and images of a major superstar are distributed, and the more ad hoc and chaotic 'matrices of transnational cultural flow' (Hannerz, 1996) through which a blues singer, a poet, a DJ, a painter or an alternative film maker may connect with diverse listeners, viewers and readers across the world. These movements are facilitated by the activity of a plethora of enthusiasts whose actions contribute to the formation of creative networks which may facilitate small-scale business practices and forms of promotion and publicity, but whose cultural industry is far from institutionalised in the manner of the major corporations.

If we focus in a little more detail on these practices and institutional interactions we can find a continual series of tensions about access and availability. This is inevitable when a finite number of books, films and recordings are released every year, a relatively small number of new art works are displayed, new plays staged and television programmes commissioned. Despite their restriction of access and participation, the media and cultural industries have been characterised as new types of industry, populated by progressive thinking, 'cultural intermediary' occupations where 'jobs and careers have not yet acquired the rigidity of the older bureaucratic professions' (Bourdieu, 1986: 151). Gaining access to work is assumed to be less dependent upon a meritocracy or assessment and recruitment according to formal qualifications. Justin O'Connor has written of how workers within the culture and media industries become ever more significant in contributing to social change in what he calls 'an a era of post-scarcity' when 'the cultural hierarchies are much more fragmented and plural' (1999: 7).

To what extent are these industries of art, culture, media and entertainment any more or less open than other types of profession? The critical questions here are about who is admitted or excluded, how this occurs, how access may vary across different arts and media industries. Anecdotally, there is much evidence (in biographies and trade magazines) to suggest that the film industry, for example, is dominated by very strong family connections. Not only are actors and actresses often drawn from very well-established family dynasties, so too are producers and directors. In a newspaper profile of the actress Sigourney Weaver, to cite one case, it becomes clear that the recognition of her talent and her subsequent success have been facilitated by the environment, economic support and cultural capital provided by a 'family background' of 'entertainment aristocracy' (Mackenzie, 2000: 11).

Researching in the late 1980s and into the 1990s, one of us has found that most of the key decision makers within the British music industry shared many features in common, and constitute a coherent class grouping (Negus, 1992; 1999). Those executives who had been in the business for 25 to 30 years and who were in senior management had been drawn from a very particular class background or habitus. Recruited into the music industry during the late 1960s and early 1970s, most senior executives were middle-class white males who had received a privately funded education at 'public schools', or attended state grammar schools, and completed studies at university. Their formative experience had been shaped during the period when rock was gaining cultural value, becoming self-consciously intellectual and respectable; a period when various elements of rhythm and blues and rock-'n'roll were 'appropriated' and 'rechristened rock or progressive music by its recently enfranchised grammar school, student and hip middle class audience' (Chambers, 1985: 84). A simultaneous expansion of the universities and institutions of cultural production provided an impetus which facilitated the recruitment into the music business of a group of mildly bohemian young people associated with the 'counter-culture'. Many of these young executives had initially been involved in booking bands, often as university entertainment officers, and a considerable number had played in rock bands. This context provided a particular series of orientations, assumptions, dispositions and values which were carried into the organisations of music production and came to dominate agendas within the expanding recording industry. Despite being presented as a fairly liberal business, populated by personnel who are 'in touch with the street', these agendas were not a reflection of the diversity of music being played and listened to in Britain. Instead they represented, in condensed form, the preferences and judgements of a small, relatively elite educated, middle class, white male faction.

The aesthetic and social consequences of this have been profound. At a decisive phase in its expansion and growth, the British music industry was re-organised around a series of dichotomies in which rock artists were favoured over pop or soul performers; albums were favoured over singles; and self-contained bands or solo artists who were judged, from a position derived from Romanticism, to express themselves through writing their own songs, were favoured over the more collaborative ways in which singers or groups of performers have, for many years, worked with arrangers, session musicians and songwriters in putting together a package. Most obviously, conventional white male guitar bands were treated as long term propositions, whilst soul and rhythm and blues music came to be treated in a more ad hoc and casual manner. These distinctions not only informed acquisition policies and marketing philosophies, they were also hierarchically inscribed into the drawing up of contracts and the allocation of investment to departments, genres and artists.

In acquiring new artists, staff in the British music industry have not been responding, in any neutral or obvious way, to the talent available or to public demand. These working practices have emerged and been shaped as a consequence of how the beliefs, practices and aesthetic dispositions of these personnel have contributed to the formation of a particular type of music industry. Whilst defying certain conventional divisions between work and leisure, these workers have used their access to the cultural industries to maintain a series of rather more traditional and enduring boundaries, social divisions and hierarchies.

If strategies of class exclusion have characterised the music industry (often naïvely portrayed as one of the most accessible and liberal of businesses), it is clear that comparable patterns can be found in other cultural industries. A case in point is presented by James Curran (2000) in his account of the frameworks of cultural values and social networks that bind together magazine and newspaper literary editors, publishers and novelists. Curran's study provides an example of how a relatively small literary network shapes the acquisition, hierarchical promotion and critical judgements made of books and authors. A range of biographical and anecdotal material suggests that this is also the case in the theatre and the fine arts.

Moving from the moment of acquisition, a further question concerns the degree to which personnel within various media and cultural producing organisations will intervene in the creative process, and the reasons they may have for doing this. This is another issue that is frequently highlighted by musicians, writers and film makers. Their first complaint usually concerns the difficulty of getting signed; their next grudge concerns the degree of 'artistic freedom' which may or may not be experienced. Here we must recognise that due to the organisation of modern production it has become increasingly impossible to produce a cultural artefact alone without the intervention, assistance, guidance, collaboration or hindrance of other people. Capitalist production is inherently social, as Marx elaborated in relation to the political economy of manufacturing in general. Adorno knew this when commenting on the making of movies, writing of novels and bolting together of interchangeable lyrics, rhythms and melodies in Tin Pan Alley songs. Benjamin recognised this too, but differed from Adorno in his more positive (if at times ambivalent) judgement of the liberatory potential of new cultural media and apparatuses, of the possibilities of turning readers or spectators into collaborators, and returning art to time (Benjamin, 1970: 224–5, 234; 1977: 98). Whatever the opportunities provided, and however they are assessed, the interlocking organisations and techniques of modern cultural production entail a necessary reliance on the institutional networks already set in place by an industry. An individual can no more realise the creation and exhibition of a movie than be able to manufacture and make function (with water and electricity) a washing machine. Hence, all judgements about the value and possibilities of creativity inevitably involve consideration of the human relationships and social processes through which an individual or group of people may have come to realise a particular creation.

This is particularly so with regard to cinema. Film has been viewed as a cultural form that has facilitated inherently collective or collaborative processes of creation. It's because of this that contemporary studios – whether Dreamworks, Disney or Universal – promote themselves as providing a creative environment when seeking to attract directors, actors and investors. The claim that film production ushered in a new type of collective creativity has been challenged by those who view the work of making films as a struggle of lone directing auteurs against the collective inertia of the studio and distribution system. Obviously enough, directors do not operate alone; film production depends upon the high degree of division of labour in the industry. As Ian Jarvie has observed: 'Films can be made or marred in such a large number of ways, and decisions made at such a number of levels in the organisation, that there is a genuine question as to whether there is sufficient centralisation of decision-making to attribute the finished product to any one individual' (1970: 26–7).

Film might be assessed as a result of its social production and the degree of collective synthesis emerging from its production, yet throughout the first century of cinema history, the predominant tendency has been to assess it as a result of individual creativity. The social production, with its complex division of labour, may at least be acknowledged, as for instance in the different categories assigned to the Academy Awards, but the habit persists of thinking that what truly makes or mars a film is the individual stamp of directorial identity. This has been articulated, at one extreme, in auteurism's cult of the personality and Romantic notions of autonomous creativity, but speaking of a Spielberg movie or an Alan Parker film is a feature of everyday evaluative discourse. As Robert Lapsley and Michael Westlake put it: 'despite the sustained and theoretically decisive critique of auteurism, mainstream discussion of cinema is still dominated by the quest for the author, its main critical concerns being to distinguish authors from the anonymous mass of directors, to establish their identity by reference to their most characteristic work and distinguishing style or thematic focus, and to pass judgement as to their respective merits' (1991: 127). The canonical status of someone like Hitchcock is to some extent the result of 'distinctive marks of an authorial, indeed a self-referential presence'

(Maltby, 1996: 437), but the conferral of status in this sense usually obscures the commercial marketing of auteurism (Karpis, 1992) and the institutional complexities of contribution and influence in a film's overall planning, production and marketing. Even relatively distinctive film directors are not immune to unwelcome interference, which can occur at any stage of the production process. The films of Orson Welles, for instance, were often carved up and rendered incoherent by the meddlers who influenced the editing process at various Hollywood studios, most notoriously during the confused editing, reshooting and rescoring that was inflicted upon *The Magnificent Ambersons*.

Far from being inimical to a film's success, either at the box office or in the critical reviews, the complex organisation of its production, as in the Hollywood studio system for instance, may be said to make possible the attainment of high professional standards in cinematic entertainment. We note here again that the self of self-expression in cultural creativity is a legacy of Romantic aesthetics that, so far as the entertainment industries are concerned, mistakes idealised instances of production or performance for the 'essence' of a cultural artefact and is responsible for 'naïve juxtapositions of art and commerce' (Jarvie, 1970: 27). This attitude frequently sets up the key issue in terms of a dualistic opposition between constraint and creativity. Cultural work of any significant kind in media organisations, such as those of music manufacture and distribution, book publishing, television production, journalism, and film production and marketing, is commonly conceived as having been achieved against the commercial constraints imposed by these organisations. For example, Duncan Petrie argues that 'filmic creativity' is 'essentially an artistic/cultural process which is structured by material constraints' (1991: 1) with 'subjective intentionality' and 'objective structuring, lying at the heart of the creative process' (ibid.: 12).

Creative freedom or professional autonomy are not pre-given entities of absolute value rigidly set against media organisations, operational routines, state censorship or market criteria. What is 'commercial' is also frequently only realised in retrospect. For example, a spokesperson for Decca Records is said to have rejected The Beatles because 'groups of guitars are on their way out', while a concert manager advised Elvis Presley, in 1954, 'to go back to driving a truck'. In 1927, the Warner Brothers president, Harry Warner, peremptorily dismissed the talkies – 'who the hell wants to hear actors talk?' – while a manager at MGM, after an initial screening of *The Wizard of Oz* to company executives, is said to have barked at its director: 'That rainbow song's no good – take it out!' As these unfortunate judgements show, it is perhaps more useful to view the commercial as a dynamic which people work towards and seek to make happen. Songs, movies and novels do not, in general, appear carrying definitive commercial qualities or characteristics. A process occurs whereby they are made commercial – and this is why modern economies employ so many people in marketing, publicity and public relations. Their aim is to connect the work of cultural producer with the lives of consumers.

Residues of Romanticism can inform a sense of creativity operating ideally as a free play of productive forces. When this is portrayed as constantly in danger of being shackled by institutional, bureaucratic and economic mono-liths, the resulting picture is crude and simplistic. It obscures the actual asym-metries of power and resources that distinguish those involved in various sectors and spheres of cultural production around the world. In addition, such a model, implying the need for (an ill-defined) freedom, would seem of little value in trying to account for creative work that has emerged from conditions of outright oppression or social exclusion.

In thinking about questions of intervention, autonomy, manipulation and artistic freedom we need a more nuanced view of the differential position of the creative artist, one which acknowledges the benefits acquired through commercial success and stardom. Not that all creative artists who sign to film agents, record companies, book publishers, or literary agents will become stars, but the imperative of stardom drives the industry due to the rewards that it offers.

When artists are struggling for recognition they're often labouring long hours, subject to all sorts of pressures and contract constraints. Whether a musician, novelist, painter or actress, they are in a weak bargaining position. They might be recording songs they don't like, wearing clothes they hate, writ-ing copy in an advertising agency, acting in roles they detest, whilst working part time as waitresses, models, warehouse operatives or office clerks. At a certain point this changes. The labour of the artist and all those other industry personnel who contribute to the creation of the artist's persona, transform that person into a commodity which accumulates ever more capital value. The film star, rock star or star author becomes a 'commodity amongst commodi-ties... the cybernetic monitor which returns all efforts to the same apparent core of meaning' (King, 1987: 149). The success of films, books, recordings, and a whole range of associated products, merchandise and events, have become ever more dependent upon the star image. The success of these chains of commodities increases or decreases the bargaining position of the star. Stars become a capital investment, worth so many millions of dollars to the budget of, say, a film or Broadway musical. They act as a guarantee – a guarantee of further investment from financial backers: that theatres will show the film; that shops will stock the book; that television and radio will showcase the band.

This leads to a degree of power and influence, unimaginable at the moment of acquisition, as the industries become organised around the stars. Not only do stars exert influence by establishing production companies, record labels, merchandising chains, restaurants, clubs, or purchasing jet aircraft,

Caribbean islands, factories or farms, or by lending money to banks (Negus, 1992; Tremlett, 1990); they also begin to wield a decisive influence over the production process (Mathews, 1999). The major film stars can negotiate contracts whereby they have script approval and the right to request changes to the script during filming, or they may have control of the final cut, over and above the director. Stars negotiate over who will *be* director. They may strive to have final approval over images used in publicity stills for films. Stars have become ever more involved in producing movies, which means they can control the financing and management of the film, leading to tensions and power struggles amongst actors and directors.

Similar tendencies are apparent in the production of music. The unknown band will be given a limited budget (which they must pay back from sales), often be allocated a producer, have extra musicians brought in to play the guitar parts, and be required to record songs that they do not wish to record. The established star performers can stipulate who will produce them, override or remix the producers' work, and pay for the best musicians to record with them. Numerous musicians own recording studios and even record labels. They can then clearly influence who records and who gets a contract. The budding novelist will often have their work cut up by an in-house editor. It may well benefit from this, but the established author will insist on the final say, even down to arguing about punctuation marks.

If we took a snapshot of the media, arts and entertainment industries at any one time, we would find most creative artists somewhere on a continuum between a struggle for recognition and a struggle to maintain elite, aristocratic star status. The dynamics of commerce and creativity will be played out differently (see also Negus, 1995). Some will be attempting to make themselves commercial, some will be seeking greater recognition for their creative effort while selling lots of books or albums. There will be a variety of tensions between autonomy and collaboration, as in one way or another they will all be working with a whole range of personnel in realising their creativity.

The Business of Owning Signs

A focus on stardom alerts us to the influence afforded by ownership and the power of investment. Ownership is a theme stressed in much writing about cultural production and the communications media. It is important, in the first instance, because concentration of media and cross-media ownership can lead to a narrowing down of social voices, limiting the representation of certain groups and constituencies, particularly those which are most socially disadvantaged and marginalised from mainstream society. A limited number of commercial or state cultural producing institutions can impact upon cultural dialogues which contribute to creativity and social change, and result in forms of outright oppression and censorship (in those parts of the world where the state dominates), or an unequal access to and power over government, social policy and public opinion from unelected sources (as in many liberal democracies).

However, the issue is not just about owning the means of producing things. It is also about owning the copyright to the sounds, words and images that are circulated across the media and various social spaces. Copyright has often been portrayed as a further form of constraint upon creativity, one beneficial to capitalism, which in turn is perceived as a system impeding the process of free appropriation which is thought integral to creativity. There is clearly a point to these claims, but they are often simplistic. Here we want to argue that copyright highlights the tension between the individual and collective, a tension which is at the heart of the commodification of creativity and the commercial organisation of cultural production. This is most apparent in the way that copyright law encodes a notion of originality and authorship. The ability to be recognised, and rewarded, as a 'creative artist' (an originator) cannot be separated from such commercial legal circumstances.

Our focus on copyright and commodification does not so much lead to an argument about the determining market constraints upon creativity, but continues our theme of the struggles through which both the creative and commercial have to be realised. A consideration of copyright highlights the role of law in cultural production: the use of laws in defining creativity, in defining originality (and the originator). It shows us how the law is used when different interests are staking a claim on the ownership of ideas, and how the law helps to transform abstract ideas into a property – the notion of 'intellectual property' as a series of rights seeks to enshrine principles that will enable the law to regulate the copying and use of ideas. As David Saunders remarks: 'In a culture as juridified as ours, the phenomenon of authorship cannot be defined independently of or prior to its legal conditions' (1992: 213). The conditions within which creativity occurs, and the ability to be recognised as an author and originator, cannot be considered separately from the legal circumstances through which they have been institutionalised.

The origins of notions about the ownership of ideas can be traced back a long way, and various authors locate them within different periods or at different points in time. However, most historical accounts agree that modern copyright law, as it exists today, was cradled in the economy of the Mediterranean during the fourteenth to sixteenth centuries, at a time when Venice was at the centre of an emergent capitalist economy and when patent and copyright laws were starting to be applied to human activities (Merges, 1995).

The reason for introducing copyright laws encapsulated a particular logic. Copyright was established to encourage inventiveness, innovation and creativity, and to ensure that the results of human creativity were made available to the public. The logic went (and still goes) something like this: to invent something, to come up with a new idea, can take considerable effort, financial expense and time. Yet, as soon as something is made available to the public, it can very quickly be copied. It can be imitated and reproduced by someone else who has not spent all that time and effort in creating it in the first place. In short, it can be appropriated.

Copyright was introduced to solve the problem of appropriation and the assumption that the existence of copying would act as an impediment, inhibiting people from coming up with new ideas. Why spend all that effort if someone else can instantly copy your creation and benefit from it? During the early days of capitalism, in the Venetian city state, this represented an attempt to regulate the so-called free, competitive, market. The laws passed in Venice in 1474 formed the foundation of the ideas about copyright which exist today. It was stipulated that any person who produced an 'ingenious device' should make it known to the authorities, so that it could be used. It was then forbidden for any other person to make and use an identical device, without the consent and license of the author, for a period of 10 years. If anyone chose to do so, then the Venetian city authorities had the right to fine the infringer and destroy their device (cited in Merges, 1995: 105).

Although this has obviously gone through numerous modifications since, having been adapted to specific circumstances, whether in Britain, France, Japan, the United States or elsewhere, this is the basis of patent law, copyright and intellectual property legislation. The principle it enshrines can be observed operating now in the music industry, the film industry and the business of book publishing. The originators are granted a limited time of exclusivity, during which the item cannot be reproduced or used without permissions being granted and payments being made to the rights holders. The idea is that this encourages creativity amongst individuals and benefits them collectively; it is for the public good, encouraging a thriving, creative, human society. Copyright arises out of the potential tension between individual and collective and attempts to balance the desire to spread culture and the need to reward authors.

If we think about this principle in terms of the institutions of contemporary media and cultural production, a key question arises: does copyright law still benefit the individual and the collective and, if so, which individuals and which collectives? For a number of writers, the answer to this question is obvious. Copyright law has been established to protect the creative efforts of authors, composers and artistic originators. This notion is central to the practices of those organisations which act on behalf of authors and composers and can usually be found in their mission statements and annual reports.

From research on copyright in the music business, Dave Laing (1993, 2003) has suggested that there can be a degree of truth in this claim, but it is only part of the story and has changed historically. Laing argues that between the 1880s and the 1930s, the process of copyright reform and changing copyright law *did* represent the predominant interests of composers, song-writers, and literary and dramatic writers. It benefited those authors who were able to influence copyright law through the various collective organisations that they formed. However, from the 1920s, with the growth of the mechanical and electronic media, a series of other parties began to have a vested interest in the way copyright was instituted. These included singers, performers (who made use of copyrighted work) and recording companies, film studios, and radio and television broadcasters. Subsequently, governments have recognised the importance of copyright to their economies and copyright has been drawn into attempts to regulate international trade.

Laing's argument implies that copyright intersects with a series of broader power struggles. How different writers conceive of such struggles will inevitably influence their judgements about the consequences of copyright law. For some writers such tensions are resolved in the interests of all, whether this entails a rather benign 'harmonious alliance' (Ehrlich, 1988) or a more fraught process of 'knowledge diplomacy' (Ryan, 1998), entailing negotiation and a plurality of interests finding common ground through diplomatic means. This process may implicate governments, lawyers, various professional groups (scientists, composers, biotechnologists), corporations (entertainment, pharmaceuticals), non-governmental organisations, universities, various manufacturers and users of technology.

In contrast, Ronald Bettig (1996) views copyright law and intellectual property legislation as tools actively used by capitalist corporations to further their interests, facilitating ever greater patterns of ownership and cultural commodification. For Bettig, relevant law enables the increasing commodification of social life as intangible ideas (sounds, words, images) are transformed into a property that can be owned. Bettig argues that the major corporations are able to control and benefit from the circulation of knowledge and ideas due to the way that, under pressure, originators must enter into deals with corporations to have their creations made and distributed (whether song publishers, game manufacturers or medicine manufacturers). Corporations also finance creations that require considerable investment, as in the production of films, the development of new or existing technologies, or the invention of new drugs. Consequently, many originators are forced to assign their rights to commercial corporations. As such corporations ultimately own the rights to so many products and inventions, it is argued that copyright has become a further means of controlling and profiting from human creative labour, not to mention the creative labour whose results have accumulated as collective knowledge in the long-established traditions of indigenous peoples. Rather than benefiting the creators and society as a whole, copyright ultimately benefits an international capitalist class who have shared predatory interests and objectives.

However, research by Steve Jones challenges Bettig's assumption that copyright legislation benefits a capitalist class united across national divisions. Jones highlights how concerted pressure from the United States government and major record companies led China to introduce intellectual property legislation in 1991. However, little effort was made to enforce it, and various factories continued to produce CDs and software. The US claimed that these practices were being actively supported by the Chinese government (supporting their own emergent capitalist enterprises). In 1994 the US threatened trade sanctions, and as a response in 1995 the Chinese government conducted a series of highly publicised raids on the manufacturers of CDs. Still the US continued to argue that 'pirate' CDs were being produced without payment of copyright and threatened further sanctions and again the Chinese government orchestrated raids.

The Chinese authorities may have had good reasons for resisting the pressure to impose copyright law. A huge amount of Chinese trade in music is of artists from the United States. In a report presented to the US government in the early 1990s, the Recording Industry Association of America claimed that this was costing the US a sum of $16 million a year. The same report argued that if China were to 'open up its markets' then the yearly sales of music could be in the region of half a billion dollars (Jones, 1996: 343). Inevitably, a large amount of that revenue would flow to the US.

Copyright is thus used by the US as a means of collecting revenue from around the world when US products are used. When cultural products from the United States flow around the world they acquire different accents. Batman and Mickey Mouse may be given a local meaning and reembedded into specific times and places, but Time Warner and Disney have been very efficient in ensuring that money is paid when these icons are used and that revenue flows to the US, and eventually to its artists, novelists and musicians.

So there are a series of tensions clustering around the way creativity is framed by a copyright system, and a range of different arguments that seek to explain its consequences and dynamics: copyright benefits the creator/author/ composer; copyright benefits a plurality of interests; copyright benefits the corporation and capitalist class; and, ultimately, copyright benefits the more powerful nations. Many of these arguments are presented in unhelpful dichotomous terms (authors versus companies; pluralism versus Marxism; West versus Third World), but taken together they point us to the complex institutional and regulatory struggles through which creative practices have to be realised, recognised and rewarded. They point to the contested space which links the creative idea or moment of inspiration to the market and the lives of the public at large.

An analysis of creativity cannot be separated from these institutional conditions. They frame its realisation even if the artist is not fully participating or is only vaguely aware of the benefits that copyright can bring. Rosemary Coombe neatly points this out:

> Various components of an individual's persona may be independently licensed. A celebrity could, theoretically at least, license her signature for use on fashion scarves, grant exclusive rights to reproduce her face to a perfume manufacturer, voice to a charitable organisation, legs to a pantyhose company, particular publicity stills for distribution as posters and postcards, and continue to market her services as a singer, actor, and composer. The human persona is capable of almost infinite commodification, because exclusive, nonexclusive, and temporally, spatially, and functionally limited licenses may be granted for use of any valuable aspect of the celebrity's public presence. (Coombe, 1998: 91)

We cannot ignore how many creative producers are acutely aware of such circumstances, actively commodifying their body and art in this way, whilst also seeking recognition and reward for their creations or requesting recompense if their work is appropriated. It is surely a naïve postmodern conceit to assert that creativity simply involves processes of 'theft' from previous forms, and that 'these are an essential part of any culture' (Lütticken, 2002). As we have argued so far in this book, there is a lot more to creativity than re-combining existing elements of culture. Equally, it is simplistic to assume that copyright can be reduced or collapsed into commodification and economic transactions. Copyright is a clue to the way people seek recognition and the will to communicate and reciprocate, no matter how this may have been incorporated into various systems of capitalism.

This is a theme we draw from the work of Jane Gaines who suggests that a focus on copyright provides an insight into the *contested* character of cultural production, reproduction and consumption. Gaines stresses the contradictory character of the dynamics involved, arguing that it is not enough to claim that consumer culture has become commodified or that cultural forms have become reified:

> Certainly there are ways in which copyright protection and its accompanying property rights *do* commodify, solidify, and tie up elements of culture. But there are also ways in which legal protection facilitates cultural circulation. Copyright's monopoly grant, whether we like it or not, *does* work as an incentive to publish and consequently to disseminate. Copyright *protection* is always and at the same time circulation and restriction. (Gaines, 1991: 122)

Gaines offers a detailed analysis of images, voices and identities, and stresses this dynamic of *circulation and restriction,* arguing that copyright makes available aspects of a common culture at the same time that it restricts the way it can be used.

Copyright encourages the creation and circulation of popular forms regardless of whether these are Superman, James Bond or the Beatles. These *can* be appropriated, used creatively and incorporated into a shared cultural life in different parts of the world. They can bring pleasure and become part of how we form affiliations with others, or how we might develop common understandings and shared experiences. They are the result of creative energies and they inspire new forms of creative effort which can be as varied as storytelling across generations, shared anecdotes and jokes in a factory canteen, singalongs in a pub, critical conceptual art in a college, or the search for new cartoon characters in children's comics.

However, when these signs are used in a way that the rights holders dislike, they can be regulated and their use controlled. The rights holders can claim back their meaning and restrict their use. If they are parodied, for example, owners can stop this occurring. Disney monitors all use of its characters around the world and can wield intellectual property law as a form of censorship. We might think that this is unreasonable, that it is an example of copyright law being used in 'the service of multimedia corporations rather than working for either artists or the public' (Lütticken, 2002). Then again, we might also think corporate insistence on copyright is justified. For example, Disney has stopped the pornographic use of its characters. Equally, Matt Groening and Fox TV filed a law-suit against a right-wing student newspaper for publishing a homophobic picture featuring Bart Simpson (Bettig, 1996). The artist Damien Hirst made a 'goodwill payment' to Humbrol Limited in order to stop legal action when he copied the Young Scientist Anatomy Set (price £14.99) for his sculpture Hymn (purchased by Charles Saatchi for £1 million). Hirst also agreed to restrictions on future reproductions. Interestingly, the original model had been produced by a commercial artist for the company Bluebird who had in turn sold the rights to Humbrol. Only a year earlier Hirst himself had threatened British Airways with legal action, claiming that advertisements for their subsidiary Go airline had been copied from one of his spot paintings (Dyer, 2000).

Here copyright is crucial to the dynamics of circulation and appropriation. In semiotic terms, copyright provides a means of returning a sign to its preferred referent. You cannot simply appropriate the image of Mickey Mouse, Bart Simpson, Snoopy or Elvis Presley. Various rights holders will seek to challenge that appropriation and re-claim the sign, the meaning. And, as meanings are poly-semantic, this is not a straightforward case of capitalist control; such an argument is one-dimensional. Yet, equally, it is clear that new texts cannot simply be created in some playful postmodern manner through the free appropriation of signs, sounds and images. This seems an increasingly quaint and naïve passing theory these days. More significantly, and on this very point, Gaines asks the questions that semiotic analysis rarely poses: who owns the sign? Who allows the image to be circulated? Who allows it to appear in another context? How do signs appear in an advert, a movie, or come to be reproduced in a textbook? Who controls their use, and what is their market value? How is this value acquired?

Gaines's work enables us to think about the links between how creative artefacts and images are produced; the social use of artefacts and images; their circulation as commodities; and their appearance in specific representations. Threading throughout, and linking these elements together, is the dynamic of commodification. This can involve the increasing colonisation of and corporate intervention into public and private life, but commodification also means making cultural forms available. It involves circulation to a wider public. In this, process, the public use of such commodities can pose a problem for ownership and control in a way that conventional political economy seems to have problems recognising. Things and objects have a social life (Appadurai, 1986) and accumulate all manner of values and sentimental attachments way beyond their appearance in the market as a commodity. This is clearly relevant to the multifaceted approach to the value of creativity which we are developing in this book.

There is a further issue lurking within Gaines's general argument. It entails a question which might appear simple, yet is central to much of the discussion in this book: What is a copy? It's a question at the heart of copyright law. It's an issue implied in Adorno's notion of standardisation and pseudo-individuality, and in Benjamin's comments on culture in the age of mechanical reproduction, along with all the subsequent attempts to grapple with debates about mass culture and the meeting of culture and industry.

As Gaines points out when thinking about this issue: the law cannot question its own categories – such as authorship, private property, and right. All it can do is maintain them in a circular manner: 'The law asks "what is an author?" and replies "An author is an originator". So, we ask: "What is an originator?" and the law responds "An originator is an author"' (1991: 15). Copyright law is used to resolve competing claims to ownership of a work. It is used to solve the riddle of originality. But it is clearly fraught with ambiguities. Gaines refers to legal sources which suggest that 'originality does not imply novelty; it only implies that the copyright claimant did not copy from someone else' (ibid.: 58), and argues that a tautology operates at the heart of intellectual property law:

All works of authorship are original. Why? Because they originate with authors...every work is an original work, regardless of whether it is aesthetically unoriginal, banal, or, in some cases, imitative. Every individual person is also a potential 'author' whose 'writings' will be as 'original' as those of a renowned or acclaimed literary figure...Copyright's minimal point of origin requirement, which considers light fixtures and belt buckles as 'works of authorship,' performs a

critique of traditional theory's notion of authorial originality. Copyright law is a
great cultural leveller. (ibid.: 63–4)

The ironies of copyright are now central to commodification and how
profits are generated through market exchange. Ownership rights (intellectual
property, so called) are central to controlling the symbol or sign, and this is
often more lucrative than manufacturing an actual product with the sign on –
but copyright is not simply a capitalist ploy. It has emerged in its current form
as a consequence of the interplay between economics and cultural formations. Capitalism works as much through the cultural as it does through the
economic. Markets are not simply created through economic transactions;
they are also created by, and operate through, cultural processes and practices. There is a reciprocal interrelationship and blurring of cultural and economic practices, and this occurs as law seeks to intervene to solve any
apparent tensions. Here we can get a glimpse of how a concern with a
particular type of creativity in Europe intersected with the legal regulation of
markets. Many theorists are concerned about the impact of the culture industries, asserting that these commercially driven, corporate institutions impact
upon and constrain the creative process, assuming a uni-directional influence.
But discourses of creativity have decisively contributed to the formation of
particular cultural industries. The culture industries certainly impact upon creativity, yet ideas and beliefs arising from the experience of creativity have continually informed, and continue to shape, the changing formations of the
modern media, arts and entertainment industries.

Despite appearances to the contrary, a study of the cultural industries
cannot, ultimately, tell us too much about creativity. What it can tell us about is,
not surprisingly, industry, business, regulatory regimes and the institutions of
production. Ironically, considering the starting point of many sociologists of culture, a study of industry and the commercial institutions of artistic production
doesn't so much illustrate the de-centring and de-emphasising of the creative
artist but, on the contrary, shows the enduring significance and continuing
importance of the creative artist within the industrial process. The industries are
organised around the artist, as the most basic analysis of acquisitions, contracts,
copyright and stardom will reveal. How we seek to analyse specific artists and
artefacts is not given – individuals will occupy quite different positions – so we
cannot generalise or apply simple models and formulas. Nevertheless, to posit
(even implicitly) the insignificance of the creative individual artist is to mis-
understand how industries operate *in relation* to artists. Rumours of the death
of the creative artist and the rise of the managerial symbol creator, cultural intermediary and creative industry have been greatly exaggerated.

4

Convention

Creativity carries with it associations of freedom, agency and the unshackling of constraints. This is a beguiling but misleading view because creativity does not operate, unbounded, in an autonomous fashion. It is usually shaped by convention. It is about giving form to the material we draw on and transform, and this cannot be done without reference to existing rules, devices, codes and procedures.

Conventions enable cultural forms and practices to be recognised and differentiated from each other. Conventions allow for agreements (and disputes) about these forms and practices and what is characteristic of them. They can be explicitly formulated and followed, as for instance in the rules of grammar, or the rules of a game. These rules are conventional to the way writing is constructed and read, or a game played and watched. More generally, conventions are tacitly acknowledged as taken-for-granted ways of engaging in, seeing, or listening to the varieties of human communication. So, for example, at the simplest level, we can easily distinguish between a friendly and a rude gesture when we are driving a car in heavy traffic.

Conventions enable communication to occur and to be understood. In regulating behaviour, they allow human interaction to occur without co-ordination problems (Lewis, 1969). This is as applicable to ballroom dancers, marching bands in parades, or lovers on a date, as it is to members of government committees, or cyclists negotiating a roundabout. Such conventions may be perceived as artificial constructs, historically contingent in their acceptance, application and use. But recognition of their artificiality should not be taken as synonymous with falseness, contrivance, or outdated barriers that stand only to be broken. These unfavourable senses developed from the late eighteenth century, and in themselves became *conventional* antitheses to the Romantic premium on spontaneity and innovation.

It is common to see convention only in negative terms. But conventions are enabling, for within them are inscribed 'the cultural arrangements that enable communication, co-existence, and self-awareness' within particular contexts and particular periods (McClary, 2000: 6). Conventions allow communication – interpersonal, artistic – and human dialogue to occur in all its varied forms. More specifically, conventions 'ratify an assumption or a particular point of view' (Williams, 1977: 179). The acceptance of conventions, however implicit, often imparts to them a compelling force, so that it may be difficult to break with them, to challenge them and move in some other direction. When this does happen, we become aware once again of their significance, and often witness people rushing to their defence for various moral, political or ideological reasons. We might think of the sanctions, both social and legislative, for defying the behaviour deemed suitable for accompanying the playing of a national anthem, or for defacing national symbols such as flags and statues of dead heroes. We're then reminded, at times strongly, of what is at stake in the conventions that run through everything we do.

Conventions are closely related to codes. All sorts of things – colours, animals, plants – become coded in particular cultures and come to signify something else. This is particularly so with regard to national identities – the British lion, the American eagle, the Chinese dragon. States of emotion may be codified – we feel 'blue', we are 'green' with envy, we see 'red'. Often such codings are governed by cultural context as, for instance, when a red flag in one context signifies socialism, in another the vicinity of danger. Codes are interpretive devices and operate as key components of communication. When combined, we can speak of the technical and aesthetic codes that operate in given cultural forms. It is through these that we cluster together various samples of expression and narration in order to better identify their common characteristics as, for example, when we refer collectively to sonnets, haikus, cyberpunk, juju, postcolonial fiction, film noir, tabloid news, and so on.

The formal features of such cultural forms often connect with more profound debates about existence and identity because of their implication in the ways people are represented, ideals abused, reputations sullied, or ethics compromised. This may result in resistance to given codes and, eventually, their transformation or abandonment. Or it may lead to the invocation of alternative codes as a means of contestation. The friction between codes and conventions is an integral feature of cultural process, and creative practice is at times generated at the most acute points of such friction.

Despite such frictions, the vast majority of creative practices involve adhering to familiar genre codes and conventions, with audiences, viewers, readers and listeners responding to these within the horizon of expectation they have of them. You don't go to a traditional folk club and anticipate a DJ and turntables. You don't take your children to see a Disney film at the cinema assuming that dominant American values will be severely critiqued. And if you take a popular romance from a bookshop shelf, you do so in the knowledge that you won't encounter passages of sadomasochistic sexual description. These different genres meet various expectations.

Genre Codes, Communities and Changes

Genre has featured as a critical concept in literary, film and music studies. In film studies, for example, it is perhaps most clearly associated with historical types of Hollywood movie, such as Westerns, horror films and musicals, but it can also relate closely to broader categories in other national cinemas, as for instance in the overarching distinction in Japan between *jidai-geki* (period films) and *gendai-geki* (films about contemporary life) (Richie, 1971). In literary studies there is a long tradition of philosophical debate about the importance and influence of general categories. The conflict between the neo-classical theory of fixed, stable genres and empiricist objections was superseded first by theories of individual creativity and then a mid-twentieth-century turn to 'New Criticism' for which 'genre' carried little conceptual value. More recently, a concern with genre has been revived as a means for thinking about the conventions channelling the writing and reading of particular works, even those which play with, play against, or play down these conventions.

Genre is an important concept because creativity is about working within, across and out from the codes and conventions of genres, in whatever media they are manifest. Our understanding of creative practice cannot then be confined to what is taken as inspirational and radically new. Even where this occurs, creativity still involves working with recognisable codes, conventions and the expectations they generate. Indeed, for much of the time it entails putting together various words, sounds, shapes, colours and gestures in a recognisably familiar and only slightly different way. Most of the time it is that element of difference which provokes a critical response, rather than any sudden dramatic change.

This is so because genres imply different criteria for creative practice and constitute tacit agreements between producers and consumers. As various studies of popular genres have shown, what the texts within particular generic categories 'have in common is in some measure responsible for the organisation of the reader's or viewer's response to them' (Palmer, 1991: 113). We respond best to thrillers, popular romances, or soap operas if we know, accept and follow the appropriate generic conventions. Such conventions have become part of our cultural know-how as readers or viewers, with certain exemplary texts at times being used as yardsticks for the evaluation of other texts generically related to them. Readers of romance fiction, for example, condemn novels that fail to conform to the required standards and characteristics (Tolson, 1996: 96; Palmer, 1991: 115; Radway, 1984: 157 ff). In this way, the audience's expectations of generic conventions can readily become normative, influencing the creative process in quite profound but often unacknowledged ways.

The notion of genre allows us to explore the interaction between textual codes and society. Tzvetan Todorov suggests that genres function as 'horizons of expectation' for readers and 'models of writing' for authors. He states that 'genres communicate indirectly with the society where they are operative through their institutionalisation...genres bring to light the constitutive features of the society to which they belong' (1990: 18; see also Jauss, 1974). As Steve Neale points out, if we use genre as a sociological, rather than a formal concept, we can think of it as implying not just 'forms of textual codifications, but systems of orientations, expectations and conventions that circulate between industry, text and subject' (Neale, 1980: 19). Far from being confined to the recognition of textual features, genre, as for instance in cinema, 'mediates between industry and audience, through particular procedures for the distribution, marketing and exhibition of films' (Tolson, 1996: 92). The rock musician and musicologist Franco Fabbri has also remarked that genres are more about 'beliefs and practice than about theory' (1982). Genres are thus not just aesthetic markers, but key categories we live with. They orient our daily activities as well as informing our judgements about effective communication and good or bad art, along with the hierarchical location of particular cultural products. Genre codes influence how we evaluate and value music, novels, films, newspapers and television programmes. It is Fabbri's concern with how genre codes are related to beliefs and experience that we wish to explore a little further here.

Fabbri initially conceives of genres in terms of 'formal and technical rules' which concern the performance and manner of making music. Such 'rules' can most obviously be found in teaching manuals, training programmes and taught courses. At the same time they may be more informally passed on via word of mouth, and patterns of learning from listening to recordings and observing performances. Many popular musicians learn by watching other artists, and by listening and copying rather than as a result of academic tuition. Similar processes occur in other art forms, such as painting, drama and dance. They may operate more directly in popular cultural forms such as film-making and the production of artwork for comics and magazines than in, say, writing autobiography or literary fiction, but conventions exert a shaping influence in every area of cultural production, regardless of the way apprenticeship operates within them. In music, different genres imply contrasting choices of musical sounds (note systems), and contrasting conceptions of time, melody and harmony. Musicians constantly signify the genre to which they belong via musical patterns, timbre, texture and particular instrumental sounds, motifs and riffs. These are recognised by audiences with the competence to assign these sounds to specific genre categories. Newspaper and periodical reviews editors of novels and films make similar correlations. In this, and in more than one sense, they follow conventions.

Fabbri also highlights how genre rules inform the postures and movements of singers and instrumentalists, the spacing of participants at a musical event and the use of the body to signify – so that, for example, punk bass players must communicate their punk-ness through their physical movements and posture. These are not strict requirements of the music they play but are conventions of effort. At the same time, genres imply certain rules of dress. We often see a poster on a wall or a photograph in a magazine and know the type of music involved without having heard the artists. We judge the clothes, the posture, the hairstyle and, sometimes crucially, the names. The first sign of a new recording artist is often the name. This signals the genre to which an artist belongs. So, for example, punk culture is associated with its rebellion against various forms of social convention, but it has social conventions of its own. That's why the names Rat Scabies, Sid Vicious and Johnny Rotten seemed appropriate stage names – they would hardly have been suitable for a jazz or country musician or a member of a boy band.

These visual and nominative aspects are directly related to the ideological beliefs that go with genres. These are often articulated in assumptions about collectivity or community and authenticity, as for example with notions of a 'rock community' that were prevalent in the 1960s and 1970s, or the idea of 'being real' in hip hop during the 1990s. Such beliefs imply some sense of belonging or shared belief system which link artist to audience and are central to attempts to imagine themselves part of a broader community or group.

Historically, many of the ideological rules of genres have depended upon exclusionary and essentialist beliefs. In many biographies of jazz and rock musicians you will frequently find quite clear views expressed about the place of women. While women have played a significant role in jazz from its earliest days, 'the popular stereotype unfairly restricts the female contribution primarily to vocal music: the classic blues singers, the 'girl vocalists' of the swing and bebop eras, and an occasional pianist' (Tirro, 1993: 189). During the early 1970s, rock developed quite clear ideological rules about the place of women. They belonged neither in bands nor in the studio, but were conceded a particular role on a tour, such as caterer, make-up specialist or groupie.

In addition, there are various essentialist ideological beliefs about who can authentically play certain types of music – who is authentic, who is real? – and, of course, the issue of 'race' and ethnicity permeates these type of debates. Early in the twentieth century, much of the debate about whether white performers could sing the blues foreshadowed later debates about authenticity in hip hop. These ideological standards and conventions also concern the use of instruments. When Bob Dylan went electric, swapping his acoustic guitar for an electric guitar in 1965 and 1966, this was seen as a betrayal by many folk fans, who saw him as having sold out to 'mass' culture. Some even considered it comparable to an act of profane transgression, as one commentator put it: 'It ... was as if all of a sudden you saw Martin Luther King doing a cigarette ad' (Filene, 2000: 184). In the second English folk music revival, sterile prohibitions outlawed the piano as a bourgeois imposition, despite its prominence in working-class culture as a staple of informal singing and dancing sessions. Some people even argued that authentic English folk songs should not be accompanied by alien guitars or banjos (Pickering and Green, 1987: 33). Similar prejudices go with the territory of many genres.

We adduce these various examples in order to make the point that different genres can imply distinct beliefs, values and ideological positions. Aesthetic identities and creative practices can form part of broader sets of social relationships and cultural practices, and through these the creative actions of production can be co-ordinated through a shared set of beliefs, values and knowledge. For example, those involved in the production of country music in Nashville have, for some years, spoken of themselves as a 'music community' (Negus, 1999). Such a music community is lived and experienced in two identifiable ways. First, it involves a geographical sense of community created as a result of living and working in one specific physical place. Hence, those working with country musicians in Nashville have enjoyed a sense of camaraderie through numerous lunchtime meetings, evening gigs, golf days and fan events, along with the socialising which occurs between peers who are employed in the same profession and share working spaces, residential neighbourhoods and leisure pursuits. In this sense, those making music in Nashville often liken themselves to a 'family' which has been created over time as a similar group of people have gradually become closer through playing in bands, producing, collaborating and competing with one another. This has led to the formation of enduring friendships and close personal ties and these have come to shape the working world of country music production in Nashville. At the same time, those involved in country music might be thought of as constituting a broader community which is not necessarily confined to the geographic borders of a specific place. Although never meeting all other 'members', the sense of community is lived as a 'known' entity that is bigger, beyond and of greater significance than the commercial country category and the organisational department or record label. This broader community would take in songwriters, musicians and producers physically located in New York State, Texas, California, Canada and elsewhere.

A slightly similar notion of genre community has been used to identify affiliative ties amongst consumers. In his study of film, Rick Altman suggests that 'genre communities' emerge due to the way that 'genre buffs more commonly imagine themselves communing with absent like-minded fans' (1999: 160). He argues that 'the farther we range from live entertainment (that is, the more we deal with separate audiences, absent to each other, yet sharing the "same" experience), the more powerful are appeals to an absent and yet implied genre community' as 'most of the time flesh-and-blood genre communities remain beyond reach' (ibid.: 160–1). Adopting such a stance, we might also think of communities formed through radio, or via the internet, establishing connections through a shared appreciation of certain novelists, painters, playwrights or actresses. This is in part a continuation of the sense of belonging created amongst fans who take it upon themselves to come together and organise themselves around the appreciation of television shows, movie stars or musicians (Lewis, 1992). A similar notion of belonging is implied in the idea that the contrasting understandings of novels are shaped by the beliefs and values of 'interpretive communities' (Fish, 1976). Even modern art has been thought of in such terms: 'The deep appeal of contemporary art may be that it can briefly make us feel, if not like a community, then at least like contemporaries of one another' (Jones, 2003: 16).

Many media and art forms are produced in such a way as to suggest a sense of absent community. Altman observes that the television laugh-track is an attempt to do this. In Christine Geraghty's (1991) study of women and soap opera she notes how a sense of community is constructed within various programmes and how this becomes part of the saga's continuing appeal. Yet it is clear that this sense of community is not only a narrative device. It becomes extra-diegetic, extending to the world outside of the fictional story and connecting with the various senses of communal feeling in the lives of the viewers.

It is important to stress the significance of this felt sense of community in the long lasting popularity of various genres (of music, television, film) because the endurance of relatively stable genres is sometimes assumed to be symptomatic of institutional inertia, aesthetic stasis and a more general lack of desire for change. Such a supposition slips all too easily into arguments about standardisation and pseudo-individuality and reminds us of the enduring legacy of Adorno, who is often a phantom presence in arguments about how standardised genre codes encourage inertia, conservatism, and the circulation of cultural forms that do not require any effort, are pacifying and do not encourage critical thought. Of course, in making these arguments, Adorno recognised that, in the uncertain and anxiety-ridden world produced by modern capitalism, there is an understandable desire for people to seek escape, fantasy and a world of reassuring familiarity. The blame for such a sad state of standardised generic patterns and predictable audience responses then usually falls on book publishers, record companies, television producers or Hollywood executives.

To make these inferences is to ignore questions about the desire for and pleasures of the familiar, of repetition and the slowly changing and unfolding, and the sense of belonging that comes with this. Although we may not be genre-monogamous in any cultural medium, as listeners, readers and viewers, we play an active part in the maintenance of genre codes, formulas and pleasurable routines. As a public we help to shape, and constrain, the activities of musicians, painters, novelists and television programmers as a result of our expectations and desire for familiarity and an enduring sense of belonging.

Such a sense of belonging – acquired through art, literature or the modern media – has been viewed as highly undesirable and potentially limiting by many modernist thinkers (such as the aforementioned Adorno) who have placed an emphasis on notions of aesthetic risk and uncertainty. Against the known representational form and familiar narrative, they have privileged the new, the shocking and the unexpected in art forms that were and still are assumed to imply or manifest some form of social critique, radical challenge and impulse forward into the new. The principle is that the new forces us to think differently. It disrupts our expectations. This does not initially suggest any sense of belonging – in fact it seeks to disrupt any cosy sense of belonging to idealised communities which may (it is assumed) serve the interests of a capitalist class or bourgeois values more generally. It is then further assumed that modernist or experimental art, music, or theatre will, in some way, facilitate progressive cultural and political change. The artist is accorded a prominent visionary and vanguard role in any revolutionary drive towards new patterns of social organisation and social relationships.

If there is such a value in art that seeks to shock and disrupt, we should also acknowledge the value of the experiences acquired from the known, the expected and the familiar. It is from known and familiar creative conventions that art contributes to the ways in which we construct our sense of self and place in the world. We cannot simply view this, as some modernist artists have, as a necessarily conservative impulse, maintaining the status quo by acting within existing aesthetic and social categories. We should try to retain an understanding and appreciation of the value of each tendency – in this case the aspiration towards some form of community, and perhaps a utopian impulse for a more united and fairer world. Of course, many modernist artists were concerned with a sense of community, but this was often articulated in vaguer and more philosophical terms than the more concrete sense of community found in movies, music, folk tales and soap operas. We might also note, as many have done, that the shocking and new can very soon become familiar and routine. Of the avant-garde, Matei Calinescu is just one writer who has observed that: 'Its offensive, insulting rhetoric came to be regarded as merely amusing, and its apocalyptic outcries were changed into comfortable and innocuous clichés' (1987: 121).

In an approach which seeks to explore, rather than resolve, these types of tensions, paradoxes and dichotomies, Fredric Jameson has argued that we should attempt to grasp, simultaneously, the ideological/manipulative *and* the utopian/transcendent potential of cultural forms. He writes that in a society 'obsessed with commodities and bombarded by the ideological slogans of big business, some sense of the ineradicable drive towards collectivity...can be detected, no matter how faintly and feebly, in the most degraded works of mass culture just as surely as in the classics of modernism' (Jameson, 1979: 148).

The idea that art forms may be manipulative and exploitative whilst simultaneously creating a sense of commonality through a utopian impulse that may, if the circumstances are right, connect with tangible collective struggles for social change, provides a way of thinking about how conventions endure and are shaped as a result of the real affiliative links amongst readers, viewers and listeners, and perhaps between artist and audience. This way of thinking not only seeks to retain the paradoxical tensions inherent in many art works and media forms but also places such potentials and contradictions in a wider context than that associated with a focus on the mediating role of the cultural industries and the formal institutions of cultural production.

We should also recognise that genres *are* formally institutionalised and used as a way of categorising and constructing commercial 'markets'. As Simon Frith has pointed out, in discussing the commercial categorisation of music, genres are used by record companies as a way of integrating a conception of music (what does it sound like?) with a notion of the market (who will buy it?). Musician and audience are considered simultaneously, as a way of 'defining music in its market' and 'the market in its music' (Frith, 1996: 76). Many industries make similar assumptions about a homology, or correspondence, between cultural form and 'market'. An assumption is made within the recording industry that different music implies different people, different cultural identities, different market segments – that the public live their lives in separate genre worlds, communities or niche markets.

If, as readers, viewers, listeners, we use genre labels in some ways as ordering and stabilising categories, they also provide the basis of delight in their subversion or commingling. For reasons of either social/ethnic division or marketing principles and procedures, we may not be commonly exposed to certain art forms, but the notion of discrete genre worlds is simplistic and unfeasible in the contemporary context of increasing social pluralisation and audience diversification. Do people who like country not listen to rap or salsa? Do people who like jazz not listen to hard rock, techno or folk? Do people who read Henry James not read James Ellroy? Do those who watch historical documentaries and soap operas on television belong to mutually exclusive audiences? Rhetorical questions of course, but market researchers make many assumptions that we do in fact slot into simple, if not monolithic, pigeonholes of taste. They operate with an abstracted model of the social world which assumes fairly fixed relations between cultural preference and social identity.

Many academic accounts of subcultures and discussions of cultural identity have pursued a similar theory of homology or correspondence. When studying youth subcultures researchers have stressed the link between musical taste and social type, with musical taste actively used to signify a sense of belonging and difference. Such examples cannot be taken paradigmatically, for they may be exceptional in their intermapping of social identity and music preference. It's not only a question of individual tastes changing and developing, but also of diversifying and being enriched by promiscuous movements between genres, against the grain of marketing expertise or peer group disapproval, and their emphasis on established cool rules and commercial rituals.

It is at this point that we begin to see not only the limitations of notions of genre community, but some of the more general limitations of the notion of genre. As Steve Neale has observed: 'There is an assumption built into nearly all genre theory that audiences and readers not only consume some or all of the genres on offer in exactly the same way, but also that they consume nothing else' (2000: 226). Genre communities are not a universal characteristic of cultural affiliation, and so shouldn't be seen as the only or even as a major communal sense of bond in people's lives. Notions of genre communities can easily imply a simple, one-track relationship between cultural producers and their public or audience, but not all cultural producers and not all audiences exist within or share one genre world or culture. There is a spurious link between the genre associated with a band, a novelist or an actor and the cultural preferences, aesthetic inclinations, and reading, viewing and listening habits of individuals. Preferences are often eclectic, and defy any simple assumptions about a direct connection between taste (or niche market), subcultural grouping, occupational genre practice and social identities. Many rock groups, for example, are a tense collusion and collision of factions, cliques and alliances, and the unit's style is often the result of a degree of antagonism, compromise and occasional synthesis.

The act of belonging to a genre community may be a strategic choice, and entail no clear link between public and private cultural preference. Or it may be a particularly temporal and temporary phenomena. Following the example we cited above, we should note that not all people who produce country music, let alone who listen to it, may maintain collective feelings of attachment (whether in their neighbourhood or across expansive space). Many people who enjoy country music singers and songs may feel a sense of extreme ambivalence to any such notion of ties of a 'country community'. Against this it could also be argued that country music is a very particular example, and that perhaps music in general is more associated with distinct patterns of genre affiliation. But even here, the relationship between musical engagement and a sense of identity may entail a sense of ambivalence or outright feeling of detachment (Negus and Román-Velázquez, 2002). So, to what extent can we claim that the public join or imagine themselves as part of a community by attending a concert, play or film, buying a book or watching a television show? Implicit in our argument here is a critique of how Benedict Anderson's original notion of the imagined community of the nation has been adopted and used to suggest all manner of 'imaginary' affiliative ties established by the mass media. Such banal assertions tend to accept the media industry's own common sense about how they construct markets and a sense of identity. They evade the question as to whether such putative links have any substantive relevance for the imaginings of the viewer, listener, reader or purchaser of a product.

Obviously it is important to have a reasonably sound understanding of particular genres so that, for example, we can follow the narrative's logic of progression in a detective story, or recognise the use of irony in comic discourse. We can quite easily engage with, understand and enjoy all manner of genres without projecting ourselves into an imaginary link to other readers, viewers, listeners, or the actors, artists, musicians or novelists involved in any particular genre. Our very knowledge of genre also allows us to take pleasure in and to recognise, and be surprised (or even shocked) by their disruption – and authors, musicians and artists continually play on this in their work. Genres and generic conventions are not fixed for all time in their formal characteristics; they change and develop. We can observe this in television game shows, the timbre and performative styles of rock or rap, in science fiction, even in the family portraits provided by high street photography studios. Genre theorists say little about the play across the codes of genres, the dynamics of these small changes, let alone more significant aesthetic and social shifts that come when genre codes are broken, prised apart or combined in previously unimaginable ways.

Cultural creativity is realised within specific regimes of representation, according to quite obvious stylistic and generic codes and conventions. Yet what occurs when creative expression connects with these regimes and conventions does not entail an endless reproduction of their antecedent patterns and meanings. If that was the case the cultural world would simply stand still. The moment of creativity occurs when writers, film makers, musicians, painters and perhaps scientists and mathematicians (Miller, 1997) wrestle with existing cultural materials in order to realise what they do not allow. A number of writers, as diverse as Edward De Bono (1996), Arthur Koestler (1964), Ulf Hannerz (1996) and Salman Rushdie (1991), have stressed how the creative act involves recombining existing materials in such a way as to bring them into new relations with each other. This involves working both within and against aesthetic genres and social canons. It can entail some considerable effort to move across genre categories, and beyond the already signified. It ultimately entails a *struggle* with *conventions* – and we turn now to how the writings of Howard Becker and Pierre Bourdieu further illuminate this process.

Recognition, Reputations and Transformations

Although having certain similarities to those who have theorised genre, Becker and Bourdieu both wish to think about the production of art in terms of some notion of a broader social space or arena. For Becker, the key concept is that of the art world, for Bourdieu it is the field of cultural production.

Becker draws the term 'art world' from vernacular usage, but he uses it specifically: 'Art worlds consist of all the people whose activities are necessary to the production and characteristic works which that world, and perhaps others as well, define as art' (Becker, 1984: 34). Art worlds are comprised of networks of people who co-operate and organise their artistic practices around a shared knowledge of conventions and agreed ways of doing things. In writing of the art worlds characteristic of certain types of writing, photography, music and theatre, Becker stresses how these are maintained through co-operation and collaboration.

He cites obvious cases of how cultural production depends upon collaboration, listing the numerous personnel who can be involved in film-making – director, producer, camera operators, editors, effects people, props, stylists, dialogue coaches and so on – through an often extensive and hierarchical division of labour. We can also think of the collaboration involved in music making or television programming. But Becker wishes to stress the collective and co-operative activities that go into such apparently individual work as poetry or novel writing as well. Using the example of T.S. Eliot's *The Wasteland* which was extensively edited, cut and added to by Ezra Pound and Eliot's wife Vivian Eliot, Becker points out that even the most apparently individual of works can be the result of collaboration (even if the poem is only attributed to one author). The artist is not alone but performs the 'core activity' at the 'centre of a network of co-operating people' (ibid.: 24–5), and within such a network Eliot considered Pound 'a marvellous critic because he didn't try to turn you into an imitation of himself' (Dick, 1972: 118).

The social character of this type of production has had consequences not only for the working lives of authors, but also for judgements about the creativity of individual authors and, in particular, their relations to editors. Publishing industry etiquette and authors' sensibilities dictate that the details of this relationship should remain a private affair, particularly the degree of intervention, collaboration or re-writing that might occur. Indeed, various familial guardians and copyright holders, and the publishing industry's own publicity people, continually seek to contribute to maintaining this secrecy. Yet anecdotes continue to surface that raise questions about what a novel is and what an author might be – in a quite different way to the death of the author, and rise of the reader, announced by Roland Barthes.

Another pertinent example concerns the dispute about the work of Raymond Carver, and the light shed upon this by the archives of the Lilly Library at Indiana University where Gordon Lish has deposited papers providing detailed evidence of his editorial interventions into Carver's narratives. Researching for a *New York Times Magazine* article, D.T. Max found the Carver manuscripts to be 'full of editorial marks – strikeouts, additions and marginal comments in Lish's sprawling handwriting' (1998: 34). He found consistent examples of Carver's original stories being re-written, particularly the endings, and a degree of intervention to the extent that some stories were cut by up to 70 per cent and substantially modified stylistically. This research has informed judgements of Carver's creative work, with some critics explaining his changing literary style in terms of his personal individual biography, while others (from examining the Lish papers) argue that this is the result of how Lish intervened more in the earlier work and less in the later writings. The exact details of this case are less relevant to our argument here than the general point that a novel, the most 'individual' of creations, can be considered a collective or collaborative creation. Having extensively revised T.S. Eliot's famous work, Ezra Pound remarked that: 'It's immensely important that great poems be written, but it makes not a jot of difference who writes them' (see Eliot, 1971).

For Becker, such examples highlight how a large part of the daily creative work within art worlds entails 'editing', and this editing involves choices – choices made by artists and by the many people who participate in these choices. This does not just apply to novels or poetry, and might include the one photo chosen for public circulation after shooting 10 rolls of film, and the one singing performance chosen for an album after recording 10 vocal tracks. These choices help give the work its final shape and suggest future directions for creativity. As mathematician Henri Poincaré is reputed to have said, 'invention is selection' (Miller, 1997: 56). And, as Gary Giddins observes in his study of Louis Armstrong: 'Every great improviser is a great editor. It's easy to run scales up and down the horn; but picking the notes that mean something is hard' (2001: 52). Becker encourages us to think about how art emerges as a result of a huge number of choices, and an acute and perceptive sense of editing, rather than appearing spontaneously.

In discussing creative choices, Becker argues that artists orient themselves according to taken-for-granted, internalised conventions. These govern the use of materials, the choice of notes or rhythms, the use of notions of perspective, of the length of a performance, or the length of a novel. Conventions are enabling – they allow artistic work to occur, and creative communication to take place. Aesthetic conventions are seldom rigid and unchanging – every performance (music, play, dance) being subtly different, every art form continually being reinterpreted. The general point here is that conventions *allow* for variations and improvisation, and for communication to be realised. They cannot simply be reduced to standardisation as Adorno explicitly argues and as might be implied in the type of genre rules model adopted by Fabbri.

Artists may adopt different stances towards conventions. For example, Becker suggests that 'integrated professionals' are those who 'know, understand, and habitually use the conventions on which their world runs', and so 'fit easily into all its standard activities'. These will include composers whose music can be easily performed according to conventional notation and on available instruments, or painters who 'use available materials to produce works which, in size, form, design and colour, and content, fit into the available spaces and into people's ability to respond appropriately' (Becker, 1984: 229).

In contrast, 'mavericks' are those who have been part of an artworld and who decide to disrupt its conventions. They may receive a hostile reception, and they may have great difficulty getting their work distributed or performed, but retrospectively they are regarded as ahead of their time – they may be seen as innovators within art worlds despite their disruption of certain conventions. Yet they still 'orient themselves to the world of canonical and conventional art. They change some of its conventions and more or less unwittingly accept the rest' (Becker, 1984: 244).

Although mavericks benefit from their position working within the conventions of art worlds, it is the integrated professional who is more likely to get economic support, a relevant response, gain resources and recognition. Mavericks may be considered odd – they may be dismissed for not doing things the right way, for writing notes that don't sound right, for not using paint or not operating a camera with the correct technique. They may in fact never be accorded any form of recognition, even posthumously. When and if recognition comes, it can go in either of two very different directions: it may merely confirm their oddness, or it may entail a re-assessment of the whole history of an art world, so hailing their creative extension of a relatively settled tradition.

Becker's categories of mavericks and integrated professionals are descriptively useful, but he doesn't really tell us much about *why* artists adopt such stances. Mavericks, for example, may be creating work guided by a coherent set of beliefs about how they are challenging artistic and social convention, or may be pursuing a more wilfully idiosyncratic and eccentric route. Becker also discusses naive artists and folk artists as 'ordinary people' working outside of the boundaries of professional art worlds. So the category of maverick is a broad one and might apply to a range of artistic motives and orientations. We can pursue this point further if we think of mavericks in relation to discussions of bohemians, outsiders and the avant-garde.

Avant-garde artists were motivated by heroic ideals which may, in retrospect, be seen as conceited and even mythical, but these beliefs explain much about why their art took the form it did and why they adopted their specific aesthetic strategies. If not as its saviour, the avant-garde artist certainly became 'the symbol of heroic resistance to all that is oppressive and corrupt in bourgeois civilisation'. This was an artist as 'an individualist and risk taker in a sheepish society...affording new insight as well as sight, a new vision of what art as life can be – a comprehensive new enlightenment' (Kuspit, 1993: 1). The Romantic overtones here are unmistakable, and extend into the figure of the bohemian whose artistic experimentation and unconventional lifestyle were designed to challenge utilitarian values and bourgeois philistinism. Largely deriving from the affluent middle class, bohemians delivered not so much a radical alternative as a radical inversion of the bourgeois self-image. The bohemian ideal sought for an amalgamation of the spiritual life represented in art with the carnal life associated with the carnivalesque body, but in the main the bohemian art world – because of, rather than despite its eccentricities, excesses and extremities – merely offered a mirror image of the bourgeois commercial world. If the bourgeoisie represented 'ambition without passion, possessiveness without depth of desire, power without grandeur, everything that was spiritually paltry and anti-vital, everything that was inadequate and pettily self-protective', bohemians turned this imbalance the opposite way in a stereotypically Romantic manner (Grana, 1964: 69; see also Campbell, 1987: 195–201; Wilson, 2000). The paradox of the bohemian lay in embodying dissidence, opposition and resistance while at the same time performing a drama in compulsive counterpoint to middle-class respectability and sanctimony. Bohemian stories 'of genius, glamour, outlawry and doom... have always been good copy', avidly consumed at the bourgeois hearth (Wilson, 2000: 3). Similarly, a category of 'outsider art' – a label applied to the creations of those marginalised through institutionalisation in mental hospitals, old peoples' homes, prisons, homelessness – has been actively appropriated, used as a source of inspiration and brought 'inside' the aesthetic canon. This has been in large part due to the way that it 'appealed to art world cognoscenti, not only visually, but because of its congruence with Romantic notions of the authentic, misunderstood, creative genius...as outsider art became fashionable, outsiders became insiders' (Zolberg and Cherbo, 1997: 2). Outsider art partly represents a challenge to the art world from without, yet its disruptive possibilities are selectively incorporated to maintain the conventions of the art world.

A consideration of how the conventions of art worlds have been challenged highlights how fragile the artistic consensus can be. It also begins to reveal some of the limitations of Becker's approach. This presupposes a sense of belonging, of affiliation to the art world and a willingness to cooperate in its conventions even as some of these are broken. Despite his attempt to ground conventions in the tangible interactions amongst art world participants, the conventions themselves can become reified as the bonds that link people. The assumption that the art world is bounded and maintained according to co-operation and agreement faces criticism similar to that raised by the idea of genre communities. In our daily lives we live with the known and the unknown. In various creative activities, the familiar and the unexpected do not exist in separate worlds, or run along parallel tracks that never meet. They continually jostle and collide with each other. Becker's art worlds collude with the tendency of genre theory towards the abstraction of certain characteristic features – detached from their living, changing context – and a process of theoretical reification whereby the bounded genre (or art world) seems to hover threaten-ingly over and around the creative practices which are being studied.

The limitations of Becker's emphasis on collaboration and co-operation, and his undeveloped analysis of the motives and the consequences of maver-icks, can be supplemented by turning to Bourdieu who provides an immediate contrast by emphasising the competitive arena within which *struggles* take place over resources and access to them. If Becker tends to do little more than relativize artistic conventions, Bourdieu relates them to how individuals and groups are positioned in relation to one another. He focuses on the power struggles that occur between individuals and groups as they compete within the 'space of position takings' which constitutes the field of cultural production. Like Becker, he conceives of creative practices as occurring within certain types of networks – but these are characterised by antagonism rather than co-operation.

Along with many other sociologists of culture, Bourdieu's analysis of the cultural field is posed against those who place an emphasis on the unique talent and peculiar life experiences of great individuals. Bourdieu's field is made up of a series of positions that are occupied by artists, whether they be poets, novel-ists, painters or musicians. These are positions adopted by individuals, but this approach emphasises the positions taken by particular genres, or sub-categories of art and literature. Bourdieu observes that different genres – of writing, of music – are not simply defined according to their own internal conventions, codes and practices, but through their relationship to other categories.

Take, for example, the field of literature. The critical and commercial status of different types of literature is visibly articulated in book shops, pub-lishers' catalogues, the teaching programmes in universities and schools, or the organisation of literature suggested in the arts sections of newspapers and magazines. How much space is devoted to a new novel by Ian McEwan or Julian Barnes compared to a new crime novel? All this will give a tangible sense of how specific genres and writers are positioned in relation to one another.

So, the crime writer or writer of spy stories occupies a particular loca-tion within the field of literary production, positioned in relation to genres such as romance, science fiction, and also in relation to modern novels and the selection of texts categorised as classics. When John Le Carré's *A Perfect Spy* was first published in 1986, Philip Roth reviewed it in *The Observer* and declared it to be the 'best English novel since the war'. There then followed a debate amongst various writers and critics within the literary field as to whether this was a novel or merely a piece of genre fiction. Was Le Carré now a modern novelist or still a writer of genre fiction (spy novels)? For some, Le Carré was using the spy form but with 'pretensions...towards writing literature' and adopting highly 'stylised' techniques, particularly in his opening chapters (Bradbury, 1990: 130–6). Yet Le Carré's work has continually communicated beyond the spy genre, using the form critically as he 'reacts against the constraints imposed by playing with, even mocking, their conventions' (Hayes, 1990: 119). Here we may be referring to debates about style, but their consequences for reputations and careers can be profound. Whilst the novelist will still make money, there is far greater prestige to be gained from assuming the position of modern novelist than that of genre fiction writer, not to mention different types of recognition, reputation and reward.

Bourdieu's point here is that the meaning of an artistic work, and the conditions of its production, can only be understood in these relational contexts. To view genres and art forms relationally is not a particularly new observation, but Bourdieu's insight is to stress the sociological struggles over position, power and prestige which underpin the production of textual forms and artistic reputations, and how the specific networks of power relations orient the strategies of artists. If you want to publish a novel, or get a record contract, or act in a movie, or display your sculpture, your chances may well be shaped by a certain talent and acquired repertoire of skills. But there are specific positions that have to be assumed in different fields in order to realise such possibilities. And as other people will be competing, the chance of realising such possibilities may be more to do with struggles over position than with any skill, proficiency or talent. It may have more to do with professional manoeuvrings, and wheeler-dealing, than the sustained application of creative skills or inspiration.

Writers, musicians and artists continually struggle to influence how their work is judged. Here both Becker and Bourdieu are concerned with the production of beliefs and values which legitimate art. Since it is not an inherent quality of the art object, the question for Becker is how art comes to be labelled as art. A key issue concerns the dynamics of distribution and the systems in place that enable art works to be circulated. If art can't get distributed, how can we ever know about it? Becker gives the example of e.e. cummings's poetry, noting that printers were reluctant to set the poetry on the page as cummings had specified, and that this held up publication. He also refers to sculptures that are too large for an exhibition space. There may be a play or musical composition which lasts too long to be performed within the formats of theatres and concerts. A rather extreme example (which draws attention to this possibility) is the current performance of Organ²/ASLSP by John Cage. This work is being played in St. Burchardi Church, Halbertstadt, Germany. Cage requested that the work be played 'as slow as possible'. Although it has sometimes lasted 20 minutes, this particular performance commenced on 5 September 2001 and will last for 639 years.

The issue here concerns art that defies conventions by being produced with little if any knowledge that it will be in a form where it may ever reach an audience. The artist is unsure whether their creativity will ultimately ever be communicated beyond their immediate 'private' world. This is a particular issue in those times and places when forms of repressive censorship are in operation. As György Ligeti has written of some of his musical works:

> All of these works were written for the bottom drawer: in Communist Hungary it was impossible even so much as to dream of having them performed. People living in the West cannot begin to imagine what it was like in the Soviet empire, where art and culture were strictly regulated as a matter of course – they had to conform to abstract concepts that were almost identical to the regulations of the National Socialists. Art had to be 'healthy' and 'edifying' and come 'from the people': in short, it had to reflect Party directives…
>
> Later, in the West, journalists often asked me the question: 'For whom do you write your music?' My experiences in the 'East' prevented me from making any real sense of this question. A banned artist does not ask questions of this kind because the products of his art never reach an audience. And so I did not write 'for' anyone, but simply for the sake of the music itself, from an inner need. (Ligeti, 2002: 3)

Hence, the lack of distribution channels, of a public arena or outlet for the work, does not halt the creative process, but it does influence the form it takes (written less with any sense of communication to distinct audiences, and more for an internal dialogue). But it still has a communicative form. Ligeti's compositions use inherited forms and ideas that people had communicated to him, and he used these in his own way in the form that had the potential to reach the public – he still composed music. The creative act, even that which might seem lone and private, is social and operates within a chain of communicated experiences.

A further issue which follows from this last point concerns the importance of those who are in a position to influence the attribution of value. Becker argues that to understand the attribution of aesthetic value we must examine how art worlds produce particular people with the authority to speak legitimately about art. The art world produces the ideas through which the art is judged. The production of art comes hand-in-hand with the production of reputations: 'All the co-operation which produces art works, then, also produces the reputations of works, makers, schools, genres and media' (Becker, 1984: 362).

Like Becker, Bourdieu observes that the production of historical and critical discourse is one of the conditions for the production and legitimation of the work of art. So, within the field of cultural production, there is another struggle going on. This is a struggle for the monopoly of legitimate discourse about the work of art. It involves continual conflict over the values by which works of art will be judged. This can involve authors, critics, entrepreneurs and academics, as well as marketing staff, publicists and public relations people. All attempt to influence the ideas through which a work of art or literature is valued and appreciated. For example, the catalogue produced by art galleries to accompany exhibitions can be seen as providing instruction on how to appreciate the art on display; it is written by an authority. Similarly, critical reviews, literary guides, and teaching texts tell us how to interpret and appreciate a novel or musical composition.

This results in what Bourdieu calls legitimation struggles – competitive battles to impose, and make stick as legitimate, definitions of what is artistic. Legitimation struggles are continually occurring in various artistic and cultural fields and, as people are positioned differently according to their ability to influence the outcome of these aesthetic disputes, for Bourdieu they are ultimately power struggles, with dominant interests seeking to impose *their* values as legitimate.

It is the way that Bourdieu links the field of cultural production to a more profound set of power struggles which, ultimately, makes him a more insightful theorist than Becker. Bourdieu emphasises how participants in the aesthetic field consistently deny their economic motivations and any desire for status and power, yet their activities continually intersect with a field of power. In the contemporary world the field of power is primarily, but not exclusively, shaped by the competition, collusion and tensions between government/state institutions and private capital/commercial interests.

At certain moments the state may exert a decisive influence in the struggles to define aesthetic meaning, attributing explicitly ideological and political anchors to art, incorporating the aesthetic into patterns of propaganda and domination. Here we might cite the *Entartete Kunst* exhibition of 1937, a collection of 'degenerate art' which had been removed from German museums and staged by the Nazi party. More recently, in 1996, the Taliban regime instituted strict forms of aesthetic censorship in Afghanistan. This most notably entailed the banning of music, but was also informed by a belief that there should be no visual representation of animate beings. Hence, cinema, television, video, family photographs and representational painting were all ruthlessly outlawed (Baily, 2001).

In somewhat less oppressive circumstances, Roger Cook (2000) has applied Bourdieu's approach to an analysis of young British artists in London during the latter part of the 1990s. A key player in the struggles to define the meaning and significance of British art during this period was Charles Saatchi, who had accumulated his wealth from the advertising agencies Saatchi and Saatchi, and M & C Saatchi. These advertising businesses had played a significant role in promulgating the neo-liberal, socially divisive, economic and political policies of the Conservative Government led by Margaret Thatcher during the 1980s, and Charles Saatchi quite actively sought to make links between these political ideas and the aesthetic beliefs in the field of art.

As Cook has suggested, viewing the field of art in Bourdieu's terms, as a series of positions, it is possible to identify two distinct poles around which a struggle for aesthetic value and influence took place. In one position he locates Damien Hirst as 'a new kind of entrepreneurial market oriented artist, fostered by the socio-political climate of Margaret Thatcher's Tory governments' (ibid.: 173), entering into 'a subversive egalitarian engagement with the everyday as a challenge to the aristocratic distanced autonomy of avant-garde art' (ibid.: 174). In contrast, Rachel Whiteread was working with a 'more purely sculptural' approach to 'the quotidian world of everyday objects', occupying a position which sought to re-assert the autonomy of avant-garde art, and create art which 'challenges the dangerous dissolution of art into the large-scale [commercial] field, or the collapse of art as an autonomous realm into the everyday' (ibid.: 173–4). It was Hirst who Saatchi most consistently championed. Cook quotes from an interview Saatchi gave to *The New York Times Magazine* in which he remarked: 'Margaret Thatcher…created an environment in Britain where people felt they could escape the role they had been pushed into…Students like Damien Hirst felt they could do absolutely anything' (ibid.: 170).

Saatchi sought to influence the meaning of art and the reputation of artists in a number of quite distinct ways. First, he acquired a huge collection of works by prominent and upcoming artists who he then promoted. A celebratory newspaper article evokes this in melodramatic tones: 'the Rolls would nose through the mean streets in Hackney and Tower Hamlets, and artists just out of college would see their entire collections at small galleries in terraced houses and warehouses bought lock, stock and barrel' (Jones, 2003: 6). Second, Saatchi displayed the art, culminating in the hugely successful and much discussed exhibition, *Sensation: Young British Artists From the Saatchi Collection*, which was held at The Royal Academy of Arts in London during the Autumn of 1997. This created controversy and huge interest amongst the public. Many minor celebrities, media personnel and pop musicians sought to associate themselves with these artists. Third, he persuaded critics, such as *Time Out* magazine's Sarah Kent, to write 'partisan catalogue introductions' (Bennett, 2003). Fourth, Saatchi strategically disposed of the work of some artists, selling them at auction and signalling 'his ability to make and break artists, even to end a historical moment' (Jones, 2003: 14). Jake and Dinos Chapman's sculpture of the physicist Stephen Hawking perched on a crag in his wheel-chair and entitled *Ubermensch* 'went for a humiliating £10,350, a tenth of the prices paid for minor works by Hirst and Whiteread'. They were subsequently dropped by their dealer, Victoria Miro (ibid.: 14). A fifth distinct way that Saatchi sought to define the meaning of art and establish reputations was through the promotion of a new aesthetic category, applied to a younger generation of artists which he labelled as neurotic realists. This was decidedly less successful. He was unable to persuade the critics and many ridiculed him, questioning his credentials as a legitimate authority on art.

Saatchi's attempt to promote a new group of artists as neurotic realists provided intimations of his precarious position within the artistic field, and raised questions about his authority and legitimacy. This became even more pronounced in the spring of 2003 when he launched a new gallery in a prominent position on the banks of the River Thames, in the somewhat unlikely location of an old London council building. *The Independent* referred to it as 'adman's art…bright and shiny, shitty and bloody, rude and jokey'. Left-wing critics, with memories of Saatchi's support for the Thatcher government, were wholeheartedly critical. Yet so were conservatives. George Walden, an ex-Tory minister, described it as 'backward, provincial and sad… There's more merit in one episode of *The Simpsons* than in his gallery'. There was also discontent about Saatchi's style of intervention into the field, with the editor of *Art Monthly* remarking: 'It's an unequal power struggle. In the end, it's all about Saatchi' (all quotes from Bennett, 2003: 16–17).

This latter point makes an explicit connection between the 'classification struggles' over artistic value and the struggle for power. In Jonathan Jones's newspaper profile of Saatchi and his activities, he asks a more general question about what art collectors seek to achieve. As he observes, most art collectors do not need money, and do not collect art as a way of making money. Instead, 'more often than not it is power the collector craves. The power to make and break reputations, to influence museums, to establish critical consensus, to change history' (2003: 14). The desire for such power is perhaps even more profound than this. Ritta Hatton and John Walker (2000: 96) suggest that 'knowledge, mastery and control…are three recurrent motives for collecting', whether this entails the accumulation of stamps, marbles or postcards. This 'mastery' – and collecting, classifying and ordering does seem a particularly male preserve – connected, in this instance, with a distinct attempt to achieve what Hatton and Walker identify as three types of power – economic, ideological and aesthetic/cultural/semiotic. As Bourdieu argues, it is ultimately a type of institutional power – political, economic, social – which informs the entire field of artistic production, influencing the establishment of reputations and struggles over economic, cultural and political resources. The conventions of creativity are continually implicated in the wielding of, resistance to and struggle for power.

Conventions and Creativity

Drawing on Becker and Bourdieu allows us to re-emphasise that the arguments we have been developing over these last two chapters entail far more than a narrow focus on the so-called culture/cultural industries. We have quite deliberately moved away from any assumption about the impact of an industry *upon* creative practice. Nor are we concerned with the way that an industry might provide a context for cultural production to take place, creating the institutional conditions of creativity. Instead, we are suggesting a far broader approach which draws from the insights gained from thinking about creative practice within an art world of co-operative interactions or a field of cultural production made up of position-takings and struggles for position. In different ways, Becker and Bourdieu move us onto a terrain of open interrogation of the grounds of consensus and the determinants of conflict as both are manifest in artistic activity and interaction. They both provide significant insights into the visible interactions *and* the less tangible structural forces through which power is manifested and contested in creative work.

The benefit of the approach taken by sociologists like Bourdieu and Becker is its countering of popular misconceptions about 'pure' art, and its demystification of traditional views of art as transcendent. What is identified, accepted and valued as art is dependent on shared social conventions and understandings which are related to the broader, divergent networks and conditions of art worlds. This clearly negates the assumption that artistic practices and texts can be explained purely by reference to the actions of talented, unique individuals. Against the notion that artists are only creating art works, Bourdieu and Becker show them to be engaging in power struggles, maintaining positions, establishing conventions and setting up boundaries to art worlds or fields.

Any new artists have to enter these fields. They have to negotiate the conventions which help to define art worlds. They cannot bend, stretch or subvert these conventions until they have first learned what they are and how they operate. We may then come to recognise their talent in what they do creatively with the conventions of their specific craft, but any deviations are meaningful only against the conventions from which they move. *Vers libres* in modern poetry made sense only in its break with recurrent metrical patterns and a set quota of syllables per line, while modern atonal music derives its meaning from the repertory of European tonality that attained conventionality in the eighteenth century and continues even now to influence musical thinking and practice.

The limitation of conventions is not that they are accepted, but that they are accepted as natural and never questioned as such. Hence, despite his sophisticated philosophical arguments about aesthetics, Roger Scruton can remark that 'conventions are fixed and timeless…rigid' (1983: 23–4). A sociological understanding encourages us to raise questions about the apparent naturalness and static character of conventions, and see instead what they entail and curtail, what consequences they have for creative practice and the reception of that practice. It allows us to tell a different story. Rendering the practice itself as something distinct from its social conventions and circumstances, something pure and sufficient unto itself, as in notions of the 'text itself' or the 'musical work', inevitably produces a negative conception of convention, as if it merely involves formula-driven production and is by definition scant in its imaginative scope. This conception is itself a historical *convention* linking Romanticism and modernist aesthetics which the most interesting advances on twentieth-century 'mass' culture critique have tried to move beyond. Giving a more positive slant to our understanding of conventions, as well as de-naturalising them, is one example of such movement.

Showing how linguistic, cultural and artistic conventions are rooted in the everyday social world can be a salutary counter to asocial and ahistorical understandings which divorce art from that world and make connections to it seem to disappear. But what we gain from the sociology of art also entails a certain loss when artistic activity is subsumed into various social grounds and determinants, as for instance when we see artists as subject to their position within a field, their economic or cultural capital, their class or family background or their determination by an industry. It's the artist as creative subject who then seems to disappear. Such approaches seem to allow for only the small steps of change, if allowing for change at all. They neglect, or quite deliberately seek to evade, or do not allow us to ask questions about how and in what ways conventions may be broken. A sociological focus on convention tends to lose sight of art in its relations of risk, uncertainty and the will to break with genre codes. If Susan McClary is right in saying that culture works by being 'always grounded in codes and social contracts, always open to fusions, extensions, transformations' (2000: 169), the trick for interpretation and understanding (and not least for creative practice) is always to keep both these vital aspects simultaneously in view. We shall now turn our attention to what this trick might involve for the concept of tradition.

Tradition

It is a common misconception to regard innovation and tradition as diametrically opposed to each other. When innovation is valued as a defining characteristic of the creative process, tradition often becomes set up against it as inevitably static and unchanging. In this view, tradition inhibits, and is seen as an impediment to be overcome.

We want to challenge this notion of tradition. As with convention in its primary negative sense, tradition shouldn't be taken as the antithesis of innovation. Rather than seeing them as deeply divided, we want to consider tradition and innovative forms and practices as informing and supporting each other. It is only by thinking about their interrelationship that we can understand processes of creativity and cultural change. Creativity doesn't emerge out of a vacuum, but builds on one or more existing cultural traditions. This is true of poetry, architecture, film-making, styles of singing and any number of other examples. In this sense creative talent requires a tradition so that it can learn how to go further within it, or beyond it. Innovation should be understood by rejecting those approaches which set it squarely against tradition and established cultural practice.

We nevertheless come to this issue with certain pre-formed views about the role of innovation in social and historical processes, and about the quality it brings to intellectual and cultural life. When a high value is placed on innovation, as has often been the case during the course of the modern period, prejudices against tradition can easily arise. This is one obstacle to the understanding of innovation and tradition we want to discuss in this chapter, but there is an equally weighty obstacle standing in the other direction. This is the attitude of opposing innovation in principle, without regard for case or context, on the grounds that it is highly unlikely it will lead to any good. Such an attitude can easily conflate what is good with what is past or what is settled into its conventional place, and so turn against the future.

We start the chapter with a consideration of the philosophies of two major figures, Edmund Burke and Friedrich Hayek, because they represent a very strong current of thinking about tradition in opposition to political, cultural and aesthetic change. Burke's writings feed into a conservative philosophy and policy on heritage, and his legacy has haunted recent discussions about the value of a range of landscapes, settings and buildings. For example, the parish church of St Mary's the Virgin in Putney is a key site in Britain's revolutionary past – it was there in the autumn of 1647 that Levellers in Cromwell's army argued their case for a radically democratic state. In an article about the significance of this church, Tristram Hunt and Giles Fraser cite Burke as the originator of the practice of elevating custom and tradition above politics and culture. They make the point that metropolitan liberals 'may sneer at local museums or visitor centres, but immigrant and marginalised communities are keen to rediscover their pasts and celebrate their ethnic or local heritage... Thanks to the metropolitan left's cultural aversion to "heritage", the historic monuments and symbols of our radical past are being sorely neglected' (Hunt and Fraser, 2003; and see Brailsford, 1976, on the Putney debates). Such an aversion leaves the stage wide open for official, establishment views of heritage – the Oxbridge colleges, stately homes and old cathedrals – and for keeping the concept of tradition conservative. This is why we begin with Burke, whose importance extends considerably beyond an argument about constitutional history. We then move on to Hayek as a more contemporary example of the reactionary defence of tradition. We devote attention to these figures because they are conspicuously absent in latter-day cultural studies, which has its own canonical agenda and preferred lines of dispute, and a predisposition to avoiding questions of custom and tradition, continuity and inheritances from the past.

Past and Prejudice

A reactionary defence of tradition arises as a characteristic opposition to the consequences of becoming modern, and the importance of the political philosopher and parliamentarian, Edmund Burke (1729–97), is that he was the first significant figure to exemplify it. While an advocate of the emancipation of the American colonies, Ireland, and India under the East India Company, he was ardently opposed to Jacobinism and the French Revolution. It was through his opposition to the events of 1789 and their aftermath that he gave the fullest expression to his sense of the value of tradition in its contribution to national stability and order.

Burke has had many political heirs, and since his own time his thought has influenced successive generations. For the contemporary conservative philosopher, Roger Scruton, Burke's significance lies in his revalued sense of tradition 'as expressing a partnership between the living, the unborn and the dead', for this 'set a context for conservative thinking which it has retained until the present day' (1991: 29). Such thinking has taken its cue from Burke in opposing large-scale transformation as a remedy for social ills and inequalities. Conservatism condemns socialists and liberals alike for seeking in such transformation 'a solution to problems that cannot be solved', and so threatening the body politic with 'the malady of agitation' (ibid.: 1). It is along lines such as this that Burke's contribution to conservative political thought has been enormous and far-reaching, extending considerably beyond the scorn for liberal do-gooders and social reformers that has been the prerogative of crusty reactionaries across the intervening centuries.

Veneration of this contribution was initiated by the later Wordsworth's praise for Burke's endorsement of 'the vital power of social ties endeared by custom'. Though in different contexts the terms are distinct, custom here can be understood as continuous with tradition. Similarly, Burke's claim for legitimacy of the British constitution, 'whose sole authority is that it has existed time out of mind' (cited in Briggs, 1965: 176), is the same as that claimed for the value of tradition. Few people would now openly espouse such a primordialist claim, but an implicit conflation of unquestioned value and assumed longevity has often enough been the basis of opposition to change, regardless of whether any appropriate distinctions have been made between custom and tradition. Burke's advocacy of the 'vital power' of tradition in cementing social ties helped develop a line of criticism setting off old against new, continuity against change.

Burke viewed tradition as the 'ancient permanent sense of mankind' (Burke, 1852: 361). The accumulation of this sense and the associated achievements contributing to it constitute a sublime inheritance running through the generations and ensuring a stable social order. By contrast, 'a spirit of innovation' represents only 'the result of a selfish temper and confined views'. For Burke, the only effective counter to this was tradition, which he defined in a classic contradiction in terms as 'wisdom without reflection' (Burke, 1978: 119). This conception of tradition presents us with an acquiescent acceptance of what has gone before. It leaves no place for reflexive practice, for creative uses of the past and creative responses to moments of innovation, challenge and change. These are quite different to the empiricist pragmatism with which Burke allied his populist conservatism. The following passage from his most famous work illustrates very well the damage of sticking to the tried and trusted:

> You see, Sir, that in this enlightened age I am bold enough to confess that we are generally men of untaught feelings; we cherish them to a very considerable degree, and, to take more shame to ourselves, we cherish them because they are prejudices; and the longer they have lasted, and the more generally they have prevailed, the more we cherish them. (ibid.: 183)

From Burke's perspective, well-established and therefore *sound* prejudices – which combine together collectively to form tradition – are to be cherished because they represent an indispensable stock of knowledge and belief, built up like a large town or city by many hands over a long stretch of time. This seems fine, but those who live and move about in them always want to know if buildings are structurally sound, never mind aesthetically pleasing, and over time some buildings need to be renovated or replaced. Burke's rhetorical formulation begs the questions of why things last, why they should be unthinkingly cherished, and why they shouldn't change. How, in any case, are we to know what to take on trust from tradition, what to critically interrogate, what to revise and renew? Burke revered the old, and unfavourably contrasted customary habits of action and the institutions which legitimated them with the quest for innovation or what he saw as chasing after mere ideals. Paradoxically, that which he revered, as for instance in the British political constitution, was revolutionary in its seventeenth-century development, so how could he have come to appreciate and cherish what had previously cast aside earlier revered traditions? It may be that Burke understood appropriate social and political change as a reaffirmation of ancient laws and liberties, and that he saw this typically English endorsement of rights by appeal to the past, rather than to abstract principles like freedom and equality, as endorsing his doctrine of traditionalism. Aside from the fact that it wasn't the rights of commoners which were in his general framework, this is a circular kind of argument. It can only approve change if it is based on, and leads back to, continuity.

In opposition to Enlightenment thinking, Burke distrusted people's 'own private stock of reason' because this would not only lead to a limited outlook, it would also deprive any individual of the resources of tradition. He advised people 'to avail themselves of the general bank and capital of nations and of ages'. From this has extended a highly restricted definition of both tradition and culture. It is consonant with Burke's diatribe against the French Revolution. There he referred to the 'latent wisdom' which 'prevails' in the inherited prejudices of tradition which people 'discover' in their empirical sagacity (ibid.: 183). Yet such 'latent wisdom' is not there, as he thought, simply waiting to be 'discovered'. It is there to be interrogated for its value in the present and in the interests of the future. Such 'latent wisdom' is not necessarily applicable for all time. Indeed, this is in part why history itself is continually being reviewed and revised.

Modifications and changes in the ways in which we view the past should remind us that alternative perspectives are always available, and that tradition, in the pluralised sense of the term, is not to be taken, unquestioningly, as 'an entailed inheritance derived to us from our forefathers, and to be transmitted to our posterity' (ibid.: 119). This is fundamentally misconceived, for nothing is unchangeably preserved throughout the ages, and traditions are only understood and valued from the perspectives of living people in the present. There is no intrinsic reason why they should be valued, and any judgements are understood from contemporary perspectives and not simply discovered in some pristine, elemental form. We may turn to traditions as particular sources or resources in response to deficiencies in the present, such as when architects continue to be inspired and influenced by the buildings of ancient Greece, Egypt or China, or when writers continue to draw on Sappho, Homer, Catullus or Li Po and Tu Fu. It is the friction between past models and conventions, and the felt urgencies of contemporary forces and pressures, that can inspire the creative process.

Burke's figurative reference to tradition as the general capital of nations and ages aptly conveys his belief that the pursuit of economic self-interest is in accord with social co-operation. Subsequently, it has become fundamental to conservative thinking that tradition, in Burke's sense of a repository of authoritative common-sense prejudices, is compatible with the market economy as an open-ended sphere of collective rationality. So understood, 'tradition is another instance of the phenomenon that is exhibited by a market – the phenomenon of tacit and collective understanding, realised through social intercourse', with neither regarded as amenable to centralised control or rational planning (Scruton, 1991: 6–7). It was for this reason that Burke defended the free-market theories of Adam Smith. His defence of Smith's *laissez-faire* economics in conjunction with his conservative defence of tradition further underscores Burke's importance in the history of conservative thought. He was, in Scruton's estimation, 'the first serious thinker to attempt a reconciliation between the ideas of economic freedom and traditional order' (1991: 29).

This line of thinking, pursuing the reconciliation of tradition and self-interest, has more recently been extended by Friedrich Hayek (1889–1992), a leading exponent of unregulated market forces, key mentor to the British Tory governments during the 1980s, and influential figure in contributions to the intellectual rationale of neo-liberal economic policies in Eastern Europe following the collapse of the Soviet bloc. As with Burke, Hayek's conception of tradition was informed by his opposition to any large-scale, collective attempts to influence the direction of social development and change. Anti-collectivism and the cultivation of competitive market dynamics through enterprising individuals are key Hayekian themes. These may not seem at first to be commensurate with his reverence for tradition, which is clearly in any particular case a collective rather than an individual achievement. It is Hayek's understanding of the epistemological basis of tradition that appears to reconcile his dogmatic individualism with his championing of a 'free' market order, despite cases of traditions being destroyed by the modern market economy. The workings of the market are never as spontaneous, haphazard and finally magical as he always claimed.

The kind of knowledge which Hayek considered crucial to social and economic life is practical and tacit, rather than the result of central planning or rational methodology. The social outcome of this knowledge as it is exercised in everyday situations and circumstances is, in Hayek's view, unintended, while any good with which it is associated has only subjectivist value. We're not only back with Burke's prejudices, with his untaught feelings which prevail because they have lasted in just that enclosed view of them, but also with Adam Smith's unplanned market benefits. Both the market and tradition exhibit what Hayek called 'spontaneous order'. Such order is the unpredictable consequence of unintegrated individual action and the exercise of popular prejudices. For Hayek, as for Burke, tradition is a central knowledge-bearing component of social order, since what enters into and is reproduced through tradition can neither be known in advance nor collectively altered, except in minor particulars. For Hayek, the accretion of knowledge within traditions is the result of an evolutionary process of natural selection, which should not be tampered with because, as with Burke's valuation of it, it has not only stood the test of time and proved adaptable to changing circumstances, but is also in itself 'usually inaccessible to critical statement' (Gray, 1984: 42).

Any attempt to develop a critically reflexive view of a moral or cultural tradition is then, for Hayek, to fall into an intellectualist trap, for any modifications made to an inherited code of thought or conduct can only be small, gradual and piecemeal. Changes to established practices occur only through these minor variations and deviations. If serious social instability is to be avoided, such changes can only be minor because the impersonal self-generating process of social order transcends the comprehension and guidance of any single individual. What has entered into and been reproduced by a tradition is for Hayek the result of a selection of 'irrational, or rather, "unjustified" beliefs which, without anyone knowing or intending it, assisted the proliferation of those who followed them' (Hayek, 1992: 75). This is directly in line with Burke's definition of tradition as 'wisdom without reflection'. Indeed, Hayek comments that tradition is 'superior to, or "wiser" than, human reason' (ibid.).

The 'proper attitude' to tradition is therefore 'one of Burkean reverence and not of reformist hubris' (Gray, 1984: 42). This is entirely consonant with Hayek's lifelong opposition to socialism and advocacy of an unhindered market system. His neo-liberalism endorsed a political arrangement that encourages the 'spontaneous' development of social process while at the same time reinforcing the 'uncreated' selection of tradition. In Hayek's view, both market and tradition arise spontaneously and serve as ways of adapting to the unknown: 'the whole structure of activities tends to adapt, through partial and fragmentary signals, to conditions foreseen by and known to no individual' (Hayek, 1992: 76). It is this haphazard adaptation as central to the self-ordering process of tradition which Hayek favoured above anything that can be produced by human ingenuity and creativity, for custom and tradition stand between instinct and reason, and what can be rationally considered, chosen and planned is, in Hayek's view, radically limited. This view is central to what Anna Elisabetta Galeotti (1987: 170) has described as Hayek's philosophical anthropology of ignorance. In Hayek's own words, 'though governed in our conduct by what we have learnt, we often do not know why we do what we do' (Hayek, 1992: 23). This expresses Hayek's notion that we enter the world socially blindfold. The blindfold we wear is tradition, and blindfolded by what we take from the past, we operate entirely by tacit skills and capacities – what he called 'knowledge of time and circumstance' as this is adapted from what is inherited (Hayek, 1949: 80). Such knowledge defines the limits of what we can properly do and know. For Hayek it follows that we cannot know the social consequences of our actions, and that any attempt to reflexively monitor and self-consciously modify the outcomes of our action is to infringe the liberty of others.

Against this, we want to argue that defining liberty as freedom from coercion by others entails a fatalistic acceptance of social inequality and injustice. To see social order as the unintended sum of innumerable separate decisions and actions, which in their collective manifestation cannot be taken as coercive, is to falsely equate public good with the private pursuit of self-interest. That of course was also Adam Smith's position, and the result is the same. The term 'public' is drained of any intrinsic positive meaning. Such a position is based on an authoritarian view of the subject. This is difficult to square – for all its appeal to unintended outcomes leading to spontaneous order – with Hayek's theory of social evolution. Hayek simply falls back on an appeal to moral tradition as a longstop to the socially destabilising effects of all-calculating, ruthless competition between 'autonomous' individuals. As Hilary Wainwright has pointed out, Hayek's arguments led him, despite his libertarian starting-point, to favour order and tradition over human creativity. His social philosophy in general, and free-market model in particular, provide for only the semblance of individual and collaborative creativity (1994: 5, 56–7). His theory of society is atomistic and his theory of knowledge asocial, for all that anyone's mental compass 'can effectively comprehend are the facts of the narrow circle of which he [sic] is the centre' (Hayek, 1949: 14). This contradicts any possibility of participating in or learning from traditions as resources of collective knowledge, fallible though they may be, or of a social order 'which recognizes the distinct role, for good or ill, of human agency and creativity' (Wainwright, 1994: 60).

The conception of tradition found in both Burke and Hayek denies us a critically reflexive perspective by claiming an exclusive reliance on established codes and procedures, the general capital of ages past. It reifies tradition as a self-ordering accomplishment occurring behind people's backs, and flies in the face of creativity's energy of renewal and its contemporary reconstitution of what is culturally inherited. It also has no way of explaining creativity in terms of big strides forward, as opposed to small movements sideways. Its populist appeal to common-sense knowledge and to conservative impulses is clear enough, but its privileging of practical knowledge and trusted prejudice results in a restrictive channelling of experience and a constrictive experience of tradition that can only be inimical to creative practice. That is why Alisdair MacIntyre defines tradition in the Burkean sense as either dying or dead. In such a tradition, creativity will be distrusted, devalued, or even dismissed entirely.

Tradition is symbolically reconstructed by successive generations, and so involves both cultural continuities and discontinuities, neither of which have an essence or core authenticity outside of their ongoing interpretation. This is the problem with Edward Shils's approach to tradition, for although he acknowl-edges that traditions are always changing, he asserts that they nevertheless contain an unchanging essence (Shils: 1981: 13–14). Shils's understanding here is not particularly different to Burke's conception of 'a permanent body composed of transitory parts' (Burke, 1978: 120).

In contrast, MacIntyre argues that a living tradition is 'an historically extended, socially embodied argument, and an argument precisely in part about the goods which constitute that tradition' (1985: 222). To participate at all adequately in such an ongoing argument means developing an understand-ing of tradition and of traditions that is critically opposed to populist forms of conservatism or the ideological uses to which tradition and heritage are put. Yet such critical opposition should never underestimate the populist appeal of a Burkean or Hayekean conception of tradition. Failure to understand this appeal leads to a common error in countering prejudice against change. This involves moving over to the other extreme and celebrating change simply for its own sake. The same folly is then repeated in inverse form: a relentlessly backwards view is exchanged for a relentlessly forwards view. Any creative practice or activity requires change if it is to remain ongoing in any dynamic sense, but this is not to cast out the need for qualified assessment in particular cases and contexts. Nor is it inconsistent with a recognition of the desire for a degree of continuity alongside change.

The Resilience of Tradition

Those of us living in parts of the world which have experienced modernity in its myriad institutional forms have, in many ways, become used to being told that we live in times of continual change. It seems then that change is an endemic feature of modern life that can have far-reaching repercussions and at the same time affect the local circumstances of our individual lives in ways which are both intensive and rapidly successive. To the extent that all cultural processes within capitalist modernity have been swept up in an ever-changing historical movement, change has become a buzzword of vitality. This generalised sense of change is often the source of an anxiety which leads to a desire for continuity in reaction to the destructive consequences of modernity's incessant movement, whether these are realised as personal loss, social instability, or environmental degradation.

Social and cultural change are often associated with innovation and creativity because of their positive connotations of growth, development and progress. These associations are clearly important, but they shouldn't imply that creativity is only significant in connection with continual renewal, which may in any case destroy or render peripheral the grounds on which certain forms of cultural creativity operate. In addition, we should be careful when accepting many of the claims made for continual change. Many changes are, when examined more closely, variations on what is familiar or apparently forgotten from generation to generation, as for example when this involves new types of social relationship, sexual mores, alluring spectacles, or styles of performance. We need to be not only more critical about the rhetoric of change associated with modernity, but also more sophisticated in distinguishing between changes that lead to an anxious desire for an unchanging tradition, and changes that are actually part of an ongoing living tradition.

Our argument is therefore directed not only against notions of tradition in the conservative thought of Burke and Hayek, but also against its conceptualisation as the necessary antithesis of modernity, with all the negative connotations of 'dead weight' it then has to carry – a reactionary closure of beliefs, a narrow constriction of outlook, and a general resistance to change. In much contemporary sociology, as well as in the field of cultural studies, tradition is either caricatured in this way, or simply neglected, as even a cursory exploration of chapter headings, book indexes and journal article titles soon reveals.

The complex of practices and institutions that are called modernity has involved an acceleration of social change as measured against the pace of change in previous historical periods. While this has always been variably experienced in different social locations, the rapidity of change has brought about an understanding of tradition that is informed by responses to modernity. Writers such as Anthony Giddens and Ulrich Beck have argued that modern societies have increasingly become characterised by a troubled awareness of the risks entailed in the contingency of personal relations, the confusion of choices in the marketplace and the possibilities of new fast-spreading diseases, violent destruction and the permeation of political conflict through terrorism into the most habitual of daily routines. It's as if 'risk society' begins where tradition ends, but this is a false polarisation suggesting that tradition is synonymous with fate and incompatible with a reflexive, individualised way of living one's life. To the contrary, for one response to a heightened sense of risk, contingency and rapid change has entailed a revaluing of tradition and attempts to enhance its symbolic value. In this sense, contemporary understandings of tradition are a response to the changes and anxieties associated with modernity.

As modernity has been experienced in different times and places, people have come to re-assess and reflect upon how a sense of history and tradition mediates their everyday lives. How people view tradition, in their families, in government institutions, in intellectual disciplines or when involved in art worlds, will tend to change as historical conditions and circumstances change. Tradition is always viewed historically, and will be characterised and valued in different ways. As we write this book, that sense of difference has perhaps never been more expansive. Most of us have now developed a much sharper awareness of the past as always in part a specific reconstruction, and of the partial ways in which that reconstruction is accomplished, whether on the page, through the screen, or inside the museum.

An expectation has developed that, as modernity advances, tradition will inevitably decline and its values diminish in significance. This has not happened. Contrary to the Enlightenment and modernist thinking, which negatively associated it with distorted or spurious forms of thinking and acting, tradition has neither disappeared as a dimension of various cultural systems nor proved incompatible with modern political, technological and cultural developments. It may seem that some traditions have dwindled and declined, their values appearing less relevant in modern times, yet how we know this, aside from very specific and finite cases, is always a perilous exercise, as is obvious from the examples of religion and ethnicity. Just as likely, if not more so, is the possibility of traditions adapting, mutating, being inverted or living on in different forms, practices or objects. Although they remain seen as traditions, their meanings and values don't remain unaltered. This is precisely why they continue to be relevant to people and continue to attract allegiance and support. Certain traditions have been relocated to alternative sites and media, or been discovered by different social groups and movements, who have used them creatively as a cultural resource that is alternative to what has otherwise been available to them, whether in their own regional class or ethnically based cultures, or in modern consumer society. Tradition as a cultural dimension has, in short, proved to be co-extensive with modernity, and it has done so in part because it has provided resources for cultural creativity and invention which modernity may appear to have foregone.

The blues provides a good example of a cultural tradition that has emerged and developed during modernity and proved adaptable to transfer from country to city, from acoustic to electrically amplified forms, and from dismissal by 1960s black power activists as accommodative and appropriated by whites to its more recent rehabilitation by a new generation of black performers like Corey Harris, Guy Davis and Eric Bibb. Its resilience as a cultural tradition is attributable to the resources it offers for extension and reinvention as well as for apprenticeship in a wide range of expressive styles and structures.

Susan McClary has described the blues as a genre 'that succeeds magnificently in balancing convention and expression' (McClary, 2000: 34). This is exactly right, but we shouldn't exaggerate expression at the expense of convention. That is McClary's point. Albert Murray also stressed this in the 1970s when he wrote of blues musicianship as being far more to do with convention and tradition than with impulse. As he put it, you don't just have the blues and then give 'direct personal release to the raw emotion brought on by suffering' (2000: 126).

The blues cannot be used expressively until you have at least a reasonable orientation with its idiomatic conventions and how these have developed within the tradition. Even when this has been acquired, the result is characterised by imitation, variation and counterstatement rather than by originality: 'It is not so much what blues musicians bring out of themselves on the spur of the moment as what they do with existing conventions' (ibid.), as they take them over and extend or actively respond to them, as did Bessie Smith with Ma Rainey's singing style, and Robert Johnson with Son House's playing style. This may chafe against the cherished notions of a commonplace romanticism about the blues, but it is only in this way that the blues tradition is extended and renewed: a 'musician must have internalised its procedures in order to participate creatively within its ongoing conversation' (McClary, 2000: 33). This is true even of those who attain preeminence in the art: 'The unchallenged supremacy of Duke Ellington is not based on pure invention but on the fact that his oeuvre represents the most comprehensive assimilation, counterstatement, and elaboration of most, if not all, of the elements of blues musicianship' (Murray, 2000: 126).

As this example of a particular cultural tradition and musical meta-genre shows, we should rethink tradition in the light of its resilience – its adaptability and extendability in modern societies – rather than seeing it merely as a residue of past social formations. This step is central to our argument in this chapter. It means understanding that we can only be original on the basis of some existing tradition, and that an abiding value of tradition lies in providing opportunities for its extension and transformation. Such an understanding is not as widely accepted as it should be because of the prevalent ways in which both tradition and innovation have been conceived. Viewing tradition simply as the antithesis of modernity is part of the same conceptual pattern as the other binary dichotomies inherited from classical sociology and anthropology.

Concepts like status and contract, *Gemeinschaft* and *Gesellschaft*, mechanical and organic solidarity, culture and civilisation, primitive and advanced ways of life, traditional and bureaucratic authority, sacral and secular associations, are all paired concepts which attempt to grasp the structural changes that have occurred in the institutional framework of a society as it becomes modern. What is characteristic about them as ways of conceptualising and analysing modern social change is that they are one-sidedly defined and interpreted as dualistic terms. They are inflexibly constituted with reference, as in the case we are considering, to tradition not only as incompatible with modernity, but also as superseded by modernity. Such concepts are therefore part of the problem when thinking about the relations between tradition and innovation. They are certainly not the solution to the problem of why some traditions have become more important because of modernity.

The assumption that there is a fundamental cleavage between traditional and modern societies has given rise to vocabularies of conceptual polarity in the analysis of social change. These either/or modes of thinking have bedevilled social and cultural theory. Radically opposing traditional and modern societies necessarily presupposes that tradition can have no viable place in modernity. The result is to make a historical myth of both pre-modernity and post-traditionality, in a chronologically opposed before-and-after scenario where tradition is what came before and what exists now is a social formation characterised by its absence. Tradition may carry weightier meanings or be given greater value in different social and historical formations but, in one way or another, traditions are present in all societies. Tradition is not what happens in one kind of society and not in another.

To argue against tradition as a general component of human society and culture is to expound the thesis that modern societies have become detraditionalised (see Heelas, Lash and Morris, 1996). This fixes tradition as the totalised opposite of modernity. The thesis restrictively narrows down our understanding of modernity to a dehistoricised sense of *not that*, which is irrevocably relegated to the past, but *this*, in all its social and cultural separateness. We're then forced to think of tradition as always inherently stable over time, from one period to the next. This again obstructs our understanding of how traditions are historically motivated, moving in dialogue with changing historical situations and conditions, and in relation to different modes of temporality, all of which change over time. Tradition is not a pre-given, singular, unchanging, abstract cultural entity.

To invoke tradition for the purposes of the present always involves the paradox that translation and transformation of the past in the form of tradition is necessary for the sake of its contemporary relevance. The necessary refiguring of tradition may then threaten to destablise that which is invoked, and enhance its quality of elusiveness. Refiguring tradition requires the recognition of difference even as it tries to reconcile past and present. Any aspect of a tradition can become changed due to the way it is passed on and re-interpreted over time, even if this appears, at first glance, to be a highly localised performative use of tradition. To take another example from the field of blues and jazz, what counts is how a musical item both relates to the spirit of its tradition and creatively stretches it into something different. It is this which makes Cassandra Wilson's regeneration (and re-gendering) of Robert Johnson's 'Come On In My Kitchen' or Son House's 'Death Letter' so powerful and compelling.

Through such potential changes in its continuities tradition can provide opportunities for innovation. It is also the ongoing argument within a living tradition about the goods that count – which songs? which books? which buildings? which ideas? – that gives it its historical extension along with its contemporary social embodiment. In whatever ways they are advanced as being of value within the present, new potentialities are creatively drawn from the relations between its different temporal aspects and from the contemporary questions that are brought to bear on its meanings and practices.

The Re-creation of Tradition

Actively engaging with tradition involves a tension, felt as a result of the changed historical conditions and circumstances through which past cultural texts, forms and practices are negotiated. Too often, in modernist approaches to knowledge, this has been viewed negatively, as if the tension is necessarily the result of populist prejudice in favour of a selective, idealised past that contrasts with a deficient present. We want to argue that as a source of creative energy it can be a productive tension as well, historically constitutive of the negotiated relationship between inherited value and new potentialities. Whatever is transmitted in tradition requires the negotiation of this tension within the changing situations in which it is received and applied. While this is true of any perspective on tradition, a creative adaptation and transformation is involved when a tradition retains vitality across the generations and periods in which it has acquired its temporal span. The vitality of a tradition lies in its potential for being applied in different ways, for becoming adaptively suited to new situations and emergent sensibilities.

So in thinking about tradition we need to overcome the idea that it consists of a single chain of meanings and values extending back, link by link, into the past. This is an inaccurate way of understanding it because of the continual, reciprocal response of old and new upon each other, in a complex interaction of emergence and residue, loss and retention, condition and consequence.

Intelligibility is possible only in its coherence within tradition, but that doesn't mean that tradition is to be defined as a mere process of serial repetition. Intelligible order is grounded in tradition, but our understanding of it is possible because of, and not in spite of, temporal distance.

Tradition is never simply passed on across time. If this was true it would stand little chance of avoiding its dissolution at the restless hands of change. Instead, we should see tradition as involving an interplay of difference and similitude, continuity and change, encounter and distance. As such it is integral to the broader process of developing a historical understanding, which is embraced by changing temporal horizons and moves with them (Pickering, 1999). That is why, when tradition acts as the bridge between memory and imagination, meaning and value, theory and practice, it is a bridge that is always being built. It can never be completed for all time because time is always moving beyond that which it seeks to bridge.

To conceive tradition in this way means that traditions only remain vital when they are being re-created. This is where the recent emphasis given to the inventedness of national traditions and the more general use of the term 'invented traditions' is rather misleading. The coinage derives from a widely influential book, edited by Eric Hobsbawm and Terence Ranger, whose argument, backed up by various case studies, is that traditions which are held to be ancient are often recent, selective, fabricated and manipulative. In his introduction to the book, Hobsbawm emphasises the purpose of invented traditions as seeking 'to inculcate certain values and norms of behaviour by repetition', implying automatic continuity with 'a suitable historical past' which is 'largely fictitious': 'In short, they are responses to novel situations which take the form of reference to old situations, or which establish their own past by quasi-obligatory repetition' (1984: 1–2). Invented traditions are not characteristic of any particular epoch or social formation but, as Hobsbawm suggests, they are likely to become more frequent during times of rapid social change when relatively settled configurations of experience and action are disrupted, damaged or destroyed. As we've seen, such change is particularly associated with Western forms of modernity. While this shouldn't be taken as implying that older traditions, or traditions outside the West, were inflexible or haven't changed over time, invented traditions, nevertheless, cluster during the modern period (ibid.: 4–5).

Hobsbawm argues that the period from 1870 to 1914 in Europe was characterised by many mass-produced traditions which succeeded in proportion to their popular resonance. David Cannadine illustrates this in his documentation of the manufacture of British monarchical ritual and pageantry as largely the product of the late nineteenth and early twentieth centuries. The general phenomenon of newly formalised traditions is equally well demonstrated in other chapters. Hugh Trevor-Roper's chapter, for example, deals with the invention of the Highland cultural tradition in Scotland, particularly around its three instances of fabrication and forgery: the kilt, the tartan and the 'discovery' of a 'Celtic Homer' and 'ancient' epic literature in Ossian. But the thesis and its general line of argument and application raise definite problems, especially in thinking about invention in its more positive, yet equally modern relation to creativity.

In Hobsbawm's characterisation, a defining feature of invented traditions is their use of the past as 'a legitimator of action and cement of group cohesion' (ibid.: 12). In some way or another, this is characteristic of all traditions in their past–present relations. It's also close to Marshal Sahlins's description of culture as 'the organisation of the current situation in terms of a past' (1985: 155). So what is especially distinctive about invented traditions? Although it is clear that they are defined by being recent, formally contrived and often used by powerful elites as a deliberate and compelling form of cultural management, their boundaries are considerably blurred in places. As 'exercises in social engineering' (Hobsbawm and Ranger, 1984: 13), they seem especially well-suited to nationalism and the construction of national cultures, the state-orchestrated rallies and ceremonials of National Socialism being an obvious example. Yet, as well as noting three overlapping types of invented tradition associated with social cohesion, institutional legitimation and forms of social inculcation, Hobsbawm refers to small-scale, informal, less public and less spectacular traditions as invented or partly invented (ibid.: 4, 9). These important analytical distinctions demand some kind of typological organisation, yet none is offered. The term 'invented traditions' also implies the existence of 'genuine' traditions, and indeed Hobsbawm acknowledges that 'the strength and adaptability of genuine traditions is not to be confused with the "invention of tradition"' (ibid.: 8). The problem is then a failure not only to differentiate fully enough among various distinct forms of invented tradition, but also to establish clearly what distinguishes genuine and invented traditions. The unfortunate consequence of both shortcomings is to reinforce the modernist prejudice against tradition as a general category, regardless of the lineage, character and credentials of any particular example.

As a historian of nationalism and nationalist movements, Hobsbawm's main line of interest is in the ideological uses of invented traditions and their associated cultural constructs (see, for example, Hobsbawm, 1997). The general thesis of inventedness is particularly effective in demystifying such uses as, for example, in showing how the notion of national tradition, based on an essentialised, deep-lying pattern of cultural heritage and stock, entails entrenched social myths that conceal time-bound forms of power relations and set up barriers to creative adaptation and change. Yet to insist too much on the construction of national identities, and the contrived inventedness of traditions in the establishment of national cultures, is to sound a clear echo of the binaries of classical sociology, thus polarising genuine and invented traditions where distinctions are far more vague and ambiguous. Such polarisation makes it difficult to dissociate officially codified traditions from how social memory informs a much broader range of cultural rituals and practices.

The analytical bluntness of a pejorative emphasis on invention serves to blur the blending of innovation and tradition which renders the term problematic. Hobsbawm is also a historian of jazz music, which has been transformed from a local idiom into many new styles and subforms as it has spread out over time and space since its initial formation in the southern United States during the late nineteenth/early twentieth century period (Hobsbawm, 1961). As we have seen in its relations with the blues, jazz can hardly be characterised as an invented tradition in the same way as the nationalist cases which clearly exemplify the category. Bhangra, a fusion of Western popular musical styles and Punjabi folk music, provides another musical example emerging from the experience of migration. Bhangra is both invention *and* tradition in its celebration of inherited Punjabi musical forms blended with reinscriptions of 'new, locally significant forms of meaning' which resonate with very specific diasporic experiences for Asian ethnic minority groups resident in various different parts of the world (Bennett, 2000: 111).

The pejorative sense of the invention of tradition also implies manipulation and mystification and should not be taken as characteristic of traditions in general. It is quite different to the inventive re-creation of tradition which is our concern in this chapter, and shouldn't be run together with it in an easy conflation. If we confuse inventedness with renewal we can inadvertently dismiss the imaginative engagement which people make with various cultural traditions, regardless of their aesthetic ranking. Artistic and cultural forms associated with tradition may speak to certain deep, perhaps only half-conscious feelings about experience or an existential sense of the worlds in which people live. This is quite tangible in the endurance of nursery rhymes, which work more through their rhythms, sounds, gestures and rituals than their semantic lyrical content, and fairy tales, which continue to provide a means of dealing with submerged human anxieties and hopes for a better world, linking the past and present to the not-yet-become (Bloch, 1988; Zipes, 1995).

While artistic forms – from the apparently most simple of children's chants to the seemingly most challenging of modernist music and art – may be manipulated by nationalism or political and religious creeds for their own ends, they are distinct from those ends even if their power to move people helps to make their manipulation effective. Hobsbawm is aware of this as, for instance, when he acknowledges that the most successful examples of invented traditions used for manipulative ends 'are those which exploit practices which clearly meet a felt – not necessarily a clearly understood – need among particular bodies of people', one example being German nationalism during the

Second Empire (Hobsbawm and Ranger, 1984: 307). Even so, invented traditions in the sense preferred by Hobsbawm assume the production of forms of collective delusion. This implies the presence of a historian or social theorist who can see through the delusion and never fall prey to such manipulation themselves. Their professional credentials in this respect are burnished by their selective use of evidence proving the duplicity of invented traditions, and by their supposition, based on virtually no empirical research or secondary evidence, that the public are readily seduced by this duplicity. In this respect, the 'invention of tradition' thesis is reminiscent of early twentieth-century mass culture critique. In its loose and generalised extensions, it has appeared as a strong throwback to such critique.

Even where this is not actually the case, the politics of representation can make it appear as such. During the early 1990s, considerable controversy was stirred up in Aotearoa/New Zealand by the press reporting of an article by a North American anthropologist, Allan Hanson (1989). For example, one front-page headline read: 'US Expert Says Maori Culture Invented' (*The Dominion* (Wellington), 24 February 1990: 1). The main import of the news story was that Maori cultural tradition, which is central to their identity and history, was invented by European colonialists in the nineteenth century, and that much of this invented material had been retained over the subsequent period. Discussion of this in the country at the time was understandably hostile. Maori scholars were angry with what was taken as a claim of inauthenticity since, not unreasonably, they understood 'invented' not in the modernist aesthetic sense of 'make it new', but as denoting falsehood and contrivance. Although newspaper coverage of the article noted that Hanson 'did not seek to denigrate Maori culture' or castigate it as inauthentic, it was felt that criticising that culture as 'invented' for political purposes, in order to enhance the assimilation of the Maoris by white settlers, nevertheless undermined Maori pride in their cultural distinctiveness, and weakened the basis of Maori land claims in the sesquicentennial anniversary of the Treaty of Waitangi. The charge of 'invention' seemed yet another piece of reactionary white revisionism in the face of Maoritanga (Maoriness). The historian Ranginui Walker pointed out that in any case Hanson's article was based on white settler writings, and didn't take into account Maori oral traditions, which were 'harboured in maraes hidden from early Pakeha view' (ibid.).

It was only on a subsequent reading of Hanson's journal article that the extent of press simplification became obvious. Academic and journalistic discourse concerning issues of 'authenticity' and 'invention' were widely divergent. As was the case with Maori cultural tradition, this can have unfortunate consequences, for 'invention' is clearly a double-edged blade: it can cut into both subaltern forms of cultural inheritance and resistance as well as the chicanery of powerful governing elites. Since it can, it calls into question the role of the outsider imposing the 'invention of tradition' thesis on indigenous peoples and their cultures. To what, by whom, and why is the thesis being applied? The anthropologist Marshall Sahlins offers a wry commentary on these questions in noting how, in the fifteenth and sixteenth centuries, 'a bunch of indigenous intellectuals and artists in Europe got together and began inventing their traditions and themselves by attempting to revive the learning of an ancient culture' and practising 'the classical virtues'. In reconstructing 'a past that was effectively irrecoverable', they 'created a self-conscious tradition of fixed and essentialised canons':

> They wrote history in the style of Livy, verses in a mannered Latin, tragedy according to Seneca and comedy according to Terence; they decorated Christian temples with the facades of classical temples and generally followed the precepts of Roman architecture as set down by Vitruvius – without realising these precepts were Greek. All this came to be called the Renaissance in European history, because it gave birth to 'modern civilisation'.

Sahlins then asks: 'What else can one say about it, except that some people have all the historical luck?' and adds, with a final comic twist: 'On the other hand, the historical lesson could be that all is not lost' (Sahlins, 2002: 3–5).

While this sketch of the Renaissance as 'invented tradition' is partly spoof, it is also deadly serious in what it says about the politics of postcolonial interpretation, whether these apply to Pacific cultures or elsewhere. These politics have been played out across the whole period of European colonial encounter and domination, often around the very conception of tradition. Nicholas Thomas has clearly identified the discrepancies between understandings of tradition among rural people in contemporary Oceania and western representations of tribal tradition. He refers to a modernity-and-tradition model being imposed on the Fijians, producing a 'thatched versus corrugated tin roofs' view of the apparent corrosion of tradition, whereas the concern for tradition among the Fijians is with social practice, values and ethics. Such tradition isn't timeless. It has changed radically over the past 150 years or so, partly as a result of colonial rule, partly as a result of opposition to the former British regime. Thomas writes that it would be quite wrong to infer from this transformation in modern times 'that contemporary rural Fijian life is not traditional', and adds: 'now customs conceived as such really do regulate social life, and, in fact, it is much more traditional than it could have been before' (Thomas, 1997: 182–3).

So, in modern Fiji, as a creative response to historical change, rural culture and identity have become, extensively and intensively, more traditional rather than less. This reactive process has to be understood in terms of interaction and self-fashioning in the face of difference: 'the process of choosing emblematic activities, dispositions, or material artefacts is indissociable from a history of encounters and what is at issue in those particular encounters' (ibid.: 187). Yet where indigenous tradition has been reified, responses to this may be negative or ambivalent as well as positive. The objectification of tradition 'is best understood not as crude fabrication or invention, but as an imaginative process in which Fijians creatively refashioned the relationships that they had the opportunity to articulate' (ibid.: 200). At the same time, 'the fact of articulation always permitted a rejection of what was customary in favour of its antithesis: this is what can be described as the negation of tradition', or as 'an indigenous modernism that repudiated the custom-bound past and various forms of obligation and constraint that epitomised it' (ibid.: 202). The invented tradition model is too blunt to be able to capture the intricate relations of this kind of cultural dynamism. As Thomas shows, we need a more sophisticated analysis of tradition if we're going to grasp how it 'can be acted upon or deployed to diverse ends' (ibid.: 208).

More broadly than this, the crudity of the invention of tradition thesis, the uncritical acceptance of it as a pioneering intervention, and its routine incantation in some writings about the modern mass media, reveal a widespread misconception of tradition and how it operates. It is easy enough to see that traditions have been used ideologically, but this does not mean that all traditions are a manipulative sham. This would be quite absurd, and yet the drift of much subsequent discussion, following the initial publication of Hobsbawn and Ranger's edited collection, has certainly moved towards this assumption. In doing this it has taken its cue from the one-sidedness of the invention of tradition thesis, the critique of manufactured continuities with a mythical past and the assumption that the public believes and buys into it. As Jonathan Friedman has remarked: 'If all culture is invention then there is nothing with which to compare a particular cultural product, no authentic foundation. It implies a serious contradiction between the often asserted commonality of cultural creativity and a discourse that consistently attributes inauthenticity to modern cultural products' (1996: 145). In its critical one-sidedness, the thesis is relentlessly modernist: secular, rationalist, objectivist, and based on a dichotomous opposition between the represented and the real. To quote Friedman again: 'it divides the world of representation into objective truth vs folk or ideological models of the world' (ibid.: 136). This divisive approach, with the clarity of exposition on one side and the opacity of delusion on the other, evades the enduring appeal of tradition and forms of cultural practice oriented towards this particular relation with the past.

So, for example, folk music in Europe and the United States is recreated tradition and would have little continuing value if this were not the case. Its meanings have been mediated by collectors and scholars with preconceptions and beliefs about the value of the music that has not necessarily been that of vernacular singers and musicians, but this dissonance is of critical importance. It shouldn't be taken as implying the same political functionality as a state ceremony or royal ritual invented *as* tradition. As tradition, folk music is not made up out of completely fabricated items even if it attempts to fix the relations of music, history and place. This particular example illustrates the dangers of the way the 'invented tradition' thesis has been taken up, not only in history but also in adjacent disciplines like anthropology and geography.

In an overview of the cultural geography of music, John Connell and Chris Gibson (2003: 37) compare the first English folk music revival of the late nineteenth/early twentieth century to English church bell ringing. They say both were seen as providing authentic sources of a medieval past. We may agree with them that this is plain nonsense, but not with their verdict that both folk music and bell ringing are invented traditions. The reasons they give for this are that their contemporary forms are different to those of two centuries ago and that 'their symbolic significance' has been 'revived and enhanced' over the past hundred years. Quite so, but this is because they are living traditions, not invented ones. The distinction is crucial, for it is in the nature of traditions that they change, are revived and enhanced, if they're to remain creatively effective and relevant to a changed present. It should also be emphasised that reducing such music to its ideological components, which is precisely the critical tendency encouraged by 'invention' as an explanatory model, is to ignore or dismiss its affective and imaginative appeal for many people. Such appeal cannot be understood simply as sentimentalism or idealisation, and though it may involve these as aspects of its production and reception, a critical understanding of folk music requires more than the exposition of its inventedness as tradition. It requires understanding how music is bound up in the complex relations between tradition and modernity, and micro- and macro-cultural worlds.

If the rhetoric of 'invention' conceals a more subtle process of institutionalisation and ritualisation and responses to it, we must recognise both the diverse interpretations possible within any tradition, and the phenomenon of cultural tradition in its pluralised manifestations, ranging from small-scale vernacular to grand-scale national traditions along with everything in between. It is only in the pluralised sense of the term that we can hope to reconcile tradition, memory and imagination as mutually dependent resources for creative practice. We need to contest notions of tradition as singular and univocal, and to see tradition in the plural not just with respect to different traditions, but to any one tradition in itself. As Hans-Georg Gadamer once put it: 'Our historical consciousness is always filled with a variety of voices in which the echo of the past is heard. Only in the multifariousness of such voices does it exist: this constitutes the nature of the tradition in which we want to share and have a part' (Gadamer, 1996: 284).

To see tradition only through one particular optic has always led to a distorted view. So with the optic of inventedness, for this ignores the ways in which traditions can operate as enabling frameworks through which present action is co-ordinated. Tradition fore-structures our understanding and provides an initiating basis for interpretation and evaluation of what we encounter and experience in the world. It is an intrinsic part of our temporal make-up, even as we critically turn against it or accept it with reservation or modification. This is why it's important to insist that traditions are not simply about the transmission of past cultural content into an acquiescent present. Particularly when most vibrant, traditions are always in the process of being recreated – or, if you like, reinvented, but without the pejorative connotations which have now come to adhere to invention in its connection with tradition. They are subject to evaluation and discrimination in terms of what they bring to a contemporary situation. Living traditions are not static but always temporally in movement, always in the process of being reshaped in adaptation to the present.

By definition, innovation alters what is already established. Bringing existing cultural elements together in a different arrangement to any witnessed before necessarily changes them. But the generation of new elements or combinations can only be recognised as new in relation to what has come before or what exists in some previous arrangement of codes, conventions, styles and practices, either within or across particular cultural formations. If this wasn't the case we wouldn't be able to assess whether anything novel is superficial or false, at least on any demonstrable grounds. We could only take innovation on its own face value and, of course, in practice we don't do that at all. It's because we look both ways when we evaluate any innovation, at what has been altered and how the alteration exceeds existing limits and limitations, that we operate with a sense of the interplay between continuity and change. However tacit our awareness of this sense in the heat of any evaluative practice, we know clearly enough that, in the longer term, processes of change are structured by patterns of continuity, and that we can only understand such patterns precisely through the ways things change, and exist, in historical movement.

We noted earlier that the creative mind can only be original on the basis of some existing tradition, yet critical value is often excessively loaded on the sense of originality. The paradox of valuing creativity for its originality is that such a quality would make it incapable of being understood. If, alternatively, originality is viewed as a matter of degree, it then loses whatever makes it distinctive as an identifiable quality. To say of some artwork that it has 'flashes of originality' is hardly an expression of unreserved approval. Indeed, such an evaluative description may herald the delivery of a more thoroughly negative judgement as, for instance, of dull conformity or lack of adventure. Evaluations of originality emphasise singularity, difference and discontinuity rather than similarity, commonality and continuity. Despite coming under critical attack over the past half century, originality is, in common judgement, a positive quality, whether this is Andrew Rissik's encomium on Paul McCartney's 'genius for song, for seamless melodic originality' (*The Guardian*, 4 November 2000: 8), or Precious Williams's praise for a Wu Tang Clan's album's 'breathtaking originality' (*The Guardian*, 17 November 2000: 8).

It is quite another matter when it comes to seeing something as stylistically hackneyed or outworn, as for example when Arthur Smith criticised the creators of the television series, *The Sopranos*, as being unable to 'disguise the stunning lack of originality of its basic concept' (*The Guardian*, 29 November 2000: 15), for here the aesthetic judgement is comparative. Total originality is incomparable because it may be unrecognisable. The very idea of it seems almost to demand the critical irony displayed by the film critic, Philip French, in writing that 'Woody Allen, one of the greatest living filmmakers and among the few whose new movies I eagerly await, has rarely made a picture tainted by total originality' (*The Observer*, 3 December 2000: 7).

An absolute sense of originality is the opposite pole to the Burkean sense of tradition as dying or dead. We don't need to fall back on a conservative defence of tradition in order to distrust the hyper-individualism of claims to originality. As we've argued earlier, written or spoken narratives in their communication of experience rely on a language which exists before and after them, and is always a public medium and resource. Any quality of newness such narratives may have is achieved through seeing what can be done with existing conventions that have been established by past usage, often within a particular tradition of storytelling or literary writing. The problem with claims of originality is when they are grand, not modest. They aspire to being definitive in their newness, yet if anything was completely original it would quite simply be unintelligible. Creativity ranges from cultural variation and counterstatement to abrupt breaks and fresh starts, but these are never absolute or total.

Creativity involves learning from what has been done in the past and learning how to take from it what can be used in the present, which thereby changes it. This reinforces our opening point that creativity does not come out of a void, and the supplementary point to which it leads, which is that talent requires a tradition. The generation of creativity through resistance to a tradition still requires knowledge of that tradition. Cultural resistance is informed by, and at least in part derives its meaning from, the tradition it seeks to transcend. There is nothing particularly new about knowing this. Hegel made the point long ago in saying that 'even if the talent and genius of the artist has in it a natural element, yet this element essentially requires development by thought, reflection on the mode of its productivity, and practice and skill in producing' (1975: 27). Cultural creativity comes with practice and the learning of certain skills, with development by thought and reflexive thinking about its modes of practice, its set parameters, its unconsidered conditions and possibilities. These can only be realised by exploring how a changed present affects a tradition and how a tradition affects a changing present.

Although the meanings and values which we find in artworks and cultural products operate in specific fields of production and performance and draw on definite genre codes and social conventions, the achievement of their communicative value implies a potential to exceed their local and immediate conditions of production. As Georgia Warnke has observed, 'cultures and traditions survive and flourish not by enforcing an endless and exact reproduction but by developing and enriching themselves and by remaining relevant to new generations' (Warnke, 1995: 139–40). Internal development, enrichment from other sources and a sense of remaining relevance depend on dialogue with difference as much as on a connection with changing times. A relentlessly backwards view insists only on continuity where there is also adaptation and extension, and a relentlessly forward view insists only on change where there is also continuity and enhanced persistence. Both views are limited.

Traditions always bear the imprint of historical time, both in what they bring from the past and how they are received in the present. Attempts at formally institutionalising existing practices as a repeatable ritual can certainly be found in various times and places. This is the kind of activity which Hobsbawm and Ranger emphasise and are primarily concerned with in their invention of tradition thesis. But it is not just formal invention that is the problem. Thinking about tradition is also difficult because it is an incessant victim of reification. So, for instance, the reduction of living traditions to an unambiguous set of received rituals can be heard in much popular, classical and world music. The many, varied, sounds that might be associated with the long musical lives of the cities of Vienna or Miami or Liverpool or Nashville – or the numerous styles that have been performed in the culturally diverse regions of Africa – are all reduced to a narrow repertoire of instrumental styles, rhythms, vocal inflections and sonic mannerisms. These are then presented and re-presented, on CDs, radio broadcasts, in magazine articles, in television programmes. In turn, they are adopted by musicians and come to be used and re-used, in a quite self-conscious way.

At the same time, audiences are encouraged to recognise these musical signifiers. This is exploited in the marketing of certain types of European classical music, in the promotion of electronic dance music and in the selling of world music. The unambiguous equation of a type of music with a specific tradition is limiting. It constrains our understanding of the meaning and movement of music in a manner very similar to that which Adorno identified in his discussion of cultural commodification earlier in the twentieth century. Adorno remarked upon how the culture industry encourages listeners to respond to music in terms of a narrow series of refrains and easily recognised, de-contexualised and abstracted 'trade marks'. The opening of a Beethoven symphony, for example, or the key moments from an opera, become something to be registered in a distracted manner before moving on to the next sight or sound. Traditions have certainly been rationalised and routinised in this way, particularly when seeking to attract tourists, visitors and advertisers. We can see and hear this in the construction of entertaining spectacles, such as when battles from the English Civil War are re-enacted, or when the Mardi Gras is celebrated in New Orleans. We can also detect it in the way that the public are encouraged to visit Dickens's London, take a trail around Mozart's Vienna or Picasso's Paris, followed by some Latin music, African dancing or Indian food. But, even here, these experiences are not simply inauthentic and falsely contrived. In some small way they always refer to the historical tradition from which they have been adapted, even if middle-class connoisseurs might aspire to a highly discerning approach and seek what is thought to be truly authentic cuisine or truly authentic forms of dance or music during their nights out.

In contrast to these strongly marked but never entirely successful tendencies to abstract, reify and package tradition, there is our experience of coming into contact with more ambiguous and less easily coded traditions and the myriad meanings and identities they generate for diverse groups of people. Kofi Agawu provides intimations of such encounters with multiple traditions when he makes an important point about considering sameness alongside questions of difference. He calls for an approach which can 'facilitate a better understanding of the peculiar juxtapositions of cultural practices that define modern Africa. It would explain how a Sierra Leonean, Nigerian, or Ghanaian can be equally moved by a hymn, a traditional dance, a local proverb, a quotation from Shakespeare, a piece of reggae, the Wedding March, and the latest Highlife music...' (2003: 235). Similarly, we may be moved by an Appalachian string band, qawwali or contemporary fado. It can be these types of encounters which provide the most exhilarating conditions for dialogue between difference and sameness, making connections with changing times and places. The vantage point it gives helps us appreciate how living traditions are often unstable and at times likely to change dramatically in character.

These two experiences of tradition – the reductively ritual and the ambivalent and unstable dialogic – should not be elided, but neither should they be treated as discrete entities. We cannot simply treat traditions as unambiguously invented and fast-frozen, nor treat them as distinct from other forms and experiences of tradition that are assumed to be more authentic, radical or in tune with lived realities. Traditions are simultaneously lived and (re)invented. Any institutional attempt to produce an unambiguous single representation will always be subject to critical assessment, reappraisal, reinterpretation and creative appropriation. This is why authoritarian states have had so many problems enforcing their singular and partial versions of national symbols, heroes and narratives. An avant-garde or radical aversion to tradition as a dead weight to be thrown off, and a conservative reverence for tradition as fixed and sacrosanct, are equally misleading. Such melancholic stances are ultimately futile in the face of how creative practice continually draws upon, transforms and animates the living spirit of tradition.

Division

As creativity has acquired its modern meanings, it has become associated with beliefs that can be construed as both elitist and essentialist. Elitist conceptions of creativity assume that only some people have the potential to be or become creative and only certain forms of creativity really matter, whilst essentialist assumptions lead to beliefs that certain types of creativity are a natural gift of biological or social inheritance.

Elitist conceptions have been pervasive in the western art tradition. Social and ideological divisions have separated groups of people even as the divisions themselves have been grappled with as points of departure for re-defining the practice and meaning of creative activity. It is here that the figure of the white, middle-class, European male becomes both stereotype and symbol of a set of questions about access, attribution and canonisation.

Essentialist assumptions about creativity have often been signalled in the use of such terms as black music, working-class or primitive art, women's fiction and Indian film. Such categories can be just as exclusive, assuming correspondences between people and creative forms. When successful, these attributions have exerted considerable power over how creativity has been conceived within different artistic areas, and informed judgements about who is capable of being recognised as a legitimate creator. They have impeded the black pianist wishing to stage an opera or play in a symphony orchestra, the woman wishing to be more than a muse to painters or composers, and the middle-class white European male wishing to play blues, jazz or hip hop.

A central feature of its modern history has involved contesting these essentialist and elitist understandings of creativity, showing how creativity does not respect social divisions and yet how such divisions have obstructed and obscured certain creative forms and practices that do not conform to attempts at fixed definition and privileged attribution. This has not been easy, and the reappraisal of the dynamics, characteristics and meaning of creativity is – as we hope we have made clear by now – a continuing process. Social living entails the continual confrontation of various divisions, attempts to overcome them, and – often despite the best intentions of those involved – the production of yet new divisions. Creativity is shaped by divisions, continually generates a process of overcoming them, and has been complicit in the perpetuation of divisions in social life.

In thinking about creativity and social divisions we need to be aware of how barriers, borders and the bridges across them assume a specific character in different places. For example, any discussion of African-American, Anglo-American and Latino/a forms of expression, along with their relationship to questions of class, race and national identity in, say, Japan, might reach quite different conclusions than studies in the United States, Britain or Africa. A performance in black face, once unambiguously perceived as a racist act, might be interpreted as a subaltern and working-class repudiation of bourgeois norms and values in the US in the nineteenth century, a display of imperialist superiority in Britain at the turn of the twentieth century, a nationalist, anti-colonial commentary in early twentieth century Egypt, an irreverent blend of cultural influences in West African concert parties during the middle decades of the twentieth century, but an ambivalent debt to black America combined with a search for a sense of Japaneseness in a globalising world in Japan during the latter half of the twentieth century (see Lott, 1993; Pickering, 1997a; Troutt Powell, 2003; Cole, 1996; Hosokawa, 2002). To consider such variations of form and cultural politics should alert us to the international or global dynamics through which certain old barriers are broken and divisions crossed, while new ones are created and reinforced.

In seeking to emphasise, albeit selectively, how a focus on the issues of social divisions can assist our understanding of the dynamics of creativity, we structure our discussion around three sets of issues. First is the way that the institutionalisation of social divisions has acted to inhibit and deny certain creative opportunities to specific groups and individuals. Second are a set of questions about whether these social divisions might imply certain different forms of creativity. Third is the question of how movement out from and dialogue across social divisions becomes possible, along with the range of tensions entailed in its facilitation of creative transformations.

Access and Attribution

In order to be recognised as a legitimate cultural producer within the European high art tradition it has been, and still is, necessary to acquire an education which provides a specific set of craft skills along with a particular type of aesthetic disposition that is mobilised when allocating value to a selective canon of art works. This is a point Pierre Bourdieu repeatedly emphasised and demonstrated exhaustively in his numerous writings on discrimination and aesthetic taste, education and the reproduction of belief, which in turn inform the struggles that constitute the fields of cultural production. Bourdieu has featured earlier in this book, and one of the key points we have taken from his research is his argument that the consecrated arts have not been open to everyone, while access has always been available to those from particular privileged backgrounds. The possibility of achieving a dominant or influential position within officially accredited fields of cultural production is informed by the ability to gain access to and accrue economic, political and cultural capital.

Hence from Bourdieu in particular (although others have also made this point) we can recognise that aspiration, ability and the will to write poetry, compose music or produce ideas is simply not enough. If the person involved is to achieve a significant place within the world of art and letters and deemed to be a recognised cultural producer occupying a legitimate position, they will require considerably more than simply raw talent. Economic power and political influence may help, but what is crucial is the ability to make use of the influence afforded by the accumulation of cultural capital – the repertoire of artistic knowledge, values, beliefs and information – and command over its application, which is necessary for the artist to gain entry into the social circles and settings required for artistic recognition. Thomas Hardy wrote of the plight of an autodidact, or self-taught, stonemason in his novel *Jude the Obscure*, set in late-nineteenth-century Britain. Jude undertook an intense process of self-education with the dream of being able to study and discuss ideas in Christminster (Oxford):

> It was not till now, when he found himself actually on the spot of his enthusiasm, that Jude perceived how far away from the object of that enthusiasm he really was. Only a wall divided him from those happy young contemporaries of his with whom he shared a common mental life; men who had nothing to do from morning till night but to read, mark, learn, and inwardly digest. Only a wall – but what a wall!

> Every day, every hour, as he went in search of labour, he saw them going and coming also, rubbed shoulders with them, heard their voices, marked their movements. The conversation of some of the more thoughtful among them seemed oftentimes, owing to his long and persistent preparation for this place, to be peculiarly akin to his own thoughts. Yet he was as far from them as if he had been in the antipodes. Of course he was. He was a young workman in a white blouse, and with stone-dust in the creases of his clothes; and in passing him they did not even see him, or hear him, rather saw through him as through a pane of glass at their familiars beyond. Whatever they were to him, he to them was not on the spot at all; and yet he fancied he would be close to their lives by coming there. (Hardy, 1929: 102)

If social class is an obvious barrier, we should immediately note that this makes Jude socially invisible to other men, the gowned university students and dons with whom he shares an incommunicable affinity. Hardy was acutely aware of the limitations placed upon working-class men with artistic and intellectual ambitions, but the gulf between manual labour and scholarly pursuits registered in this quotation is one between classed men, not between men and women, whether across the class divide or within a particular class. The whole question of creativity has been riven not only by class but also by gender.

The social categories of gender and social class intersect in various ways, and while historically they have defined the denials and limits of creativity, these are not simply imposed from outside. They can be internalised as part of who people believe they are or are able to become. So, for example, working-class men in the late nineteenth and early twentieth centuries had at times to hide their interest in music, literature or painting if they were to avoid the attribution of effeminacy. Although employed as a colliery blacksmith, Sid Chaplin, from the north-east of England, had to write under pseudonyms during the three years of his mining apprenticeship and make his writing 'a secret occupation' because it was regarded as 'somehow feminine'. A working man's masculine identity in the pit communities of Northumberland and Durham was founded in 'his muscular strength and ability, or agility', whereas 'writing was very effeminate, so I said nothing about it'. Here, class and gender in their internalised combination were experienced as obstacles to Chaplin's aspirations. Even as a closely guarded clandestine activity, his writing involved 'a terrible jump' in his cultural expectations and self-identity: 'I think I went to the pillar box about six times before I parted with my first piece, and then I felt rather relieved when I never heard about it again' (Pickering and Robins, 1984: 143). The relief was not only to do with feelings of self-worth, but also with the anxiety that if found out, he'd be stuck with the attribution of effeminacy.

The struggles of working-class autodidacts in the era of industrial capitalism were, of course, largely male struggles, but middle-class women faced equally difficult obstacles in their aspirations to creative expression. Here we confront the gendering of creativity itself. If writing poetry or short stories was 'somehow feminine' for working-class men, somewhat paradoxically, across class lines during the same era, creativity as a middle-class cultural value became increasingly male-oriented. In the early nineteenth century, for example, the poet Robert Southey declared that 'literature is not the business of a woman's life, and cannot be', while, for Gerald Manley Hopkins in the late nineteenth century, 'the male quality is the creative gift' (cited in Gilbert and Gubar, 1984: 3, 8). Masculinising the arts reduced the threat of their association with femininity and effeminacy, and by the time of modernism the exclusion of women from literary and musical creativity was highly advanced (see, for example, McClary, 1991: 17–18; Citron, 2000: 50). This didn't mean that middle-class women in the nineteenth and early twentieth centuries ceased to produce art or engage in cultural production. But it did mean that they were barred from various cultural institutions because of their gender, with only a token few being included as honorary members or granted occasional participation as guests of men. A deeper injury was that their engagement in writing, painting or composing entailed risks to their moral reputation and social standing. A woman's artistic creations were treated as if gender made a crucial difference to her identity and the value of what she produced.

In Britain, the assumed difference in the identity and value of women's involvement in artistic and cultural practice stemmed from the stereotypical ideal of femininity prevalent in the Victorian and Edwardian periods. This ideal, whose repudiation has required over a century of struggle, placed women tendentiously in positions of peripheral support and appreciation rather than of dynamic involvement in the creative practices that were held in greatest esteem. The social critic and writer on art and architecture, John Ruskin, encapsulated the ideal in his lecture 'Of Queens' Gardens':

> The man's power is active, progressive, defensive. He is eminently the doer, the creator, the discoverer, the defender. His intellect is for speculation and invention… [Woman's intellect] is not for invention and creation, but for sweet ordering, arrangement, and decision. She sees the qualities of things, their claims, and their places. Her greatest function is Praise: she enters into no contest, but infallibly adjudges the crown of contest. (Ruskin, 1907: 135–6)

This was not the only view of women's place and function: Mary Wollstonecraft and John Stuart Mill, for example, represent alternative, early feminist conceptions of gender difference. But the Ruskinian ideal was strongly echoed by others – Thomas Carlyle considered a woman's purpose in life to be 'a beautiful reflex' of her man – and its influence was enormous, with cultural institutions and practices playing a considerable part in its power and reach (Wolff, 1990: 16–18). The Ruskinian ideal was closely related to the dichotomy of male/public and female/private realms and the celebration of domesticity as a cherished haven in a tempestuous world. The stereotypical 'angel in the house' – in Coventry Patmore's famous phrase – was the saint at the centre of this haven, with her binary counterpart, the whore or 'fallen woman', banished to the street outside (Patmore, 1885; see also Christ, 1977). Whether as Dora Spenlow or Agnes Wickfield in Dickens's *David Copperfield*, Esther Summerson in Dickens's *Bleak House*, or Rosie Mackenzie in Thackeray's *The Newcomes*, 'the angel in the house' was intended as the epitome of moral refinement, spiritual grace and physical virtue, the domestic exemplar and guardian of traditional values in a rapidly changing industrial age – one whose main role in life was to support men and endorse all they did: 'Man must be pleased; but him to please is woman's pleasure' (Patmore, 1885: 73).

The biological essentialism of this gender model, and its accompanying notion of men and women belonging to separate spheres, relegated women's creative practices to certain lower-grade genres and to domestic activities such as needlework or piano playing. Yet, paradoxically, piano playing provided women with the opportunity to demonstrate a high level of artistic accomplishment by playing solos or accompanying themselves singing, certainly within the bourgeois home. Piano lessons became part of a young woman's education and women became central to a middle-class piano culture that developed in Europe during the late eighteenth century, with publishers producing a considerable amount of sheet music for the 'female market of amateur players' (Parakilas, 2001). However, while all but one of Haydn's keyboard works were dedicated to women pianists, and several of Mozart's piano sonatas and concertos were tailored to the female pianists he had in mind when composing, 'the piano concerto's identification with virtuosity and public performance eventually assured its status as a vehicle for the male professional – most often the composer himself' (Parakilas, 2001: 87).

Over time, creative virtuosity became increasingly a male preserve. With painting, for example, women became confined within particular genres such as portraiture, landscapes and still-lives – flower painting being one of the most common 'female accomplishments' – and usually exhibited as amateurs rather than as artists (Wolff, 1990: 24–5; see also Seed, 1988). One reason for this restricted subject matter was the exclusion of women from the study of anatomy (women were not allowed access to life classes and so denied the opportunity to learn the techniques of painting nude models). These techniques were a prerequisite of being able to produce history painting, commonly regarded as among the noblest of fine art genres in the early nineteenth century and based on the representation of human figures in historical, mythological or biblical settings. As Marcia Citron has noted, women's exclusion from access to the nude (male and female) resembled their exclusion from classes in music theory and orchestration, and 'this at a time when music was valued for its complexity and size' (2000: 61). With fine art, though, the problems of discrimination and restriction were compounded by the expanded painterly representation of the female nude from the late eighteenth century, so that women were present as an image, 'with the specific connotations of body and nature, that is passive, available, possessable, powerless', while men were absent from the image but dominant in discourse, point of view and social position (Parker and Pollock, 1981: 116).

The domestic ideology of the period, along with the bourgeois expectation that women (or rather, ladies) should not participate in what Ruskin called man's 'rough work in the open world' (1907: 136), meant that women became associated primarily with the decorative or 'lesser' arts, and so dissociated from what had become elevated into the 'greater' arts of architecture and sculpture and the 'higher' genres of visual art. William Morris was one of the few to rail against this greater/lesser, high/low dichotomy, though more from a political objection to the consequent downgrading of the popular arts rather than from a perspective in gender politics (see, for example, Morris, 1979: 31–56). These aesthetic confinements and dissociations were part of the broader ideology of sexual difference and the gendered demarcation of social role and place which developed out of industrialism and were later consolidated by the spread of suburbia, and the growth of male-dominated bureaucracies and professions. Sean Nixon's (2003) research, completed in London during the 1990s, would suggest that such assumptions about men and women were still pervasive in the 'cult of creativity' which informed the recruitment, management and rewarding of advertising practitioners at the end of the twentieth century.

While this was always a complex, partial and never complete series of divisions (see, for example, Davidoff and Hall, 1997; also Hall, 1981), gender barriers were nevertheless pervasive and extended, in greater or lesser degree, up and down the social scale. They were not simply reproduced, directly or passively, in the creative practices of men and women, but they certainly exerted a considerable influence over what was regarded as proper and appropriate in those practices. Creativity became associated particularly with men – the doers, the discovers, the inventors – while the opportunities for creative work for women were both fewer than for men, and hedged about with constraints, as was the case with nineteenth century women writers: 'women through most of the nineteenth century were barred from the universities, isolated in their own homes, chaperoned in travel, painfully restricted in friendship. The personal give-and-take of the literary life was closed to them' (Moers, 1977: 64).

The broad, if never complete, establishment of creativity as male, particularly in the mid-nineteenth to mid-twentieth century period, was a major strand in the development of the secularised conception of creativity which we have dealt with in this book. The problems of attribution and access to which it led for women's art and women's cultural practice were nevertheless rooted in various religious assumptions and values within the Judeo-Christian tradition, where a primary gender was asserted right from the beginning. A male God was Lord of all creation, and man was created in God's image. In other traditions, such as Mayan, African and ancient Greek cosmologies, fertility and the creation of life were symbolised by female deities, but in western cultures it was men who inherited God's mantle of creativity:

'I said it was impossible for a woman to become an artist – I mean a *great* artist. Have you ever thought what that term implies? Not only a painter but a poet; a man of learning, of reading, of observation. A gentleman – we artists are the friends of kings. A man of stainless virtue. A man of iron will, indomitable daring, and passions strong, yet kept always leashed in his hand. Last and greatest, a man who, feeling within him the divine spirit, with his whole soul worships God!'

Vanburgh lifted off his velvet cap and reverently bared his head; then he continued, 'That is what an artist should *be*, by nature'. (Craik, 1850: 161, cited in Parker and Pollock, 1981: 83)

The biological function of women as child-bearing has also been used at various times to discount their cultural ability to engage in artistic creativity – Parker and Pollock (1981: 6–7) cite the sculptor Reg Butler attributing the creativity of female art school students in the 1960s to 'frustrated maternity'. Women reproduce, men produce; women's bodies are the vessels of procreation, men's minds are the engines of intellectual and artistic creativity. 'Men bring forth ideas, paintings, literary and musical compositions, organisations of states, inventions, new material structures, and the like, while women bring forth the new generation' (Barron, 1968: 221). These distinctions not only reinforced the dualisms of nature/culture and body/mind by associating women with the former and men with the latter, but also privileged symbolic creation over physical re-creation. Symbolic creation produces 'lasting, eternal, transcendent objects', whereas physical re-creation is delimited by biological fallibility and human finitude (Ortner, 1974: 14; also see Gilbert and Gubar, 1984, chapter one on the metaphor of literary paternity).

Women were thus set apart from artistic creativity just as they were from intellectual pursuits, commercial enterprise and work (unless they were servants or women of the labouring classes). Lack of income might force women to write, as it did initially with Frances Trollope, the Brontë sisters and Mary Ann Evans, but the suspect activity might then be disguised by the adoption of male pseudonyms – we still know the latter as George Eliot, despite the fact that she produced some of the most imaginative portraits of provincial England available to us. The force of male prejudice against women artists or writers remained formidable. For example, the left-wing American critic Granville Hicks could easily dismiss such female writers as Willa Cather, who 'could do nothing but paint pretty pictures', and Edith Wharton, whose work 'ended in romantic trivialities' (1935: 219, 226). Even in the face of such remarkable novels as *My Antonia* and *The Age of Innocence*, the implication that men were the true creators remained strong.

To the extent that women and creativity were taken to a great extent as a contradiction in terms, female writers and artists either regarded what they did as naturally inferior because of their gender, or had to struggle against internalising male judgements of their 'innate' capabilities. This was an unequal struggle because men – or rather, a privileged coterie of men – commanded the intellectual and academic criteria and definitions of hierarchical values in art, music and literature. As Rozsika Parker and Giselda Pollock have argued, while the retrospective feminist celebration of women's work in the crafts is justified, it doesn't displace those authoritative values or the historically defined role given to women in the nineteenth and early twentieth centuries (1981: 58; and see Parker, 1984). Within this period, the status of an artist increasingly determined the way their art was seen, with artistic exceptionality or genius becoming an exclusively male possession. Such was the force of existing social stereotypes that any claim to such a possession by a woman, or even of independent consciousness, would have been to court distrust, censure and infamy. That is why Marie Bashkirtseff could only rail against those 'idiots who think that my painting is the amusement of a woman of the world' (Parker and Pollock, 1981: 109).

A further barrier which has confronted women who wanted to write, paint or compose music has been their relative lack of suitable precursors in the face of canonical male authority. While the contemporary female writer may feel that 'she is helping to create a viable tradition which is at last definitively emerging' (Gilbert and Gubar, 1984: 50), female writers in the past have not had the benefit of appropriate validating paradigms of aesthetic convention, creativity and self-creation as artists.

To some extent this continues to be the case. In Harold Bloom's formulation, the dynamics of artistic creativity arise from an 'anxiety of influence' and an heroic Oedipal struggle to overcome one's male precursors. While this is a dubious model in itself, it is inapplicable to a female artist when her male precursors 'incarnate patriarchal authority' and endorse the social stereotypes which deny 'her subjectivity, her autonomy, her creativity': 'Thus the "anxiety of influence" that a male poet experiences is felt by a female poet as an even more primary "anxiety of authorship" – a radical fear that she cannot create' (ibid.: 48–9).

Marcia Citron has noted that this anxiety for female artists in the past often translated itself into deference to male views and judgements, and an ambivalence about women's relationship to the creative process. She traces this among a number of women composers, such as Fanny Hensel (1805–47), and Clara Schumann (1819–96), who noted in her diary: 'I once believed that I had creative talent, but I have given up this idea; a woman must not wish to compose – there never was one able to do it' (Citron, 2000: 56–7; see also Reich, 1985: 228–9). There is great pathos in these words, but who was speaking here, and to whom? It is difficult, perhaps impossible, to say. The problem goes deeper. It not only included undervaluing personal achievement, or losing belief in a sense of personal creative ability, or exaggerating personal singularity as a female artist. It could also entail a dislocating confusion about their identity *as* artists. For female musicians of this period, the lack of autonomous female precursors or contemporaries might lead, as it did with Clara Schumann, to 'a split sense of selfhood: a strong subjected self when it came to performing, a self tending toward objectified Other when it came to composing' (Citron, 2000: 56). Once again, men produce, women reproduce – in this case the male-created musical score – so providing a convenient means of 'displacing the threat of female creativity' (ibid.: 71). The problem with the musical canon is, indeed, that 'there is still no fully formed female tradition to relate to' (ibid.: 67; cf. Halstead, 1997). The musical canon has been a male-dominated tradition.

Innovation and Illumination

The male-oriented metaphoric destruction of previous stylistic paradigms, in the progress-bound sense of artistic development, derives from nineteenth-century Romantic aesthetics (and in some versions from Enlightenment notions of linear historical development). Through its extension, the model has also lent endorsement to the modernist premium placed on creative innovation. This requires what the novelist Anthony Burgess described as 'a strong male thrust' (cited in Gilbert and Gubar, 1984: 9). Machismo gender bias aside, innovation is, as we have noted earlier, not only a difficult quality to identify and assess. When used as an absolute criterion of aesthetic worth, it also relegates other forms of creative work to the sidelines, making them seem somehow deficient. This has affected how, for example, the work of female painters and sculptors has been viewed for at least two reasons. Firstly, as Lucy Lippard has pointed out, some women artists have consciously reacted against avant-gardism and retrenched 'in aesthetic areas neglected or ignored in the past', while others have not been concerned with adopting the persona of artist-as-rebel but have continued to work 'in personal modes that outwardly resemble varied art styles of the recent past' (Lippard, 1976: 6). Secondly, until fairly recently avant-gardist criteria of innovation have been established by men and largely associated with them, so that a major question for feminist criticism becomes whether women's creative work requires a different conception of innovation and originality, one concerned not so much with radical stylistic challenges as with creative practice itself and the contexts in which it occurs.

A similar premium on the provision of illumination, on new insight and vision, has been a central cultural value in North Atlantic societies over the past century or so. As we noted in chapter one, in response to the rise of an instrumental rationality, the creative imagination became revered as the fount of innovation, insight and an intensified vitality of sense. Charles Taylor locates the realised quality of a heightened, more vibrant quality of life most particularly in epiphanic works of art. These bring us 'into the presence of something which is otherwise inaccessible' (1989: 419). An epiphany can be described as an illumination of meaning which 'either fosters and/or constitutes a spiritually significant fulfilment or wholeness' (ibid.: 425). Whether directly or vicariously, through an engagement with an artwork or cultural product, it is an intensely felt example of the kind of sharply focused experience in which, however temporarily, there arises a sensation of acute insight or being at one with an idea, emotion or perception. The sense of illumination and self-fulfilment accompanying this feeling or apprehension remains closely connected with the idea of creativity. Why else do writers go on blackening paper? This may happen out of an habitual obsession, but for most writers routine and repetition would hardly supply a sufficient explanation of why they are habitually driven to their desks.

For Taylor, epiphanies occur in two ways. The first connects people as artists, audiences, or readers with that sense of spiritual fulfilment, significance or wholeness exemplified by Wordsworth's poetry or Constable's paintings. This experience frees them from the debased, mechanistic routines of the workaday world. With its second manifestation, 'the locus of epiphany has shifted to within the work itself', as in much modernist poetry and non-representational visual art. The sense of fulfilment remains, but it is identified and felt in the 'translucence' of the artistic or cultural product.

Many writers and critics have valued the qualities of epiphanic artworks for more or less the same reasons as Taylor. The literary sense of epiphany as it was developed by James Joyce borrowed from Aquinas the three components of integrity, symmetry and radiance. An epiphany for Joyce – or his young pseudonymous hero, Stephen Daedelus – combines the apprehension of the integrity and symmetry of a scene, fragment of speech, gesture or object in the discovery of its radiance, so that 'the soul of the commonest object, the structure of which is so adjusted, seems to us radiant' (Joyce, 1966: 215–18). This formulation should remind us of the retention of a spiritual dimension in aesthetic ideas about creativity, and not just those of high modernism. Taylor finds it exemplified in Wordsworth's poetry, and the description given by Wordsworth of an epiphanic perception on first entering London is just one example of an earlier celebration of the momentary revelation of something divine in everyday life (Wordsworth, 1969, Book VIII: 144–5). Wordsworth's term for such moments was 'spots of time', and they are of course closely related to Dewey's 'moments of fulfilment'. Their value in experience is that they bring perception and understanding together in an exact vision as in the realisation of *an* experience out of the welter of everyday events and episodes.

The privileging of epiphanic insight and illumination as an aesthetic model can seem to result from a quality in (or attributed to) particular works of art that refuse space for alternative interpretations, experiences and traditions. Even if they are not held up above all other forms of cultural production, both of the forms of epiphany identified by Taylor seem exclusively western and so may be identified as another variant of cultural elitism. This is a tricky issue. With literary culture, for example, certain books transform how we feel and think, while others do not, and we cannot treat this distinction wholly in terms of the issue of who decides what is 'great' literature and whose definitions of 'greatness' stick. What makes this issue more complicated is that it may suggest that the 'common reader' cannot make such decisions, or can only parrot the definitions they have internalised. A history of working-class auto-didacticism based on the assumption that its subjects were simply class ventriloquists would clearly be deeply compromised and flawed. While the question of class influence is always relevant, it shouldn't be taken as denying the ability of ordinary people to articulate those encounters with literary texts which they have found transformative.

Many 'common readers' in the past may have believed that only canonical literature 'could produce epiphanies' and 'only great books could inspire them to write' (Rose, 2001: 371), but this does not absolve Taylor from the charge of confining his discussion of epiphanic artworks to those of the western high literary tradition. The sources of selfhood in the modern period do not belong exclusively to this tradition. Martha Nussbaum has pointed to Taylor's lack of attention to African, Asian and Latino/a traditions, all of which, in various ways, have contributed to 'the sense of self of most Americans and many Europeans'. Many citizens in the West define their identity quite centrally in terms of those traditions rather than those of Europe or North America. Moreover, in a globalised world, questions of cultural identity and social justice cannot be confined to western aesthetic and ethical sources (Nussbaum, 1990). This confinement of focus is true more specifically of Taylor's account of 'authentic' art as well. He draws almost exclusively on high cultural art and aesthetics, with the epiphany of translucence being not far away from a reified 'text in itself', and the 'life and works' paradigm of literary or artistic creation, which we critiqued in chapter two.

The spiritual dimension in the semantics of creativity clearly lives on in epiphanic art, yet not just the art of high culture. It is found in popular culture as well, as when people speak of a sense of revelation or of being emotionally transfixed on first hearing a particular popular song. It may be that for certain people 'a kind of piety…still surrounds art and artists in our time', and that this comes from 'the sense that what they reveal has great moral and spiritual significance, that in it lies the key to a certain depth, or fullness, or seriousness, or intensity of life, or to a certain wholeness' (Taylor, 1989: 422). Even more than in the early twentieth century, such piety seems now to be characteristic of a social minority with a high stake in the cultural capital associated with a rarefied sense of aesthetic value. The distance of such aesthetics from the everyday world of majority populations only exaggerates the sense of that world as out of joint, forsaken or spiritless, as a heartless world where instrumentalism and commercialism are dominant. This may be a convenient distancing strategy, but it tells us nothing of value about popular aesthetics.

The tradition of aesthetic value which runs from Romanticism through to much modern art is not the only locus of cultural authenticity. People use whatever sources are available to them for entry into realms alternative to the everyday world they live in. Often, an alternative source of creative vitality has been encountered and embraced through an exoticised cultural relationship. So, for example, during the early twentieth century, many white European and North American people discovered this source in 'black music', from an initial encounter with black spirituals through to an enthusiasm for blues and jazz. The romantic white response to black styles and idioms as more authentically expressive, exhilarating and hip is paralleled in the source of inspiration which many modernist painters found in African and other non-western art, often labelled as primitive.

These were not the only responses, nor did they necessarily preclude a deeper apprehension of the expressive power and aesthetic complexity of blues and jazz. For example, Simone de Beauvoir wrote of her passionate, if indiscriminate attachments at this time to African-American music, citing such songs as 'St James Infirmary' and 'St Louis Blues': 'Because they were born of huge, collective emotions, common to each and every one of us, these songs touched us individually, at that point of deep intimacy common to us all. They dwelt in our hearts, nourishing us just as certain words and cadences of our own tongue did' (1973: 139). Gary Giddins (2000) has remarked on how Bing Crosby, Al Jolson, Frank Sinatra and Elvis Presley all discovered something about their own sense of self and performing identity through an engagement with black forms that suggests an enduring, albeit continually modified, minstrel tradition and its ambiguous relationship to African-American cultural forms. As Giddins first observed in 1976 when assessing the significance of Bing Crosby within the US popular music tradition:

> Jolson, Crosby, Sinatra, and Presley operated against the annealing influence of the black-music continuum. Each responded to the black images and styles in his respective decade, so that Crosby's admiration of Jolson was crucially tempered by his idolisation of Armstrong, Beiderbecke, and Waters; Sinatra's debt to Crosby was mitigated by his involvement with Billie Holiday and Tommy Dorsey; Presley's response to the white pop tradition was shaped by his involvement with blues and rhythm and blues. Which is not to derogate the minstrel impulse as a purely negative phenomenon. Minstrelsy is not an aberration but a continuing tradition in popular American culture. Economically and socially, minstrelsy is more often than not unjust; aesthetically, it is the key with which some of our more intelligent white performers unlocked the doors to their own individualities. (2000: 17)

So the significance of blues and jazz in the development of modern popular music cannot be reduced to questionable (sometimes essentialist) notions of racial expression. There has always been some more profound crossover involving movement beyond the parameters of black music's labelled ethnic origin and racial stereotypes. In criticising the absence of such protean musical forms as blues and jazz from Taylor's account, Nussbaum observes that they are, 'in Taylor's own sense, "moral sources" of enormous depth and power':

> How many of his readers, when they think about love or pain, owe as much to Trollope or Eliot or Holderlin as they do to Bessie Smith or Billie Holiday? And is the vision of suffering, joy, endurance – and justice – that unfolds in the searing, broken cadences of Holiday's last recordings any less worthy of close philosophical scrutiny than the forms of art and literature that Taylor does discuss? (Nussbaum, 1990: 32)

A sense of communicated experience and the creative expression of suffering, joy, endurance and justice is for many people associated with both non-western and popular sources such as these, rather than with those that constitute Taylor's own. While Taylor's analysis of the sources of modern identity is wide-ranging and rewarding, it fails to show how people have moved promiscuously between canonical works and popular culture. That has been true of the past two centuries, though perhaps especially so over the past 50 years. Such movement has often been the source of cultural creativity, and it is related also to the interactions and hybridities which have resulted from mobility, from movement between places and cultures. Creativity is not necessarily a consequence of being bound organically to one place. Such a close bind may just as often be experienced as entailing a sense of confinement, inhibiting creativity as much as it may also foster it.

Moving Out and Moving In

In one of his many reflections on how the geographical and attendant cross-cultural movement and meeting of people can profoundly facilitate and shape the creative process, Salman Rushdie has written:

> The crossing of borders, of language, geography and culture; the examination of the permeable frontier between the universe of things and deeds and the universe of the imagination; the lowering of the intolerable frontiers created by the world's many different kinds of thought policemen: these matters have been at the heart of the literary project that was given to me by the circumstances of my life, rather than chosen by me for intellectual or 'artistic' reasons. (2003: 6)

Rushdie's observations, part celebratory, are in keeping with his other pronouncements about the cultural value of mixing and a hybrid aesthetic. But he also makes a more critical point about the contradictory tensions which link liberation and restriction as a result of the crossing of various frontiers:

Anyone who has crossed a language frontier will readily understand that such a journey involves a form of shape-shifting or self-translation. The change of language changes us. All languages permit slightly varying forms of thought, imagination and play. I find my tongue doing slightly different things with Urdu than I do 'with', to borrow the title of a story by Hanif Kureishi, 'your tongue down my throat'. (ibid.: 6)

Rushdie foregrounds language, but the same language may be used in different cultural contexts. It may take on quite different cultural resonances, connecting with all manner of historically accumulated associations of class, region, accent, gender and race, and becoming articulated with various non-linguistic, non-representational forms of gesture, colour, or sound (codes which are integral to an understanding of culture and creativity, and yet often overlooked). To write in English should be understood within the context of this type of understanding of cultural divisions. We shall pursue the consequences of this a little further with an extended reference to those writers associated with 'West Indian' literature in the middle of the twentieth century, whose artistic work resulted in the London of the 1950s sometimes being referred to as 'the literary capital of the West Indies' (Donell and Welsh, 1996; Griswold, 1987).

To refer to London in the 1950s in this way could be construed as misleading for reasons that we hope will become clear in what follows. Such a casual claim assumes clear links between culture, place and identity. It assumes that the piece of land you are born on organically defines your identity and your culture, and that you then carry this identity with you and take it somewhere else. Hence, it *detaches* the notion of the West Indies from the geographical Caribbean region, but simultaneously re-connects it to another place in terms of a notion of origins: London becomes part of the West Indies because people have come to the city from the Caribbean. There are also intimations of an essentialist unity to identities here, as if we can talk of a West Indian literary identity that is shared by the various participating groups.

One point we wish to stress is that people are not simply born to a culture in which they continue to participate by reproducing it through artworks locally or in another part of the world. A further misleading assumption is that art forms with a specific cultural identity are simply created by those 'within' the group. Nelson George (1989; 1998) has effectively scotched this assumption in noting the Jewish contribution to African-American forms of music. Internationally, as Patria Román-Velázquez's (1999) study of Latin Americans in London demonstrates, Latin identities are created anew in different locations, continuous with history but in relation to a new set of circumstances. In any case, it was not only Latin Americans who contributed to a 'diasporic' Latin identity. Local British musicians, entrepreneurs, DJs and dancers also played a part in the 'making of Latin London'. Thus, Latin identity is not an exclusive collective sense produced and reproduced by Latin Americans. Hence, if London became a literary capital of the West Indies in the middle of the twentieth century, this cannot simply be explained in terms of certain essentialist characteristics of particular people who have dispersed from the Caribbean Islands.

A further issue here concerns the presumed similarities of selfhood and creative practice that go unexamined in such arguments. The labelling of people is not the same as the creative acts of those people. Just because someone is categorised as Latin, Turkish, Jewish or West Indian doesn't necessarily always mean that this is integrally tied to their music, poetry, painting or films.

If there is any value in claiming some place as the symbolic centre of a literary or other artistic formation, it may be that this lies only in signalling the significance of that place – here the English metropolis – in the institutionalisation of West Indian literature, and in the creation of a certain Caribbean identity in Europe as various writers were inspired to move to London. Crucial to such migrations were the colonial education systems which provided knowledge, a celebrated corpus of literature, and a particular disposition and orientation towards the English language and literary canon. C.L.R. James has written one of the best accounts of just such an educational background in early-twentieth-century Trinidad, where he absorbed the public school code through literature and cricket, and intellectually 'lived abroad, chiefly in England' (1980: 71).

Many young people travelled from the Caribbean as students in receipt of scholarships, but with a variety of motives. A few wished to leave the Caribbean permanently, to 'escape' in the manner which V.S. Naipaul seemed to desire. Others left wishing to expand their knowledge or to receive recognition, with the eventual aim of returning to the Caribbean at some future date (see Walcott, 1998; Lamming, 1960; Nettleford, 1993; Walmsley, 1992).

It is worth noting the ambivalent social status of these writers as they searched for a means of expression. Although finding themselves in a subordinate position, frequently subject to racial prejudice, they were in a somewhat privileged social location compared to many working-class and women writers in Europe. In discussing George Lamming, Alan Sinfield (1989) has observed that the vast majority of people in Europe had no stake whatsoever in the tradition of literary canonical texts which had shaped these writers' formative aesthetic experiences. Bridget Fowler (1997: 142) has highlighted the considerable economic and social constraints during this period which impeded the ability of women writers to become 'bohemian exiles'.

The writer's ambivalent position becomes pronounced if we consider the very use of the preferred label of 'exile', as opposed to immigrant or expatriate. This term established very specific associations and was integral to the strategies through which a position could be found. It was part of how writers were called upon to legitimate themselves within the literary metropolitan world. As Rob Nixon has written in a study of V.S. Naipaul:

> For reasons of publishing, audience, and education, there was a substantial pressure on Caribbean authors of Naipaul's generation to move abroad if they wished to survive as writers. Liberally interpreted, this pressure could be read as a form of coercion. But…I would contend that *exile*, in the domain of literary history, possesses a very specific genealogy that by this stage has less to do with banishment and ostracism than with a powerful current of twentieth-century literary expectations in the West. Writers domiciled overseas, regardless of the circumstances of their removal from their native lands, commonly imagine and describe themselves as living in exile because it is a term privileged by high modernism and associated with the emergence of the metropolis as a crucible for a more international, though still European – or American – based culture. The phrase *in exile* resonates with a sophisticated anxiety that fits tidily with a certain conventional perception of the writer's lot in society. (1992, 24–5)

Nixon has a point. There is a voluminous literature devoted to the impact of exile upon the twentieth-century novel, particularly in Europe. In many discussions of literary style, exile seems almost to have become a determining category, without which the writings of figures such as Joseph Conrad, Henry James, James Joyce and Vladimir Nabokov are inexplicable. Exile, used in this way, becomes an act of existential choice, part of embracing a certain literary persona, as it was for many writers from the United States who travelled to Europe during the 1920s. This chosen exile was very different to enforced exile or escape in the face of oppression, such as the German Jewish artists and intellectuals who left Europe during the 1930s, many relocating to the United States. After World War Two, African-American writers like Richard Wright, Chester Himes and James Baldwin lived in exile in Paris (Campbell, 2003), but despite the racism they experienced while growing up in the United States, the conditions of their exile hardly compare with those of Osip Mandelstam or Nâzim Hikmet.

So, the term exile is elastic in meaning, and the experience of exile is diverse and multidimensional. The proceedings of a conference of writers in exile, held in New York in 1987, are in one sense a long and winding argument between themselves about the very meaning of exile for creative writers (Glad, 1990). At the end, many voices had been heard, but no consensus reached. It is because its meaning is so diffuse that the celebration of exile as a creative modernist impulse (imbued with residues of Romanticism) lives uncomfortably alongside the testament of those many refugees and emigrés fleeing political persecution for whom exile has been nothing whatsoever to do with the creative process. Many people have been exiled, but not all have been creative writers. Imposed exile may be quite *detrimental* for literary expression, or art may emerge as a response to the very trauma of such an experience.

So we might concur with Nixon that a degree of scepticism about the value of the term exile is now appropriate. But it is one thing to note an apparent fit of literary persona within modernist discourse – the experience may be quite another story. Nixon is perhaps too dismissive of the real anxieties and experiences that authors wish to signal through the use of this term.

Abdelrahman Munif suggests a flavour of what's involved in the experiences of emigré authors, when he writes of the double-bind they find themselves caught in, wanting to win favour in the host country while trying to prove, sometimes too earnestly, that their hearts are still with the people of their own country. The writer is torn between regaining their 'homeland through writing – to the point of obsession! – or losing it – to the point of amnesia!' (1991: 110). There is the danger of nostalgia, or of failing to recognise that as writers in exile change, so do their home countries, showing up the whole idea of country as 'an ever-shifting memory of the past and dream of the future' (ibid.). These temporal dislocations may extend also to the language in which they write, for in the present they strive to inhabit another people's world of words, and yet in the past this adopted language sustained the interests of their colonisers: 'Although learning that language offers deliverance for the writer – or the illusion of deliverance – as a bridge between two cultures for the transmission of a message, the exiled writer knows that the language he is using has also served, historically, as the intellectual edifice on which the colonising culture hangs its claims and assumptions of superiority' (ibid.). The complex task of such writers is then to learn how to inhabit this edifice without giving house-room to such claims and assumptions.

In negotiating the experiences of exile, writers may derive some support from sympathetic critics, broadcasters and small-scale publishers. The writers, intellectuals and artists who began travelling from the English-speaking Caribbean to Britain from early in the twentieth century became part of, and contributed to, distinct literary networks. These were facilitated by the establishment of small circulation magazines, journals, and radio broadcasting, particularly a BBC programme entitled 'Calling the West Indies' (1938), which soon changed its title to 'Caribbean Voices' (1946) and began to provide an outlet for writers and poets (even if not initially envisaged for this purpose, it was to entertain and educate the troops based overseas). Up to its demise in 1958, the series featured all the nascent literary talents of the Caribbean: Lamming, Selvon, Mittelholzer, Salkey, Naipaul, Keane and Braithwaite. For Edward Braithwaite, it was 'the single most important literary catalyst for Caribbean creative and critical writing in English' (Jarrett-Macauley, 1998: 141–59).

Creative artists from the West Indies contributed to the formation of metropolitan literary circles, to the institutions of broadcasting, publishing, criticism and poetic performance. Such an influence was formative in setting the genre boundaries and informing the commissioning strategies that would subsequently lead to the promotion of other types of 'world' literature. These writers sought publishers, and in the emergent post-colonial context became an attractive proposition to a publishing industry seeking to take advantage of a growing market for West Indian literature. Mike Phillips has even remarked that 'for a long time it was easier for a black writer living in the Commonwealth to be published in Britain than for a black person born and brought up in London or Birmingham' (2001: 146).

Yet these writers from the Commonwealth occupied an ambivalent position. Not fully integrated within or belonging to host networks, their involvement with the publishing industry was by no means a straightforward process. Like many artistic creators they had a range of personal motives and agendas. We can explain neither their art nor their engagement with the career of writer in terms of coercion by an imperialist capitalist industry, or exertion of their own free will and their ambition to succeed. The formation of English language Caribbean literature as a commodity resulted in a number of tensions. Authors such as Rex Nettleford and George Lamming argued that in entering into these types of literary relationships and in creating such literature the writer began to construct a very different Caribbean form of writing, one that (in part) was being produced to appeal to readers who were not geographically located in the Caribbean. To quote Rex Nettleford:

> The question of 'the market'…cannot be ignored. Who does the Caribbean writer really write for?…for the Caribbean readership still growing but yet to offer the critical mass which brings profits? Is he addressing the more affluent North American suburban class or the intelligentsia?… Does he write for the British literati with a long tradition of playing patron to sibling talents from the outposts of empire? (1993: 56)

In a lecture on emigration to Britain, following his eightieth birthday in 1981, C.L.R. James spoke of the two-way perspective enjoined on Anglo-Caribbean people – representing and speaking of the country they are living in while representing and speaking of the colonial or post-colonial territory they have come from (Busby and Howe, 1984: 48–9). Nettleford adds to this by raising concerns about the rupture between the literary arts and oral traditions, asking whether a 'scribal writ' had been imposed as part of a process of 'colonial conditioning'. He suggested that through increasing literacy, writers in exile became removed from the very traditions they sought to maintain and represent. Derek Walcott also touched on such aesthetic consequences in referring to how 'postures of metropolitan cynicism must be assumed by the colonial in exile' (1998: 58) in order to avoid a sense of isolation. The writer cultivates a different persona, and in writing creates something anew, removed from what they appear to be representing. This is the process of shape-shifting or self-translation referred to by Rushdie, which extends into the inexorable two-way change noted by Munif, so that representation is then always one step removed from that which it styles itself as authentically seeking to express.

At the core of these arguments is the insight and anxiety that a Caribbean or West Indian aesthetic had been shaped by the interests of the metropolitan literary intelligentsia, and by the desire and pressure to sell books to the major book markets constructed by commercial publishers. These are markets which then, and now, do not prioritise the Caribbean.

Once again, the issue is more complex than simply the small size of the market and its lack of sales potential when judged by publishers in London. The market for books in the Caribbean has been decisively influenced by the imposition of examination systems which have required the serious study of particular texts. According to Keith Q. Warner, 'many Caribbean writers suffer the misfortune of being associated with the works that had to be studied under trying examination conditions in earlier times and experience a definite drop in their readership among the non-school-going public' (1992: 45). For this reason the type of modern literature created by these authors was frequently not associated with the experience of reading for pleasure. This argument itself carries many assumptions about a specific homogenous reading experience, as if reading for pleasure was far removed from the 'classics'. But it does point to how writings returned to the Caribbean within a very specific literary, serious, scholarly context.

The complexities of book reading in general, let alone of the specific authors under discussion here, have received little critical attention. In Wendy Griswold's (1987) rare study of the critical reception of West Indian novels, she considers the reviews of George Lamming's books and notes that while his earlier works were reviewed more positively in the Caribbean than in the United States, his later work was reviewed more favourably in the United States than in the Caribbean. Her analysis of critical responses to his work in Britain suggested that these were apparently constant. Although she emphasises the early lack of enthusiasm on the part of US reviewers, Griswold does not take her interpretation of these contrasts much beyond the implication that Lamming's books gradually became less oriented to or in sympathy with the sentiments of a Caribbean readership. Such findings might be tentatively interpreted as supporting Nettleford's point about the new type of reader being addressed by the displaced writer or, at least, a distancing on the part of the author from questions of a distinct West Indian identity.

Yet there is clearly a complex dynamic which links readers to writers via critics, educational establishments and commercial publishers. Insights from Bourdieu's (1993, 1996) studies of literary production in France would suggest that, apart from writing novels, authors engage in a range of struggles for position and conflicts over the production of aesthetic beliefs and literary reputations.

Just how a writer's style might change within this nexus is an interesting and under-researched issue, but it is clearly more complex than a straightforward accommodation to metropolitan values. Through its very presence such literature can contribute to changing artistic perceptions and may facilitate a transformation of metropolitan literary values, adding new dialects and innovative styles that extend the use of the English language (Griffiths, 1978). One obvious aesthetic impact of this is that English literature, or being a British writer, is no longer the preserve of 'an ethnically specific designation' (Nixon, 1992: 43).

The cultural form, the identity of the writer, the identity of the literary circles and the identity of the publishing industry are all transformed during these movements, as creativity occurs across the frontiers of culture, language and ethnicity. For this reason, we must stress that a discussion of creativity and social divisions should adamantly refuse the assumption of an unchanging racial, gendered or class position. People move and change. Creativity not only entails the transformation of aesthetic materials, it can also entail the transformation of individuals, groups and values, and the ways these are represented.

Such transformations cannot be glibly celebrated as facilitators and harbingers of new hybrid social identities and aesthetic forms any more than they can be roundly condemned as inauthentic responses to various patterns of domination. In thinking about and attempting to understand how creativity is realised through social and geographical movements which constitute some form of exile, we should be attentive to the enduring tensions arising around and through such divisions. We should also be aware of the various struggles (for recognition, economic reward, power and influence) which inform the transformations of literary style and convention.

The writers we have been discussing, who left the Caribbean, shared a similar education and a set of acquired middle-class mores. Their orientation to literature and the process of becoming a writer was not incompatible with that of those they found in metropolitan London. In certain respects they were indeed in a superior position to the black British writers (as Phillips suggests) or to many of the white working class in Europe (as Sinfield observes). The dispositions and knowledge of these exiled writers allowed for their acceptance in metropolitan literary London, facilitating various creative dialogues.

What soured such dialogues was the unanticipated racial labelling which greeted these writers, almost instantly. The realisation that in London they were, pejoratively, black, disrupted their sense of belonging or full participation in the middle-class literary world. The experience of finding oneself labelled black, and stereotyped accordingly, would subsequently lead to further and different types of dialogue. The middle-class Caribbean writer suddenly had something in common with black working-class musicians and film makers due to the way that race and racism impacted upon the realisation and recognition of creativity. The aesthetic disposition, creative choices and sense of belonging were transformed through racism and the struggle against it.

The more general point emerging from this is that any discussion of social divisions should understand how movement allows for dialogues to take place, and how this can be disrupted, leading both to new divisions and possibilities for new dialogues. In the case we've been referring to, such movement occurred amongst a certain type of educated intellectual, but similar patterns might be found in the movements undertaken by working-class and rural musicians who moved from various regions of Latin America to New York City between the 1940s and 1960s and who contributed to the development of jazz styles and salsa. This doesn't mean that movement is always from what is thought of as the periphery to centre, even though proportionately this may be so. It can also entail movement the other way, as for example with Gauguin, who left France for Tahiti and 'the simple life' in his quest for an intensity and directness of artistic expression that he felt had become lost in Europe under centuries of accumulated tradition. His desertion of his family for the sake of this quest raises the moral question of its justification in the interests of artistic creativity. As Bernard Williams has commented: 'While we are sometimes guided by the notion that it would be the best of worlds in which morality were universally respected…we have, in fact, deep and persistent reasons to be grateful that that is not the world we have' (obit., *The Guardian*, 13 June 2003).

The decision to move away, consciously and self-reflexively, can be seen as a deliberate attempt to overcome the limitations of background and upbringing, the injuries of social division, or the strictures of social and aesthetic conventions. This is a modernist creative strategy, though it is one that has subsequently become something of a postmodern caricature as the globalising entertainment industry packages exile in ever more forms of world music, world literature, world cinema and world news. Against this we can cite the Czech philosopher Jan Patočka's conception of the creative writer as trustee 'of the meaning of that life which is infrangible and personally accomplishable' (Vladislav, 1990: 20). The attempt at removal, at being out of step and moving away, re-locating and reinventing the self, is how numerous creative artists have sought some form of liberation from the barriers of class, race, gender, or sexuality. This has allowed for forms of creativity which comment upon, re-present, intervene in and display the instability of divisions and potentials of change. Creativity has followed and arisen as a response to such movements. In conversation with the Chilean writer, Antonio Faundez, Paulo Freire offered this observation:

> Wherever exiles finally settle, they tend to experience from the moment they arrive the ambiguous feeling of freedom on the one hand, at having escaped

from something threatening, and on the other of having suffered a tragic break in their history. Learning to live with that ambiguity is difficult but it has to be done… If they do succeed, then their time of waiting in exile, actively waiting, will become for them a time of hope. (Faundez, 1989: 11)

The skill is to turn loss and irresolvable ambiguity into hope and artistic triumph. In this perilous shift lies the enigma of creative arrival and travel from the local and particular towards another enigma, the universal.

7

Genius

For many years, social and cultural theorists have tended to avoid or oppose the identification and recognition of exceptionality with which genius is associated. The very notion is often rejected as inherently mystifying or elitist. While we may be able to critically dismiss certain aspects of the idea of genius as no longer valid, this should not lead to a wholesale rejection of the concept. We want to encourage an approach which can think of the activity and its judgement as distinct, without collapsing them – as if the idea of genius only arises as an ideologically laden value judgement and not in a very exceptional human achievement to which the act of according value is just one response.

The epithet genius is a medieval inheritance from Latin, denoting an attendant inner spirit assigned to every person at birth, governing their fortunes and determining their character. By extension, the sense of genius as guardian spirit was applied to specific groups, or to a particular place, as in the term *genius loci*. The Roman attribution of genius was thus widespread, and although as a guardian spirit within any particular family it was conceived as being embodied in the paterfamilias, it was not confined to a few singularly endowed individuals elevated above the broad mass of citizens.

The modern concept of genius is characterised by a move away from this spiritual sense of a guiding light through life that is available to all, and from its broader association with the whole spectrum of human endeavour. This has involved a shift from a relatively inclusive to a relatively exclusive meaning of the term. The basis for this shift was laid in the seventeenth century by the combination of the Latin sense of *genius* with another Latin word, *ingenium*, referring to an innate ability or talent. Genius still referred to a quality possessed by a person, rather than a specific category of person, but by the end of the eighteenth century, genius had become the designation for a distinct human type. This was one (invariably male) possessed by an inner spirit or daemon impelling him to strive towards the dizzy heights of artistic achievement. Such heights came to be conceived as the creation of an original imaginative vision of the world, and an original style or character of artistic expression. Hence the exclusivity, which then helped to harden other social divisions over the course of the next two centuries. Genius became an extraordinary single individual, raised above time and responsible for the finest of the fine arts. The genius was perceived as someone acutely innovative, original and superior, set apart from ordinary mortals, and as a creator *ex nihilo*, seeming to be close to the very forces of creation.

Art was the primary site for the transposition of religious conceptions about the origin of the world into secular ideas about originality, and those of creation into the modern sense of creativity. The artist – and above all the artistic genius – was the chief beneficiary of this transfer, becoming the new modern paradigm of individual development as self-creation. The more everyday life was conceived in opposition to self-creation and the search for originality, the more artists were elevated above mundane affairs and ordinary folk, at least during the Romantic period, and in less dramatic ways ever since. In their most exceptional moments of creativity artists were considered to be divinely inspired, and those granted the prodigious creative powers of the genius were considered, above all, as the fittest agents for the gradually secularising transition of creation from God to Man, producing, in Coleridge's conception, 'a repetition in the finite mind of the eternal act of creation' (Coleridge, 1910: 159). In this sense, artistic creativity was an intense reaction to the modern disenchantment of the world, with an artwork conceived as 'a presence which opens onto the infinite', so that, in Roberts's crisp formulation, 'modern art is the continuation of the sacred by other means' (1994: 173). This transcendent conception of creativity and art brought the individual and the universal into an apparently paradoxical relation, with the power of genius being that of reuniting the universal and particular in an original vision of the world. It was the belief in this power which helped reduce the sense of exceptionality to a single individual, representative of a distinct personality type.

While various examples from earlier periods or other places can be identified, it was within European Romanticism, and especially Romanticism in its British and Germanic contexts, that our continuing ideas about genius were first developed and consolidated. The shift in reference to genius as an exclusive category of person was accorded its greatest value in this specific historical epoch and geographical region, but particular notions of creativity, artistic expression, fine art and the figure of the artist spread beyond it, and continue to remain influential both within Europe and beyond. So, for instance, it was because of the expressivist realisation of artistic vision discussed in chapter one that the sense developed of exceptional creative powers arising, in analogy with natural growth, as the result of innate capabilities. These exceptional powers were then ascribed to singular, gifted individuals for whom the category of genius seemed ideally suited. Creative geniuses became exalted above and beyond any cultural form, genre or tradition in which they worked, as well as over everyday life and mundane practical skills.

The changed meanings and values associated with the category were thus connected with a transformed understanding of creativity as the outpouring of natural impulse, a spontaneous expression of a new sense of subjectivity and individuality. The initial shift is signalled in two works dealing with the subject of genius which were published in the third quarter of the eighteenth century by Alexander Gerard (1774) and Edward Young (1759). Both offered organic images of the creative process and refigured genius into a celebration of uniqueness. The ideas in these accounts influenced such contemporary figures as Herder, Goethe and Kant, and have remained influential ways of thinking about exceptionality. In Kant's *Critique of Judgement*, for example, genius is defined as 'the innate mental disposition (*ingenium*) through which nature gives the rule to art' (1982). As an innate predisposition, genius is beyond conceptual thinking in its originality, but as an exemplar is also responsible for forming or radically changing the ground rules of artistic expression within a cultural tradition. Kant neither attributes genius to an inner daemon (or in more modern terms, the forces of the unconscious) nor counters that notion by simply emphasising years of hard toil, but what he delineates is artistic genius as a conflux of sublimity and reason. This has remained central to our understanding of the originality of genius.

The tension between an originality which *cannot* be known intellectually, and the consequent evidence of it which can *only* be known intellectually, has characterised ways of thinking about innovation and exceptionality throughout the modern period.

The Ideology of Genius

From the late nineteenth century onwards, it seemed that this tension could be resolved by applying new scientific methods to questions of genius and creativity. Aside from the questionable empirical procedures involved, the positivist explanation of genius assumed that it is an objectively measurable phenomenon that was distinct from any historically variable and culturally specific values.

For Francis Galton, such objectivity was not in doubt. Nor was the innate capability of genius. In an influential study (1869), he viewed genius as a hereditary phenomenon, running in particular families, and almost exclusively through the male line of descent. In direct connection with this view, Galton laid the basis for eugenics, the doctrine of improving a population by controlled breeding for desirable inherited characteristics. The oppresive side of this logic meant that good literature is pre-eminently a question of good breeding, and genius a product of natural selection. Such evolutionist and racist notions have now been discredited, largely because of their popularity under Nazism, though they have remained implicit where selective sterilisation has been practiced or the right of people with disabilities to have children has been denied. Galton's ideas survive in standardised measurements of intelligence such as IQ tests, a key staple of twentieth-century British and North American psychology. In the United States, IQ tests were used from the start as a technique for identifying children with the genetic potential for genius.

'Gifted' may be today's preferred term for such potential, but giftedness was initially used as a synonym for genius. It inherits the Galtonian link between gene and genius, even if that link is no longer exclusively male. The genetic transmission of intelligence and talent, unconnected with social arrangements and opportunities, remains a common idea. It continues to inform certain aspects of the academic curriculum when undergraduate discussion of the relationship between individual and society is conducted in the terms of 'nature or nurture', coined by Galton himself.

Race-thinking affected another conception of genius in the late nineteenth and early twentieth centuries. This involved recycling the Romantic association between madness and genius. Creativity, genius and madness have been sporadically associated in western culture since Aristotle's time – as if peaks of cultural productivity are dependent on mental instability, if not illness – but following the Romantic revaluation of 'madness' as a source of true insight, the association attained the status of a truism (Gilman, 1988: 219–20). It acquired even greater resonance in the late nineteenth century because of anxieties concerning racial hygiene and degeneration. For example, Cesare Lombroso (1891) and others considered genius and madness as analogous on the basis of their departure from normality. Normality in this period was, at least in part, a racialised notion. As an aberration from normality in this sense, creativity seemed confirmed in its association with pathological conditions.

So, for example, from the satanic figure of the Jewish genius, the association spread out into the antisemitic stereotypes and myths of the early twentieth century. In response to this, Freud attempted to eliminate stereotypical Jewish distinctiveness from his discussions of creativity, and instead examined exceptional talent and creativity in the development of particular outstanding individuals. In his writings on Leonardo da Vinci and Michelangelo, for example, Freud viewed creativity as displaced sexual energy, a sublimation of the id into the realms of fantasy and the aesthetic. It is this idea which lies behind Josef Breuer's statement in *Studies on Hysteria* (co-written with Freud in 1895): 'Goethe did not feel he had dealt with an experience till he had discharged it in a creative artistic activity' (Gilman, 1991: 139). This approach not only makes male sexuality the wellspring of artistic creativity, it also makes creativity dependent on sexual repression. So for Freud, creativity was akin to neurosis and shared the same aetiology. Over the twentieth century, this became a stock cliché: the image of the artist who is not sexually fulfilled, and who sublimates libidinous energy into artistic creation.

An obvious objection to equating sexual repression with creative expression is that such repression may be apparent without any necessary manifestation of creativity. Even if we partially accept this type of psycho-pathological explanation of genius (or the behaviour which might be conducive to genius), we're still faced with the fact that although many people might be diagnosed or labelled in this way, they don't necessarily produce the art or literature of Michelangelo or Dostoevsky. A different stereotype could be produced, with sexually frustrated males sublimating their energies into stamp collecting, record collecting, train spotting or obsessive support for a football team.

The permeation of the category of genius with stereotype and myth has been challenged in various ways by artists themselves. Instead of the pathological association of artistic creativity with madness and mental derangement, social deviancy and racial degeneration, a positive identification is made with creative departures from normality. Particularly, but by no means exclusively, among the avant-garde common associations have been with children and childhood play, with primitivism and 'native' art, and with clowns and clowning. These associations have figured in two major ways. First, as a variable alternative to utilitarian values, bureaucratic rationality, the work-ethic and crass commercialism. Second, as a romanticised ideal in relation to the established order because the assumed raw, unspoiled vitality was considered superior to stereotypical bourgeois cultural norms and, more significantly, regarded as close to the redemptive forces of creativity itself (see Ritter, 1989; Pickering, 2003 for art and the clowning tradition). Taking up just one of these cases, 'primitivist' art from Africa or Oceania became a source of inspiration within modernism because its creative vigour was seen as supplying precisely the qualities European art seemed to have lost – 'intensive expressiveness, clarity of structure and a forthright simplicity of technique' (Gombrich, 1967: 428). It also represented a radical compensation for what Klingender (1972) called cashbox aesthetics. Such art spoke to a sense of lack in white subjectivity as well as in high European culture, but its positive evaluation did not alter its aesthetic ranking. It was still seen as resulting from anonymous craft skills rather than from individual artistic creation. Even today, the products of individual artistic creation in economically privileged countries are displayed in art galleries, while the artworks of so-called primitive or undeveloped societies remain largely relegated to museums of ethnology or anthropology. The ideology of creativity continues to divide the West from the Rest.

As we have seen, the divisions associated with creativity have invariably stemmed from essentialist social identities and elitist sources of authority and power. While these were formed around such structuring conditions as social class, gender and ethnicity, so they led to various intersections across spatial and temporal boundaries. The male appropriation of the mantle of creativity meant that attempts by women to engage in artistic work could pose a serious threat to their ascribed femininity, even to the extent of seeming to unsex themselves. This was paralleled in the racialised fixity of difference, over the same period, so that along with Africans and those of African descent, high cultural creativity was denied to other non-white peoples of the world, who were viewed as either socially backward, or stuck somewhere, backwards in time. This denial informed the dominant stereotypes of such people (Pickering, 2001). For example, even in the late twentieth century, the Asian American stereotype in North America was of someone 'characteristically timid and docile', without the 'traditionally masculine qualities of originality, daring, physical courage, and creativity' (Chin and Chan, 1972: 68–9). Masculinity in white American society has conventionally meant 'aggressiveness, creativity, individuality, just being taken seriously' (Kim, 1982: 198). The capacity for expressive power was accorded to African Americans in song, music and dance, but the ascription of racial inferiority and confinement to specialist roles or lesser artforms went hand-in-hand because originality and innovation were attributable only to the exclusively white, male category of genius.

Serious consideration of African Americans as painters, poets or composers did not begin until the twentieth century was considerably advanced. While this meant that the consequences of racism for cultural identity and practice began to be addressed, critics and commentators often evaded the usual difficulties of analysis and assessment by treating the exceptional creativity associated with genius as an enigma or paradox. An example of this is provided by Gary Giddins who, in the opening of his study of Louis Armstrong, moves continually, almost obsessively between statement and counterstatement:

> Genius is the transfiguring agent. Nothing else can explain Louis Armstrong's ascendancy. He had no formal training, yet he alchemized the cabaret music of an outcast minority into an art that has expanded in ever-widening orbits for seventy-five years, with no sign of collapse. He played trumpet against the rules, and so new rules were written to acknowledge his standards. His voice was so harsh and grating that even black bandleaders were at first loath to let him use it, yet he became one of the most beloved and influential singers of all time. He was born with dark skin in a country where dark-skinned people were considered less than human and, with an ineffable radiance that transcends the power of art, forced millions of whites to reconsider their values. He came from 'the bottom of the well, one step from hell', as one observer put it, but he died a millionaire in a modest home among working-class people. He was a jazz artist and a pop star who succeeded in theatre and on records, in movies and on television. Yet until he died, he travelled in an unheated bus, playing one-nighters throughout the country, zigzagging around the world, demanding his due but never asking for special favours. He was an easy touch and is thought to have handed out hundreds of thousands of dollars to countless people down on their luck. Powerful persons, including royalty and the Pope, forgave him a measure of irreverence

that would have been unthinkable coming from anyone else. Admirers describe him as a philosopher, a wise man, someone who knew all the secrets of how to live. (1988/2001: 4–5)

According to this account, it was Armstrong's genius which allowed him to enter the narrative myth of the American dream – ascending from humble origins to life at the top among the rich, famous and influential. Such is the way that the story of talent is often told in the United States, though the tale is given a further mythical twist by adding that he remained humble even when he'd reached the heights. Giddins also highlights the way that any consideration of the exceptional ability which goes by the name of genius must negotiate the codes, conventions and expectations of genre, the legacies of tradition and the oppressive force of social divisions. In this respect, the description fits Kant's conception of genius as someone who gives the rule to art, and it is this capacity which explains Armstrong's ability as a musician to escape the minstrelized racial pathology of 'nigger'. Genius potentially transcends such barriers, communicating experience across frontiers.

Not all who have an interest in critically according value to cultural forms would agree with the idea of Armstrong's genius. It is the exclusivist tendency in labelling genius within a particular high art European tradition which has prompted many – not least feminist writers – to be highly suspicious, if not avowedly opposed, to the very category. Their suspicion at the exclusivity is not dimmed by the continuing influence of the Romantic masculinity of genius whereby exceptional ability enables a male artist to gain access to a 'feminine' or 'primitive' mode of consciousness. It's because we share this suspicion that we have highlighted the development of the idea of genius as culturally exclusive, as psychologically pathological, and as ideologically supportive of social divisions and the historical disenfranchisement of such categories of people as women, the working class and African Americans. These are all aspects of genius which have been derided and rejected, but this doesn't mean that the term genius no longer has critical value. It seems to us that there's a vital issue which the ideological critique of genius doesn't seem to answer, and this is how genius is constituted as a particular moment of creativity, presuming for now that it does occur and cannot be dispelled as simply another cultural myth. This brings us back to the sharp divergence between two approaches to creativity which we have highlighted throughout the book.

The Explanation of Genius

The divergence is particularly marked in respect of genius. The first approach explains creativity in terms of the long course of learning, acquiring knowledge, and attaining competence and skill, that is required before a sufficient level of proficiency is reached at which creative acts can occur. Michael Howe offers an example of this kind of explanation of genius when he writes that, like 'ordinary men and women, major authors have had to invest large amounts of time and effort in order to become unusually skilled'. He goes on: 'Their heavy dependence upon training and preparation is one of the many aspects of human experience that creative geniuses share with other people' (Howe, 1999: 175). In contrast, there is an approach which locates the sources of creativity as lying beyond rational principles and procedures. The emphasis is on some form of inspiration, or alternatively on some value in creative practice that arises without any undue intellectual application, formulae or method. A revised version of this is provided by Gabriel García Márquez. When asked about inspiration, García Márquez distanced himself from the influence of Romanticism before refining that influence by defining inspiration as a struggle which entails a reciprocity and interflow of writer and theme:

> It's a word that has been discredited by the Romantics. I don't see it as a state of grace nor as a breath from heaven but as the moment when, by tenacity and control, you are at one with your theme. When you write something, a kind of reciprocal tension is established between you and the theme, so you spur the theme on and the theme spurs you on too. There comes a moment when all obstacles fade away, all conflict disappears, things you never dreamt of occur to you and, at that moment, there is absolutely nothing in the world better than writing. That is what I would call inspiration. (García Márquez and Apuleyo Mendoza, 1988: 34)

Here García Márquez is acknowledging the opposition between these different approaches whilst also attempting to move beyond them. The contrast between these two approaches goes back a long way – Plato and Aristotle were perhaps the first to give them clear expression – but it deepened enormously as a result of Romanticism. It did not originate with Romanticism, but the oscillation between these two contrasting senses of creativity is distinctively modern. They inform and support the two main myths about genius that have developed in parallel. Peter Kivy has characterised them as the possessor and the possessed.

The possessed is the passive genius whose inspiration acts as a conduit for what is delivered by some external agency: 'There is no "source" in a mental act of will. There is just the passive recipient of brilliant invention from "we know not where": from "nowhere"' (Kivy, 2001: 21). The possessor, by contrast, is an active genius who achieves artistic excellence through self-will and determination, the extent of which itself produces an aura of exceptionality. The difference is between 'a genius to which creation happens and a genius who makes creation happen' (ibid.). An early eighteenth-century formulation of this difference, discussed by Kivy, is that offered by Joseph Addison, who compared 'natural' and 'cultivated' forms of genius. The 'natural' genius is a sort of 'primitive' who creates 'without the assistance of art or learning', who is 'nobly wild and extravagant', a breaker of rules, original rather than derivative, and producer of sublime rather than beautiful works. 'Cultivated' geniuses have by contrast 'formed themselves by the rules, and submitted the greatness of their natural skills to the corrections and restraints of art' (ibid.: 23–7). The myth of Beethoven's apparent possession (despite the evidence of hard work, and constant re-drafting in his notebooks) and J.S. Bach's seeming ability to be able to compose exceptional music via a methodical routine, are examples that are often cited as an illustration of this distinction.

These opposed characterisations of genius have come to infuse various other contrasting aesthetic distinctions, such as invention vs. skill, art vs. craft and imagination vs. method, as well sublimity vs. beauty and originality vs. rule. Modern conceptions of art, aesthetics and culture are riddled with these dichotomous oppositions. We've argued throughout this book that such contrasting terms should not be treated as opposed to each other but as mutually dependent. Their value and significance would be seriously reduced without the other with which they are paired. It is the divergence between the two contrasting senses of creativity that is an obstacle to understanding, particularly where the contrast itself remains a key point of differentiation among various conceptions and theories of creativity. The sharp divergence between the apparently ordinary and the exceptional leads to the false alternatives of abstract metaphysical speculation as opposed to a narrow analytical focus on mere variation in aesthetic and cultural conventions. This is quite different to a critical aesthetic that works with an explanatory *tension* between complete genius and a more occasioned conception of what genius involves, in an interflow of artist and theme where inspiration leads to a moment of innovation that changes a cultural tradition through its lasting value and significance. It is towards this kind of critical aesthetic that we're attempting to move.

Remembering that *exceptional* cultural achievement arises out of arduous toil and preparation is one way to offset organicist and absolutist conceptions of genius, regardless of whether these are applied to writing, musical composition, painting or dancing. If we don't keep in mind the protracted acquisition of knowledge and aptitude, the term 'genius' will mean *nothing other* than exceptionality, and so will remain in diametrical opposition to what is taken as ordinary, what is downgraded as mere talent, or what is assigned to rational method and procedure. Yet it remains difficult to think beyond such conceptions when the dominant meanings configuring the term seem to demand that exceptionality always be considered as completely unique. Exceptional, usually, because only a privileged minority possess the 'innate' capability of genius. The naturalisation of creative genius remains a commonplace, as in the glib incantation that poets – or footballers, dancers and actresses – are born, not made. This takes us no further than the notion of creativity as simply the outpouring of spontaneous impulse.

As we have continually argued, the opposition between artistic vision and humdrum, mechanical life can only diminish our understanding of the range and scope of the creative process. The problem we continually encounter is that any attempt to grapple with this process seems inevitably to run up against a whole series of dichotomies and conflicting perspectives. These cannot simply be resolved at a theoretical or conceptual level, for they have their source in the tangible, sensory experiences that coincide with the creative act. Yet when confronted with these divergent meanings, there's a tendency for many writers to attempt to resolve them by prioritising one or the other. This may, for example, be done either by claiming that only a select few – Plato, Dante, Hegel – are truly creative (Steiner, 2001), or by arguing that all everyday actions are potentially creative and adopting a dismissive or sceptical stance towards any notion of exceptionality (Willis, 1990; Joas, 1996). For us, the separation of these positions serves only to reinforce and perpetuate another unhelpful, and still pervasive dichotomy: that of elitism/populism.

The Reputation of Genius

During the latter part of the twentieth century, an intellectual move from cultural elitism to cultural populism was paralleled by a similar move from biologism to constructivism in explanations of genius. While polar swings such as these can perpetuate their originating dichotomies, the obvious question to ask of the resulting critical position on genius is whether any greater understanding has been achieved. We can explore this question via a particular and highly instructive example.

For Tia DeNora, creative genius can only be explained by reference to its acceptance as a cultural resource both initially, and then by succeeding generations. Beethoven's rise to eminence, for example, provided a cultural resource for the development of high musical aesthetics during the early nineteenth century. His rise has to be understood sociologically in terms of the 'mobilising resources, presentation devices, and practical activities that produced Beethoven's cultural authority' (DeNora, 1997: 189), for otherwise we could fall prey to the mystical notion of his individual, charismatic gift, as others have done. For DeNora, originality is beside the point, for genius presumes a 'natural' hierarchy of talent, 'as if this distribution existed outside of our attempts to frame questions about it' (ibid.: 190). Genius is thus, through and through, an ideological category. It is ideological because it covertly reproduces hierarchical structures of power and obscures the social conditions and struggles within which reputations and sources of cultural authority are produced. The question becomes not who has creative talent, or who is a genius, but what talents become recognised and legitimated *as* creative in specific social circumstances.

DeNora's study of Beethoven is of considerable interest in what it says about the social context and cultural politics of Beethoven's Vienna. Her general position, which is considerably indebted to Becker and Bourdieu, is that artistic reputations are historically produced, and that cultural authority may be reinforced by various social and political investments. This is certainly a salutary counter to stock notions of hereditary powers or sublimated energies, but the problem with the theoretical framework she imposes on cultural creativity is that it is seen entirely as the consequence of social conditions and forces. In assuming that works and performances are valued solely for reasons connected to social power and privilege, the clear imputation is that the reputation of genius is only a matter of social fabrication, as if there were nothing more to genius than the politics of its construction.

In seeking to demystify the Romantic myth of Beethoven as archetypal genius, DeNora argues his genius away. For Peter Kivy, this is the result of a narrow sociological formalism. Beethoven's music, his most significant achievement, is ignored by DeNora, or at least severely downgraded in favour of attention to social interests and intrigues in the historical context within which Beethoven lived and worked. Objecting to this reductive account doesn't mean that we have to revert to a socially immune 'text in itself' conception of music or an ahistorical 'life and works' approach to musical composers but, as Kivy remarks, if you want to evaluate, say, debates about the degree to which Beethoven's Seventh Symphony may be judged incoherent or not, you should examine the symphony, 'not the motives of its supporters or detractors' (2001: 196). So the problem is one of analytical imbalance as well as crude methodology, and it appears to have come about because of a critical elision of textualism and elitism.

This is either a straightforward misconception or a sleight of hand. Concern with the workings of a cultural text doesn't preclude concerted attention to the social contexts of its production and reception. These are different aspects of cultural analysis, but they're certainly not incompatible. So it would be glib to charge Kivy with being a latter-day elitist because of his defence of listening to the music. Likewise, it would be fatuous to accuse him of simply reproducing the ideology of genius by asserting a belief in creative exceptionality and greatness. His critique of DeNora cannot be dismissed so easily, and not only because he does attend to the blocked or unacknowledged creativity of disenfranchised groups. The significance of his critique is that DeNora's denial of the phenomenon of genius has become orthodox in cultural studies and the sociology of art and music.

We can distil from Kivy three key objections to DeNora's argument against genius (2001: 175–217). Firstly, to say that genius is nothing other than a social and political construct makes it an empty concept – there are no geniuses, only the politics of genius. This leaves us with the unresolved problem of how exceptionality may be explained. Secondly, DeNora deconstructs genius and the appreciation of genius not by contesting value, but by contesting motive, as if musical appreciation is only and entirely a matter of self-interest – or in Kivy's lampooning take on this: 'Scratch a music lover and you will, inevitably, find a status seeker or social climber beneath' (2001: 208). This reduces all musical aesthetics, including the aesthetics of popular music, to acts of bad faith. Thirdly, it is important to distinguish, as clearly as one can, between artistic and cultural production on the one hand, and its critical acceptance and celebration on the other. They cannot simply be conflated as – in Bourdieu's terms – the evidence of social and cultural capital. In Beethoven's case, this is an impoverishment of historical imagination. It fails to address the question as to why his music endures beyond the time and place in which he lived, or how it connects with huge numbers of people. Is this only due to the social and political construction of belief in his genius, and nothing to do with the music and the actions of its maker? Kivy's response is to say that if genius is explained solely as constructed reputation, anyone can become a genius if they're given the right connections and the requisite publicity. This is rationality running away with itself.

In noting these critical points, we have no wish to deny that the idea of genius has been and can be used to legitimate a restrictive and socially divisive canon, to justify the existence of educational institutions and practices privileging a small minority, and to rank male and female cultural achievements according to unjust criteria. But the fact that the great praise and attention accorded to various individuals, and the artworks or products associated with them, may have served certain ideological interests doesn't mean that they or their achievements are utterly subsumed by these interests. As Kivy carefully notes, it is important to distinguish between mythical representations of genius and the claim that genius is a myth. Blanket dismissal of the notion of genius means that the question of exceptionality is avoided altogether. To treat it merely as a reified bourgeois category, or to see it solely as the product of a repressive aesthetic canon, is an evasion of the problems posed by genius. The idea and value of genius as exceptionality exceeds its sociological critique.

In cultural studies and the sociology of culture, genius is often critiqued, or dismissed entirely, because of an overriding concern to reconceive creativity as a more general phenomenon than that advanced in conventional aesthetic canons. While this is self-evidently laudable, it has created a huge obstacle to thinking about exceptionality in cultural creativity. It is one thing to argue against elitism, but quite another to attribute creativity, equally, to everyone. This is misleading – flattening the concept into insignificance. A second dubious step is to selectively approach genius only in terms of the most fallacious uses to which the term has been put in the past. If creativity has become recognised as ordinary, as an ability that we all have, why should we not also acknowledge the extraordinary? Is the concept of genius invalid in a democratic society, an undesirable legacy from an inegalitarian age?

Kivy makes the crucial point that critiquing the elitism of social class, race and gender doesn't necessarily entail the denial of exceptionality. He asks: 'why in the world should I not recognise the eliteness of genius?' He accepts the genuine difficulty which genius poses for feminist sociology but wishes to make clear that it is not so much the concept of genius which has historically excluded the female genius, 'but rather the insidious (and false) characterisations of women that prevent them from falling under that concept'. So for feminism 'to deny the eliteness of its own genius is to give over to the enemy' (Kivy, 2001: 232, 237). A.C. Grayling has recently made the point that discerning and appreciating marks of quality in an artistic or cultural object is not in itself a mark of elitism, Eurocentrism, exclusivity or opposition to demotic and non-western cultural traditions. Such discernment and appreciation are not 'the special endowment of any class, or ethnicity, or of either gender' (Grayling, 2002: 5). Marks of quality include fineness of observation, skill in production, psychological acuity, wit, insight and inventiveness. These can be found in folk and popular cultures as well as in artistic and literary canons. Engaging and being engaged by them isn't necessarily equivalent to cultural snobbery.

We can illustrate this issue further by reference to Adorno, whose critical insight and intellectual acumen we have drawn on elsewhere in the book. Jürgen Habermas, when recalling his time working in the Frankfurt Institute of Social Research, remarked: 'Adorno was a genius; I say that without reservation'. This is as unequivocal a statement as could be made. Habermas based it on the grounds that Adorno 'had a presence of mind, a spontaneity of thought, a power of formulation that I have never seen before or since'. Habermas spoke of being 'unable to grasp the emerging process of Adorno's thoughts; they emerged, as it were, finished. That was his virtuosity'. He also added that it was denied Adorno, 'in a clearly painful way, ever to be trivial', and yet his genius 'did not stand in contradiction to his egalitarian convictions. By all notable standards, Adorno remained anti-elitist' (Habermas, 1992: 122–3).

There are a couple of immediate features that make these memories of Adorno interesting. First, we have one of the most critically regarded sociologists in the recent European tradition invoking the term genius, and in a manner which could be construed as contributing to an Adorno myth – did Adorno's thoughts really emerge as any more 'finished' than Beethoven's compositions? This is perhaps a salient example of how a lack of sociological reflexivity informs discussions of creative exceptionality, coming as it does from one of the most astute and challenging of social theorists. A second point concerns the way that Habermas links Adorno's genius to his anti-elitism. Anyone who is familiar with the way that Adorno's work has been caricatured in some of the more simplistic introductory sociological and cultural studies textbooks, will know that Adorno has often been lazily labelled as an elitist. This is a complacent claim which bothers itself with neither the conceptual problem of exceptionality and elitism for cultural and social theory, nor with the paradoxes and intricacies of Adorno's life and writings. Adorno sometimes provokes anxiety because there is a certain type of sociological squeamishness when it comes to this issue, informed as it is by an often unquestioned posture towards notions of democracy, equality and sociology's own presumed pro-gressive credentials.

An unwillingness to reflect on some of these epistemological presuppo-sitions and how they inform the disciplines of sociology and cultural studies leads to the kind of sociological argument advanced by DeNora, which seems either to confuse aesthetic judgement with political analysis or, worse, to col-lapse aesthetic judgement into political analysis. Whenever these moves occur, they diminish the scope of the sociological imagination.

Sociology can provide important insights into how ordinary people's actions are constrained by historically established patterns, conventions and limits within which everyday interaction occurs. But it has also to negotiate the unconventional and at times surprising interpretations of the already estab-lished, the movement beyond existing limits. In social studies of art and culture, such moments are often ignored. In arguing against the notion of genius as natural endowment and uniqueness incarnate, the inclination of many sociol-ogists is to identify the material conditions and contexts of everyday cultural practice in which creative processes occur, and the necessarily public forms of their communicability, including those of cultural markets, through which they become distributed and known. These may be necessary analytical steps, even if somewhat predictably conventional, but methodologically they have limits. Such an approach tells us little about the passionate attachments and reflexive identifications which people make with art and cultural products, whether these are painting, dance, or popular music. As one particular branch of social analysis, the sociology of art has remained largely disengaged from these attachments and identifications. It has told us everything about art except why we enjoy it.

It is curious that far more attention has been paid to the pleasures and gratifications involved in the consumption of popular culture and the media. The emphasis has invariably been on how these relate to the quotidian and to the rhythms and textures of everyday life. Yet, inevitably, part of the enjoyment of creativity involves the identification, and celebration, of exceptionality. We can witness this in the museum and the gallery, at the rock concert and in the symphony hall, at the theatre and on the television screen. In sociological aesthetics, though, our appreciation of exceptionality is sharply diminished, if not absent.

The issue of genius lurks threateningly behind the recent critical obsession with questions of literary and artistic canonicity. It is almost as if by confining explanation to ideological factors – patriarchal values, say, or the privileged interests of social elites – the problem will go away. Ideologically powerful though they are, literary and artistic canons are only one aspect of the problem. Their critique doesn't provide a comprehensive answer to the question of how and why historical variation occurs in relation to the concomitant sense of creative expressions seeming to speak to us of common experiences, however problematic both variation and commonality may be.

The difficulty of the question is particularly felt when what is assessed as exceptional is critically in the frame. In the face of exceptionality, we should acknowledge the strong temptation to forget the questions attendant on historical contextuality and think instead in terms of the 'common notion that the creation of great works of art is independent of the social existence of their creator, of his or her development and experience as a human being among others' (Elias, 1993: 50). Added to this is a complementary notion which regards the maturation of genius as occurring independently of the life-experience of the individual concerned, as if it is the result of some mysterious inner process.

Despite these difficulties, the reluctance to address the question of exceptionality – and the potentially intricate ways that this connects artistic creator with appreciative viewer, listener and reader in anything other than ideological terms – is a major shortcoming in the sociology of art. In exploring the dynamics of art, creativity and cultural production, we may look to such sociologists as Janet Wolff, Howard Becker and Pierre Bourdieu, but what we find is that exceptionality is evaded or avoided. It's been sociologised away. It has either been rejected as ideological, or concealed within an analysis of the consensual codes and conventions of art worlds, or barely acknowledged amidst struggles for position and recognition across different fields of production (see, for example, Wolff, 1981; Becker, 1976, 1984; Bourdieu, 1983, 1993).

The Rehabilitation of Genius

There are a few exceptions to this pattern of neglect. One sociologist who has attempted to grapple directly with the question of exceptionality and explicitly with the notion of genius is Norbert Elias in his unfinished work on Mozart, edited and published posthumously. As with Bourdieu (and others), Elias considered social context to be crucial to any understanding of 'a "genius", an exceptionally gifted creative human being' who, in this particular case, was 'born into a society which did not yet know the Romantic concept of genius, and whose social canon had no legitimate place for the highly individualised artist of genius in their midst' (1993: 19). For Elias, the changing social relations between the producers and consumers of art works are of central importance. For Mozart this involved composing during the breakdown of aristocratic patronage and the emergence of freelance artists facing an anonymous and atomised public as their market. Unlike the emphasis Bourdieu places on the objective relations of fields, and the external contexts within which artists are formed, Elias argues for a need to bring together such an external 'he-perspective' with that of 'an I-perspective...the standpoint of his own feelings' (ibid.: 7).

Whether or not Elias manages to achieve this in an admittedly fragmentary unfinished work is debatable, but he does offer pointers to the importance of experience via the social-psychological emphasis he places on a process of sublimation. He doesn't use this term in the conventional Freudian sense. He uses it to mean the ability of an individual to self-reflexively monitor and control the spontaneous and free-flowing fantasy and dreams of their autonomous mental play and to harmonise these with aesthetic conventions and the social canon without losing their spontaneity. This process of sublimation must, at some point, communicate to a public as it reinterprets the established patterns and limits to which it is in some way aligned. This is an obvious enough point, but the ways in which what is, initially, historically specific and locally known moves across and between place and period, to be recognised by later generations in quite different locations, is not so easily settled. As Elias noted, this 'open question' is too often 'disguised as an eternal mystery' (ibid.: 54). This sense of mystery – or rather of mystification – is a corrupt extension of certain aspects of Romantic thought, but it does stem from the positive accent which Romanticism placed on creative human agency in the communication of experience.

In this conception, the poet, for instance, responds to the world with creative imagination and conveys this in a particular assemblage of words, rhythms and figures of speech that synthesises the tension between experience and a particular expression of it. A further aspect of this conception is that his or her experience is then re-created by readers with sufficient sympathy and involvement to enable them to share that experience. In so doing the reader not only grows in imagination and feeling, but also, to some extent at least, shares in the creative powers of the poet. The reader's 'grasp of the author's words within the context of writing is constantly affected by their sense of themselves and their own current context of reading, and *vice versa'*

(Sell, 2000: 144). This is why the poetry of Henry Vaughan can still speak, movingly, to present-day atheists, since the 'human qualities they find in his response to circumstance may positively inspire them in their own very different lives' (ibid.: 145). Idealisation or mystification can begin at any point in this conception of the communication of experience, but it is in this conception that Romanticism provides us with the first fully developed example of the theory of an active audience. The disavowal of an ignorant and fickle public by various modern writers, artists and composers, and the ascendancy of mass culture criticism in the early twentieth century, were then part of a long detour on the road to reactivating the audience – whether this involves viewers, readers or listeners of particular cultural forms – and seeing them as negotiating with texts and performances on their own social and individual terms.

Just as the conception of an active audience in contemporary media and cultural studies arose in reaction to an earlier mechanistic view of the audience in the effects tradition of mass communication research, so the conception of an active reader in Romantic thought arose in reaction to an earlier mechanistic rationalism, with its attendant empiricist and utilitarian outlook. Both emerged as correctives, and yet both can lead to an idealised view of reader/viewer/listener activity in the process of cultural consumption. So, for instance, Paul Willis (1990) stresses the symbolic creativity of young people in recoding and transforming the meanings of consumer products in such a way as not only to underwrite the ideology of consumer sovereignty, but also to erase the distinction between symbolic value and the social. We may then need to bend our thinking about the active audience back towards a notion of conditioned frames of improvised action, though we should not do so at the expense of a creative sense of agency.

A creative and yet conditioned sense of agency is precisely what is appealing about Elias's conception of sublimation as a process which allows the mind its autonomous play while accommodating this within a specific genre or stylistic framework. Here is the interplay between play and convention that helps an artwork or cultural product to achieve communicative value. Elias refers to this as crossing the bridge of de-privatisation, by which he means that the imaginative play and daydreaming of the artist are subordinated to 'the intrinsic regularities of the material, by means of which the artist's feelings and vision can be communicated to others'. The painstakingly acquired creative know-how of the painter, musician or writer is drawn on to harness the stream of mental play and fantasy to certain devices and conventions while retaining the spirit of inventiveness. In spontaneously fusing fantasy and framework, imagination and convention, the tensions arising between them have constantly to be reconciled if artistic or cultural production is to achieve a concrete expressive form to which people can respond. The resolution of these tensions results in cultural products that combine

I-relevance with 'you-, he-, she-, we- and they-relevance' (Elias, 1993: 58–62). When this happens, a cultural product attains communicative value, and Elias summarises its most exceptional moments in the following way:

> The pinnacle of artistic creation is achieved when the spontaneity and inventive-ness of the fantasy-stream are so fused with knowledge of the regularities of the material and the judgement of the artist's conscience that the innovative fan-tasies emerge as if by themselves in a way that matches the demands of both material and conscience. This is one of the most socially fruitful types of subli-mation process. (ibid.: 60–1)

This coming together of mind and material 'as if by themselves', with the expression seeming utterly right and appropriate to the experience, is what happens in the phenomenology of being 'possessed', when artists speak of the picture painting itself, the poem writing itself, the song falling from the sky. The pinnacle to which Elias refers is communicative value at its highest point, leading people to feel that the expression is complete and beyond further improvement, and providing them with the link from an everyday conception of creative acts to a clearer understanding of exceptional creative acts.

The saxophonist Charlie Parker has often been cited as an example of someone at one with the material they're playing, aware of what they intended to do and seeking constantly to wrestle with existing cultural materials in order to move beyond them. In Ken Burns's series of television documentaries, simply entitled *Jazz,* Parker is referred to as a genius by both Wynton Marsalis and Gary Giddins.

Both speak of Parker the person as a genius, but acknowledge the par-ticular moment for which the genius label is usually applied. This is Parker's realisation during one performance – which seems obvious now only in retro-spect – that he could 'fly' away from the root notes of a chord yet still return to them. The notion that improvisation could be based upon the possibilities suggested by the underlying chord changes rather than the existing melody, and that this allowed frequent movements into the upper register, opened up a whole new range of possibilities and changed the course of jazz and popular music. Giddins refers to this as 'the revelation that became the basis of his music' (1998: 264). The inspired moment when this realisation came to Parker is conventionally dated to the night when he was engaged in a practice jam session at Dan Wall's chili joint prior to his main performance of the evening. As Parker recalled:

> I remember one night before Monroe's I was jamming in a chili house on Seventh Avenue between 139th and 140th. It was December 1939. Now I'd been getting bored with the stereotyped changes that were being used all the time at the time, and I kept thinking there's bound to be something else. I could hear it sometimes but I couldn't play it.

Well, that night I was working with 'Cherokee' and, as I did, I found that by using the higher intervals of the chord as a melody line and backing them with appropriately related changes, I could play the thing I'd been hearing. I came alive. (ibid.: 264)

Parker's explanation provides an insight into the quite conscious way that he was searching for a manner of overcoming the existing conventions. His telling comment is that he could hear it, but he couldn't play it until that quicksilver moment when he suddenly slid through the difference between hearing and playing and so dispelled it. He came intensively alive, as if freed from what had previously constrained him. That moment didn't simply appear, as if from nowhere. Since his teens Parker had carried around a notebook in which he would make constant entries, often after watching other performers in concert. He became a great fan of Art Tatum, and there is surely some resonance between Tatum's flourishes and Parker's flying. Parker learned from other performers, Coleman Hawkins among them. That was all part of the preparation for this moment. It occurred on an ordinary everyday occasion, and previous to it was all the accumulated time spent on becoming proficient enough in his art to arrive at that feeling of dissatisfaction with the then regularised structure and style of playing, and to have intuitively ascertained 'something else' fresh beyond it. Without its many antecedent steps he might not have reached that vital shift in his mode of playing where the improvisation then took him.

This changed everything. It was a moment of genius. It not only became etched into Parker's memory. It also charted a completely new direction in the history of jazz and popular music. In this sense it was extraordinary. Parker was in that moment both the possessor and the possessed, a musician who had become totally absorbed in what he was trying consciously to achieve, and so at one with the endeavour that he produced an instant of magic. Such moments of inspiration – and again we have to resort to metaphor to attempt to describe them – are deeply embedded in the struggle to find just the right form of expressive communication for what the artist wants to say, play or convey. They don't come from outside, as if by a touch from a divine finger.

A similar moment of metamorphosis occurred some 25 years later during Bob Dylan's almost accidental realisation that the long rambling rage-driven poem that he had 'vomited' out could be condensed and brought together with a driving 4:4 rock beat. It led to *Like A Rolling Stone*, a six-minute single that changed enormously the way that people perceived the possibilities offered by the pop song. Dylan has often referred to this number as his breakthrough, and for the poet Mark Ford it is infused with 'a kind of artistic exhilaration at the possibilities suddenly discovered within a seemingly exhausted genre' (Ford, 2002: 133). This didn't happen overnight. Indeed, there are now various official and unofficial recordings of Dylan working on this song where it has a quite different form to that which it ultimately came to have. For example, an earlier version was in waltz-time; the eventual time signature only came with a later studio take. So work on the song could have faltered, failing to coalesce in its final landmark form. It could have ended in these preparatory efforts rather than paving the way to its revolutionary achievement, even if in retrospect we can see how they helped move Dylan forward to what he was striving to create, with no (settled or guaranteed) direction home.

The volatility of genius is not only subject to the vagaries of critical judgement and the contingencies of historical forces and conditions that affect such judgement. It is also subject to the flawed trials and false starts that are always involved in the process of creativity. Added to this, those to whom the label genius has been applied have not always been assured of their own ability to achieve the aims they have set themselves, and have suffered from the denial of praise or have doubted what George Eliot called the 'attitudinising deference which does not fatigue itself with the formation of real judgements' (1994: 55). These remarks closely relate to Eliot herself, yet critically she is now commonly praised for her literary fiction, especially in *Middlemarch*, which 'has achieved a unique status as both paradigm and paragon in discussion of the novel as a literary form' (Lodge, 1981: 218). Felicia Bonaparte, for example, remarks upon Eliot's 'genius for imagining the inner lives of other people', arguing that what distinguishes her exceptional talent from other contemporary novelists was the way her insights

> were so radically new at the time that they caused a revolution in psychological analysis and the creation of fictional character...Freud had not yet begun to do the work that was to make his name but the ideas that were to become the field we now call psychology were already in the air...Eliot was not, as some have maintained, the first to put the action within the consciousness of her characters. Many writers had done that, long before the Victorian age. The fact, however, that her narratives keep circling through those subjective states that place us, for a time at any rate and without corrective lenses, inside her characters point of view, entitles her to be considered the first true psychological novelist. Eliot was also one of the first to conceive of her characters – in a fluid, modern way – as 'a process and an unfolding', to quote her own description of it, rather than, as Dickens was doing, as entities with a solid core that remains in essence the same. (Bonaparte,1997: xxii–xxiii)

While Eliot's fictional characters display a broad social range, in the provincial English life which formed her material, it was her sympathetic intensification of the ordinariness of human action and interaction, her imaginative power of connection with the commonplace, which was exceptional. This quality was realised in varying ways over a long period of work, rather than being manifest in a moment of revelation, but as we have emphasised, such moments should be understood in the context of the longer span of toil and struggle which make them possible. While genius may often be narrated in terms of exceptional moments of often dramatic insight, these are firmly embedded within an extended process of becoming at one with and synthesising from existing elements.

The Genius of Genius

Moments of genius are sometimes referred to as strokes of genius. These are one way in which genius can be manifested, and they are less regular than the process of sublimation referred to by Elias. This is similar to what Ralph Waldo Emerson called the 'dream power' of the poet. Emerson brought the two together when he described dream power as 'transcending all limit and privacy, and by virtue of which a man is the conductor of the whole river of electricity' (1983: 466). Metaphors of electric connection are a close relation to the conception of creativity as being possessed, taken over, transformed into a vehicle for the transmission of some external (or unconscious) force.

As we've seen, Kivy contrasts this manifestation of genius with the more regular form evinced by someone like J.S. Bach, writing a cantata a week, 'each one a little gem', and combining this, week-in week-out, with fairly humdrum activities (Kivy, 2001: 241). The contrast is undeniable, but these activities were entirely compatible with Bach's regular production of his little musical gems, which took form in the time set aside for them through what were obviously intense powers of concentration. It is this more regular process of creative work that is involved in other areas of cultural production, such as for instance the writing of a novel like *Middlemarch* or *Madame Bovary*. We can refer to a range of creative processes from the revelatory epiphanic moment of possession to the dedicated and at times prolonged activity of the possessor, not in terms of their mutually exclusive opposition but as varying instantiations of what we refer to as genius. What we want to insist on here is the way such exceptionality depends upon a longer process of *becoming*, from which the exceptional creative act that is termed genius can emerge. In this way, the ordinary is not at odds with the exceptional, but continually open to the possibility of becoming exceptional.

However, while creative genius does not originate beyond human activity, equally it does not proceed simply from regularised conditions or methods. Nor are obsessive powers of concentration a sufficient condition for genius. To illustrate this, Kivy uses the example of a man spending a lifetime of single-minded concentration building a scale model of London out of matchsticks. There must be added to obsession a drive towards the breaking of limits accompanied by a will to communicate this to others. This drive can produce exceptional artworks or cultural products, in the entire range of genres, forms and performances rather than in any falsely separated area of creative work, but it also entails the possibility of failure and a degree of risk – whether this is conscious or not for those involved. As Max Beerbohm once said of the English music hall performer, Dan Leno: 'Only mediocrity can be trusted to be always at its best. Genius must always have lapses proportionate to its triumphs'.

The occurrence of lapses, mistakes, moments of failure or misjudgement are in some way true of many figures to whom genius has been attributed. These are often forgotten or overlooked, particularly in light of the exceptional triumphs of someone's creative work. They suggest that we should move away from the conventional sense of genius as an ontological condition or rarefied individual form of identity. We should abandon the sense of genius as an entire person. This sense is shared by all the approaches we have referred to, but it is an assumption that has attained the status of an unquestionable truth. The sense of creative power identified with a rarefied state of being leads to an absolute conception of genius and innovation which we've argued against throughout this book. It would be impractical, even undesirable, to return to the Roman idea of genius, particularly because the term has become so firmly inscribed into a modernist understanding of innovation. But we should perhaps think of the possibility of moving towards a less rarefied and reified sense of how we might want to apply the term genius.

Our preference is for an understanding of creativity which embraces both the ordinary and exceptional in terms of their productive tension. This is as true of works and performances to which genius is attributed as it is of those which are evaluated as relatively minor. The need to consider creativity in its more mundane forms doesn't require the relinquishment of some conception of exceptionality. It is the whole range of meanings and associations which must be engaged with, rather than a more selective version that simply swings to the polar opposite of elitist notions. Throughout this book our claim has been that approaching creativity as the communication of experience and the attainment of communicative value allows us to grasp the mutually constitutive relation between the ordinariness and exceptionality of creativity.

It is through this relation that cultural artefacts move between specifically local moments of production and recognition and patterns of reception and assimilation, which are broader both geographically and historically. If communication is about going outwards from self to other, we're still searching for a more comprehensive vocabulary for explaining how everyday localised creativity is able, in certain ways at certain times, to achieve connections across different times and places, and so be seen as referring to particular experiences to which many different people can collectively relate. The task is to try to understand how an artistic text or cultural product comes to exceed its initial integration with one specific context while still retaining an association with that context. It is one thing to recognise that the meanings of artistic and cultural products are related to particular social, political and historical conditions and circumstances, but quite another to assert that they are reducible to such conditions and circumstances. That would negate their aesthetic value entirely. Such value obviously changes from generation to generation, and from place to place, but some works of art and certain items of popular culture seem to attain, relatively easily, the renewal of their licence to pass between generations and locations. Moving across time and space in this way means that what is taken from artistic and cultural products is subject to historical and social variation, in ways which enrich their cumulative meanings and symbolic significance.

To think about such movement across different temporal and spatial contexts doesn't presuppose a search for some universal principle. It is about trying to engage analytically with the dynamic process which connects cultural practices together to form meta-cultural frameworks of comprehension, meaning and communication. Bestowing critical acclaim on someone's exceptional achievement is certainly not to imply that they have created universal, transhistorical works of art which we share simply because we are human. Yet we still need to recognise that many people, across divergences of time and space, *do* engage with such art, whether it is music, poetry, literary fiction or drama. It is not because they project a shared sense of identity, or because a common meaning is shared between creator and listener. It is because their particular modes of expression allow all sorts of people a point of entry which enables participation in the work, and activates some connection between what is performed and what is lived. These connections are something to be celebrated, but not mystified.

Creative talent is in part the result of hard work, experimentation and continual effort spent in perfecting a craft – most creative artists produce their fair share of mediocre work. Their achievements are also the result of a will to draw from and to push against existing forms and conventions, and an equally passionate desire to communicate beyond immediate temporal and spatial boundaries. As this occurs, they are indeed ordinary and exceptional and we can appreciate their creativity as both an ordinary and exceptional experience. It is this which leads us to argue that creativity should be thought of as the communication of experience which always involves gradations of movement between the mundane and exceptional, between novelty and innovation, and between the immediate and distant. This movement is what we celebrate, and understanding it may give us even more to celebrate.

If exceptionality is to be understood, it cannot be isolated from the ordinariness of human life, and not only because exceptionality is defined exclusively in contrast to what is ordinary. Isolating it in this way can lead to the myth of monumental greatness, conceived in terms that are abstracted from any sense of changing biographical circumstances, social relationships, economic imperatives, stylistic conventions and historical traditions. We may say that an artistic product has proved to have lasting value *because of* these very particular circumstances, rather than due to the way that it might simply transcend them. Our feelings are engaged, sympathies awoken, bodies moved and our taken-for-granted ways of thinking are transformed as they are stimulated by a specific form, artefact or product from a quite particular time and place. It is the way this connects with our sense of difference and sameness that allows us to make contrasts and comparisons, weigh up the relations of continuity and change, consider similarities and disparities, and ultimately allow this creative form a valued place in our lives. It is through the way that genius emerges out of the ordinary experience of human endeavour that we can come to a deeper understanding of our changing world and our changing historical identities.

Bibliography

Adorno, T. and Horkheimer, M. (1979) *Dialectic of Enlightenment*. London: Verso.

Adorno, T. (1990) 'On Popular Music', in S. Frith and A. Goodwin (eds) *On Record*. London: Routledge.

Adorno, T. (1991) *The Culture Industry: Selected Essays on Mass Culture*. Edited by J. Bernstein, London: Routledge.

Adorno, T. (1994) *The Stars Down to Earth*. London: Routledge.

Agawu, K. (2003) 'Contesting Difference, A Critique of Africanist Ethnomusicology' in M. Clayton, T. Herbert and R. Middleton (eds), *The Cultural Study of Music*. New York, London: Routledge.

Altman, R. (1999) *Film/Genre*. London: BFI Publishing.

Amis, M. (2000) *Experience*. London: Jonathan Cape.

Appadurai, A. (ed.) (1986) *The Social Life of Things: Commodities in Cultural Perspective*. Cambridge: Cambridge University Press.

Armstrong, I. (2000) *The Radical Aesthetic*. Oxford, UK and Malden, MA: Blackwell.

Babcock, B.A. (1993) 'At Home: No Women are Storytellers: Ceramic Creativity and the Politics of Discourse in Cochiti Pueblo', in S. Lavie, K. Narayan and R. Rosaldo (eds) *Creativity/Anthropology*. Ithaca: Cornell University Press.

Baily, J. (2001) *'Can You Stop the Birds Singing': The Censorship of Music in Afghanistan*. Copenhagen: Freemuse.

Barber, L. (1999) 'Simply Divine', *The Observer*, 28 February.

Barron, F. (1968) *Creativity and Personal Freedom*. London: D. Van Nostrand Co.

Baudelaire, C. (1972) *Selected Writings on Art and Artists*. Harmondsworth: Penguin.

Beauvoir, S. de (1973) *The Prime of Life*. Harmondsworth: Penguin.

Beck, A. (ed.) (2003) *Cultural Work: Understanding the Cultural Industries*. London: Sage.

Becker, H. (1976) 'Art Worlds and Social Types', *American Behavioural Scientist*, 19: 703–18.

Becker, H. (1984) *Art Worlds*. Berkeley and Los Angeles: University of California Press.

Benjamin, W. (1970) *Illuminations*. London: Jonathan Cape.

Benjamin, W. (1977) *Understanding Brecht*. London: New Left Books.

Bennett, A. (2000) *Popular Music and Youth Culture*. Basingstoke and London: Macmillan.

Bennett, T. (1998) *Culture: A Reformers Science*. London: Sage.

Bennett, O. (2003) '... so why has everyone got it in for Charles Saatchi?' *The Independent on Sunday*, 20 April, pp. 16–17.

Benstock, S. (1987) *Women of the Left Bank: Paris, 1900–1940*. London: Virago.

Bentham, J. (1962) *The Works of Jeremy Bentham*, Vol 2. New York: Russell and Russell.

Benzon, W. (2001) *Beethoven's Anvil: Music in Mind and Culture*. Oxford: Oxford University Press.

Bernstein, J. (1991) 'Introduction', in T. Adorno *The Culture Industry: Selected Essays on Mass Culture*. Edited by J. Bernstein, London: Routledge.

Bettig, R. (1996) *Copyrighting Culture*. Boulder, Co: Westview Press.

Bloch, E. (1988) *The Utopian Function of Art and Literature*. Cambridge MA: MIT Press.

Bonaparte, F. (1997) 'Introduction' to Eliot, G. *Middlemarch*, Oxford: Oxford University Press.

Boorstin, D. (1992) *The Creators*. New York: Random House.

Bourdieu, P. (1977) *Outline of a Theory of Practice*. Cambridge, London, New York and Melbourne: Cambridge University Press.

Bourdieu, P. (1983) 'The Field of Cultural Production, or: The Economic World Reversed', *Poetics*, 12: 311–56.

Bourdieu, P. (1986) *Distinction*. London: Routledge.

Bourdieu, P. (1990) *The Logic of Practice*. Cambridge: Polity Press.

Bourdieu, P. (1992) *An Invitation to Reflexive Sociology*. Cambridge: Polity Press.

Bourdieu, P. (1993) *The Field of Cultural Production*. Cambridge: Polity Press.

Bourdieu, P. (1996) *The Rules of Art*. Cambridge: Polity Press.

Bourdieu, P. and Passeron, J.C. (1977) *Reproduction in Education, Society and Culture*. London and Beverly Hills: Sage.

Bowland, E. (1995) 'The Irish Woman Poet: Her Place in Irish Literature'. in C. Morash (ed.), *Creativity and its Contexts*. Dublin: The Lilliput Press.

Bradbury, R. (1990) 'Reading John le Carré', in Clive Bloom (ed.), *Spy Thrillers: From Buchan to le Carré*. Basingstoke: Macmillan. pp. 130–9.

Brailsford, H.N. (1976) *The Levellers and the English Revolution*. Nottingham: Spokesman Books.

Briggs, A. (1965) *The Making of Modern England*. New York: Harper.

Burke, E. (1852) *Works and Correspondences*, Vol. IV. London: Rivington.

Burke, E. (1978) *Reflections on the Revolution in France*. Harmondsworth: Penguin.

Busby, M. and Howe, D. (eds) (1984) *C.L.R. James's 80th Birthday Lectures*. London: Race Today Publications.

Calinescu, M. (1987) *Five Faces of Modernity: Modernism, Avant-Garde, Decadence, Kitsch, Postmodernism*. Durham: Duke University Press.

Campbell, C. (1987) *The Romantic Ethic and the Spirit of Modern Consumerism*. Oxford and New York: Basil Blackwell.

Campbell, J. (2003) *Exiled in Paris*. Berkeley, Los Angeles, London: University of California Press.

Chambers, I. (1985) *Urban Rhythms, Pop Music and Popular Culture*. Basingstoke: Macmillan.

Chin, F. and Chan, J.P. (1972) 'Racist Love', in R. Kostelanetz (ed.), *Seeing Through Shuck*. New York: Ballentine Books.

Christ, C. (1977) 'Victorian Masculinity and the Angel in the House', in M. Vicinus (ed.) *A Widening Sphere: Changing Roles of Victorian Women*. London: Methuen.

Citron, M. (2000) *Gender and the Musical Canon*. Urbana and Chicago: University of Illinois Press.

Clare, A. (1992) *In the Psychiatrist's Chair*. London: Heinemann.

Clark, T. (1997) *The Theory of Inspiration*. Manchester and New York: Manchester University Press.

Clarke, J., Hall, S., Jefferson, T. and Roberts, B. (1977) 'Subcultures, Cultures and Class', in S. Hall and T. Jefferson (eds), *Resistance through Rituals*. London: Hutchinson.

Cole, C.M. (1996) 'Reading Blackface in West Africa: Wonders Taken for Signs', *Critical Inquiry*, 23, Autumn, pp. 183–215.

Coleridge, S. (1910) *Biographia Literaria*. London: J.M. Dent & Sons.

Connell, J. and Gibson, C. (2003) *Sound Tracks: Popular Music, Identity and Place*. London and New York: Routledge.

Cook, R. (2000) 'The Mediated Manufacture of an "Avant Garde": A Bourdieusian Analysis of the Field of Contemporary Art in London, 1997–9', in B. Fowler (ed.), *Reading Bourdieu on Society and Culture*. Oxford: Blackwell.

Coombe, R. (1998) *The Cultural Life of Intellectual Properties*. Durham: Duke University Press.

Cowper, W. (1857) *The Poetical Works*. London: John Kendrick.

Craik, D. (1850) *Olive*. Oxford: Oxford Library.

Curran, J. (2000) 'Literary Editors, Social Networks and Cultural Tradition', in J. Curran (ed.), *Media Organisations in Society*, London: Arnold, pp. 215–39.

Dash, M. (1989) 'Introduction', in E. Glissant, *Caribbean Discourse: Selected Essays*. Charlottesville: University Press of Virginia.

Davidoff, L. and Hall, C. (1997) *Family Fortunes*. London and New York: Routledge.

De Bono, E. (1996) *Serious Creativity*. London: HarperCollins.

DeNora, T. (1997) *Beethoven and the Construction of Genius*. Berkley: University of California Press.

Dewey, J. (1925) *Experience and Nature*. Chicago: Open Court Publishing Company.

Dewey, J. (1980) *Art as Experience*. New York: Minton, Balch.

Dewey, J. (1938) *Logic: The Theory of Inquiry*. New York: Henry Holt.

Dick, K. (1972) *Writers at Work*. Harmondsworth: Penguin.

Donnell, A. and Welsh, S. (eds) (1996) *Reader in Caribbean Literature*. London: Routledge.

Dreyfus, H.L. (2001) *On the Internet*. London and New York: Routledge.

Dreyfus, H.L. and Dreyfus, S.E. (1986) *Mind Over Machine*. Oxford and New York: Blackwell.

Dyer, C. (2000) 'Hirst pays up for Hymn that wasn't his', *The Guardian*, 19 May, p.1.

Ehrlich, C. (1988) *Harmonious Alliance: A History of the Performing Right Society*. London: Oxford University Press.

Elias, N. (1993) *Mozart: Portrait of a Genius*. Cambridge: Polity.

Eliot, G. (1994) *Impressions of Theophrastus Such*. Iowa: University of Iowa Press.

Eliot, T.S. (1971) *The Wasteland: A Facsimile and Transcript of the Original Drafts including the Annotations of Ezra Pound*. London: Faber & Faber.

Emerson, R.W. (1983) *Essays and Lectures*. New York: The Library of America.

Engel, C. (1866) *An Introduction to the Study of National Music*. London: Longman.

Ettema, J. and Whitney, D. (1982) *Individuals in Mass Media Organisations: Creativity and Constraint*. London: Sage.

Fabbri, F. (1982) 'A Theory of Music Genres: Two Applications', in P. Tagg and D. Horn (eds), *Popular Music Perspectives*. Gothenburg and Exeter: IASPM.

Fabbri, F. (1985) 'Patterns of Music Consumption in Milan and Reggio Emilia from April to May 1983', in P. Tagg and D. Horn (eds), *Popular Music Perspectives 2*. Gothenberg and Exeter: IASPM.

Fabbri, F. (1989) 'The System of Canzone in Italy today' (1981) in S. Frith (ed.), *World Music, Politics and Social Change*. Manchester: Manchester University Press.

Faundez, A. (1989) *Learning to Question: A Pedagogy of Liberation*. New York: Continuum.

Filene, B. (2000) *Romancing the Folk: Public Memory and American Roots Music*. Chapel Hill and London: University of North Carolina Press.

Finnegan, R. (1997a) 'Storying the Self: Personal Narratives and Identity', in H. Mackay (ed.), *Consumption and Everyday Life*. London: Sage.

Finnegan, R. (1997b) 'Music, Performance and Enactment', in H. Mackay (ed.), *Consumption and Everyday Life*. London: Sage.

Fish, S. (1976) 'Is there a text in this class?' *Critical Enquiry*, 2 (3): 465–86.

Fletcher, W. (1990) *Creative People: How to Manage Them and Maximise Their Creativity*. London: Century Hutchinson.

Flyvbjerg, B. (2001) *Making Social Science Matter*. Cambridge and New York: Cambridge University Press.

Ford, M. (2002) 'Trust Yourself: Emerson and Dylan', in N. Corcoran (ed.), *Do You, Mr Jones? Bob Dylan with the Poets and Professors*. London: Chatto & Windus.

Fowler, B. (1997) *Pierre Bourdieu and Cultural Theory*. London: Sage.

Friedman, J. (1996) *Cultural Identity and Global Process*. London: Sage.

Friedman, J. (2001) 'The Iron Cage of Creativity', in J. Liep (ed.), *Locating Cultural Creativity*. London and Sterling, Virginia: Pluto Press.

Frith, S. (1996) *Performing Rites: On the Value of Popular Music*. Oxford: Oxford University Press.

Frith, S. and Horne, H. (1987) *Art into Pop*. London and New York: Methuen.

Gadamer, H.-G. (1996) *Truth and Method*. London: Sheed & Ward.

Gaines, J. (1991) *Contested Culture: The Image, the Voice and the Law*. Chapel Hill: University of North Carolina Press.

Galeotti, E.A. (1987) 'Individualism, Social Rules, Tradition: The Case of Friedrich A. Hayek', *Political Theory*, 15 (2): 163–81.

Galton, F. (1869) *Hereditary Genius*. London: Macmillan.

García Canclini, N. (1995) *Hybrid Cultures*. Minneapolis and London: University of Minneapolis Press.

García Márquez, G. and Apuleyo Mendoza, P. (1988) *The Fragrance of Guava*. London and Boston: Faber & Faber.

Garnham, N. (1990) *Capitalism and Communication: Global Culture and the Economics of Information*. London: Sage.

Geiger, G.R. (1974) *John Dewey in Perspective*. Westport, CT: Greenwood Press.

George, N. (1989) *The Death of Rhythm and Blues*. New York: Omnibus.

George, N. (1998) *Hip Hop America*. New York: Penguin.

Geraghty, C. (1991) *Women and Soap Opera*. Oxford: Polity Press.

Giddins, G. (1998) *Visions of Jazz*. Oxford: Oxford University Press.

Giddins, G. (2000) *Riding on a Blue Note, Jazz and American Pop*. New York: Da Capo Press.

Giddins, G. (2001) *Satchmo: The Genius of Louis Armstrong*. New York: Da Capo Press.

Gilbert, S.M. and Gubar, S. (1984) *The Madwoman in the Attic: The Woman Writer and the Nineteenth Century Literary Imagination*. New Haven and London: Yale University Press.

Gilman, S. (1988) *Difference and Pathology*. Ithaca and London: Cornell University Press.

Gilman, S. (1991) *The Jew's Body*. New York and London: Routledge.

Glad, J. (ed.) (1990) *Literature in Exile*. Durham and London: Duke University Press.

Glissant, E. (1989) *Caribbean Discourse*. Virginia: University Press of Virginia.

Gombrich, E.H. (1967) *The Story of Art*. London and New York: Phaidon.

Goodman, N. (1968) *Languages of Art*. London: Oxford University Press.

Gracyk, T. (2002) 'Music's Wordly Uses, or How I Learned to Stop Worrying and To Love Led Zeppelin', in A. Neill and A. Ridley (eds), *Arguing about Art*. London and New York: Routledge.

Grana, C. (1964) *Bohemian versus Bourgeois: French Society and the French Man of Letters in the Nineteenth Century*. New York: Basic Books.

Gray, J. (1984) *Hayek on Liberty*. Oxford and New York: Basil Blackwell.

Grayling, A.C. (2002) 'A Question of Discrimination', *Guardian Review*, 13 July, pp. 4–6.

Griffiths, G. (1978) *Double Exile: African and West Indian Writing Between Two Cultures*. London: Marim Boyars.

Griswold, W. (1987) 'The Fabrication of Meaning: Literary Interpretation in the United States, Great Britain, and the West Indies', *American Journal of Sociology*, 92 (5): 1077–117.

Habermas, J. (1984) *The Theory of Communicative Action*, Vol 1: *Reason and the Rationalisation of Society*. Boston: Beacon Press.

Habermas, J. (1992) 'A Generation Apart from Adorno: An Interview', *Philosophy and Social Criticism*, 18 (2): 119–24.

Hall, C. (1981) 'Gender Divisions and Class Formation in the Birmingham Middle Class, 1780–1850', in R. Samuel (ed.), *People's History and Socialist Theory*. London: Routledge and Kegan Paul.

Halstead, J. (1997) *The Woman Composer*. Aldershot: Ashgate.

Hannerz, U. (1996) *Transnational Connections*. London and New York: Routledge.

Hanson, A. (1989) 'The Making of the Maori: Culture Invention and its Logic', *American Anthropologist*, 91, pp. 890–902.

Hardy, T. (1929) *Jude the Obscure*. London: Macmillan.

Hardy, T. (1967) *Thomas Hardy's Personal Writings*. Edited by H. Orel. London and Melbourne: Macmillan.

Harrison, C. and Wood, P. (eds.) (2001) *Art in Theory, 1900–1990*. Oxford and Malden, MA: Blackwell.

Hasse, J. (1995) *Beyond Category: The Life and Genius of Duke Ellington*. New York: Da Capo.

Hatton, R. and Walker, J. (2000) *Supercollector, A Critique of Charles Saatchi*. London: Ellipsis.

Hayek, F. (1949) *Individualism and Economic Order*. London: Routledge.

Hayek, F. (1992) *The Fatal Conceit*. London: Routledge.

Hayes, M. (1990) 'Are You Telling Me Lies David? The Work of John le Carré', in C. Bloom (ed.), *Spy Thrillers, From Buchan to le Carré*. Basingstoke: Macmillan. pp. 113–129.

Heelas, P., Lash, P. and Morris, P. (1996) *Detraditionalization*. Cambridge, MA. and Oxford, UK: Blackwell.

Hegel, G.F.W. (1975) *Aesthetics*. Oxford: Oxford University Press.

Hesmondhalgh, D. (2002) *The Cultural Industries*. London: Sage.

Hobsbawm, E. (1961) *The Jazz Scene*. Harmondsworth: Penguin [published under the pseudonym of Francis Newton].

Hobsbawm, E. (1997) *Nations and Nationalism since 1780*. Cambridge and New York: Cambridge University Press.

Hobsbawm, E. and Ranger, T. (eds) (1984) *The Invention of Tradition*. Cambridge, London and New York: Cambridge University Press.

Hosokawa, S. (2002) 'Blacking Japanese: Experiencing Otherness from Afar', in D. Hesmondhalgh and K. Negus (eds), *Popular Music Studies*. London: Arnold.

Howe, M. (1999) *Genius Explained*. Cambridge and New York: Cambridge University Press.

Hughes, M. and Stradling, R. (2001) *The English Musical Renaissance, 1840–1940*. Manchester and New York: Manchester University Press.

Hunt, T. and Fraser, G. (2003) 'Revolutionary Putney', The *Guardian*, 19 February.

James, C.L.R. (1980) *Beyond a Boundary*. London, Melbourne, Sydney, Auckland, Johannesburg: Stanley Paul.

Jameson, F. (1979) 'Reification and Utopia in Mass Culture', *Social Text*, 1, Winter, pp. 130–48.

Jameson, F. (1991) *Postmodernism, or, The Cultural Logic of Late Capitalism*. London: Verso.

Jarrett-Macauley, D. (1998) *The Life of Una Marson 1905–65*. Manchester and New York: Manchester University Press.

Jarvie, I. (1970) *Towards a Sociology of the Cinema*. London: Routledge & Kegan Paul.

Jarvis, S. (1998) *Adorno*. Cambridge: Polity Press.

Jauss, H.R. (1974) 'Literary History as a Challenge to Literary Theory', in R. Cohen (ed.), *New Directions in Literary History*. London: Routledge.

Joas, H. (1996) *The Creativity of Action*. Cambridge: Polity Press.

Jones, J. (2003) 'He's Gotta Have it', *The Guardian G2*, 4 April, pp. 2–6/9–12/14/16.

Jones, S. (1996) 'Mass Communication, Intellectual Property Rights, International Trade and the Popular Music Industry', in E. McAnany and K. Wilinson (eds), *Mass Media and Free Trade: NAFTA and the Cultural Industries*. Austin: University of Texas Press.

Joyce, J. (1966) *Stephen Hero*. London: Four Square.

Kant, I. (1982) *The Critique of Judgement*. Oxford: The Clarendon Press.

Karpis, R.E. (1992) *Hitchcock: The Making of a Reputation*. Chicago: University of Chicago Press.

Kavanagh, P. (1964) *Self Portrait*. Dublin: The Dolmen Press.

Kennedy, M. (2001) 'And now, a few words from our sponsor: just give us a mention', *The Guardian*, 4 September, p. 4.

Kim, E.H. (1982) *Asian American Literature*. Philadelphia: Temple University Press.

King, B. (1987) 'The Star and the Commodity', *Cultural Studies*, 1 (2): 145–61.

Kivy, P. (2001) *The Possessor and the Possessed: Handel, Mozart, Beethoven and the Idea of Musical Genius*. New Haven: Yale University Press.

Klingender, D.D. (1972) *Art and the Industrial Revolution*. London: Paladin.

Koestler, A. (1964) *The Act of Creation*. London: Hutchinson.

Kuspit, D. (1993) *The Cult of the Avant-Garde Artist*. Cambridge: Cambridge University Press.

LaCapra, D. (1994) *Representing the Holocaust*. Ithaca and London: Cornell University Press.

Laing, D. (1993) 'Copyright and the International Music Industry', in S. Frith (ed.), *Music and Copyright*. Edinburgh: Edinburgh University Press.

Laing, D. (2003) 'Copyright', in *Continuum Encyclopedia of Popular Music of the World, Volume 1 Media, Industry and Society*. London: Continuum.

Lamming, G. (1960) *The Pleasures of Exile*. London: Michael Joseph.

Lapsley, R. and Westlake, M. (1991) *Film Theory: An Introduction*. Manchester: Manchester University Press.

Lewis, D. (1969) *Convention: A Philosophical Study*. Cambridge MA: Harvard University Press.

Lewis, L. (ed.) (1992) *The Adoring Audience: Fan Culture and Popular Media*. London: Routledge.

Ligeti, G. (2002) 'György Ligeti on his Orchestral Works', CD booklet accompanying *The Ligeti Project II*, Teldec Classics, 8573-88261–2.

Lippard, L. (1976) *From the Centre*. New York: Dutton.

Lippmann, W. (1965) *Public Opinion*. London: The Free Press/Collier Macmillan.

Lodge, D. (1981) '*Middlemarch* and the Idea of the Classic Realist Text', in A. Kettle (ed.), *The Nineteenth-Century Novel: Critical Essays and Documents*. London: Heinemann.

Lombroso, C. (1891) *The Man of Genius*. London: The Contemporary Science Series.

Lott, E. (1993) *Love and Theft: Blackface Minstrelsy and the American Working Class*. New York and Oxford: Oxford University Press.

Lütticken, S. (2002) 'The Art of Theft', *New Left Review*, 13, pp. 89–104.

MacIntyre, A. (1985) *After Virtue*. London: Duckworth.

Mackenzie, S. (2000) 'In a Galaxy of Her Own', *The Guardian Weekend*, 22 April, pp. 10–15.

Maltby, R. (1996) *Hollywood Cinema*. Oxford: Blackwell.

Mathews, T. (1999) 'They're not just rich and famous. They're in charge', *The Guardian Review*, 19 November, p. 2.

Max, D.T. (1998) 'The Carver Chronicles', *New York Times Magazine*, 9 August, pp. 34–40/51/56–57.

McClary, S. (1991) *Feminine Endings*. Minneapolis and Oxford: University of Minnesota Press.

McClary, S. (2000) *Conventional Wisdom*. Berkeley, Los Angeles and London: University of California Press.

McEwan, I. (2002) *Atonement*. London: Vintage.

McRobbie, A. (1998) *British Fashion Design*, London: Routledge.

Merges, R. (1995) 'The Economic Impact of Intellectual Property Rights: An Overview and Guide', *Journal of Cultural Economics*, 19, pp. 103–117.

Miège, B. (1989) *The Capitalization of Cultural Production*. New York: International General.

Miller, A. (1997) 'Cultures of Creativity: Mathematics and Physics', *Diogenes*, 177, pp. 53–72.

Mitchell, D. (1975) *Gustav Mahler: The Wunderhorn Years*. London: Faber & Faber.

Moers, E. (1977) *Literary Women: The Great Writers*. New York: Doubleday Anchor Press.

Morris, W. (1979) *Political Writings*. London: Lawrence & Wishart.

Morrison, B. (2001) *Creativity, Newness and Healing*. London: Goldsmiths College.

Munif, A. (1991) 'Exile and the Writer', in P. Mariani (ed.), *Critical Fictions: The Politics of Imaginative Writing*. Seattle: Bay Press.

Murray, A. (2000) *Stomping the Blues*. New York: Da Capo Press.

Neale, S. (1980) *Genre*. London: British Film Institute.

Neale, S. (1990) 'Questions of Genre', *Screen*, 31 (1): 45–66.

Neale, S. (2000) *Genre and Hollywood*. London: Routledge.

Negus, K. (1992) *Producing Pop: Culture and Conflict in the Popular Music Industry*. London: Arnold.

Negus, K. (1995) 'Where the Mystical Meets the Market: Commerce and Creativity in the Production of Popular Music', *The Sociological Review*, 47 (2): 316–41.

Negus, K. (1999) *Music Genres and Corporate Cultures*. London: Routledge.

Negus, K. and Román Velázquez, P. (2002) 'Belonging and Detachment: Musical Experience and the Limits of Identity', *Poetics, Journal of Empirical Research on Culture, the Media and the Arts*, 30, pp. 133–45.

Nettleford, R. (1993) *Inward Stretch, Outward Reach, A Voice From the Caribbean*. London: Macmillan.

Nixon, R. (1992) *London Calling: V.S. Naipaul, Postcolonial Mandarin*. Oxford: Oxford University Press.

Nixon, S. (2003) *Advertising Cultures: Gender, Commerce, Creativity*. London: Sage.

Nussbaum, M. (1990) 'Our Pasts, Ourselves', *New Republic*, April, pp. 27–34.

O'Connor, J. (1999) 'Popular Culture, Reflexivity and Urban Change', in J. Verwijnen and P. Lehtovouri (eds), *Creative Cities: Cultural Industries, Urban Development and The Information Society*. Helsinki: University of Art and Design.

Ortner, S. (1974) 'Is Female to Male as Nature is to Culture?', *Feminist Studies*, 1 (2): 5–31.

Palmer, J. (1991) *Potboilers*. London and New York: Routledge.

Parakilas, J. (2001) *Piano Roles: A New History of the Piano*. New Haven: Yale University Press.

Parker, R. (1984) *The Subversive Stitch: Embroidery and the Making of the Feminine*. London: The Women's Press.

Parker, R. and Pollock, G. (1981) *Old Mistresses: Women, Art and Ideology*. London: Harper Collins.

Patmore, C. (1885) *The Angel in the House*. London: George Bell & Son.

Petrie, D. (1991) *Creativity and Constraint in the British Film Industry*. London: Macmillan.

Phillips, M. (2001) *London Crossings*. London and New York: Continuum.

Pickering, M. (1997a) 'John Bull in Blackface', *Popular Music*, 16 (2): 181–201.

Pickering, M. (1997b) *History, Experience and Cultural Studies*. Basingstoke and London: Macmillan, and New York: St Martin's Press.

Pickering, M. (1999) 'History as Horizon: Gadamer, Tradition and Critique', *Rethinking History*, 3 (2): 177–95.

Pickering, M. (2001) *Stereotyping: The Politics of Representation*. London: Palgrave.

Pickering, M. (2003) 'The Blackface Clown', in G.H. Gerzina (ed.), *Black Victorians/ Black Victoriana*. New Brunswick, N.J. and London: Rutgers University Press.

Pickering, M. and Green, T. (1987) 'Towards a Cartography of the Vernacular Milieu', in M. Pickering and T. Green (eds), *Everyday Culture*. Milton Keynes and Philadelphia: Open University Press.

Pickering, M. and Robins, K. (1984) 'The Making of an English Working-Class Writer', in J. Hawthorn (ed.), *The British Working-Class Novel in the Twentieth Century*. London and Baltimore: Edward Arnold.

Potter, D. (1993) *Potter on Potter*. Edited by G. Fuller. London: Faber and Faber.

Radway, J. (1984) *Reading the Romance*. Chapel Hill: University of North Carolina Press.

Reich, N.B. (1985) *Clara Schumann: The Artist and the Woman*. Ithaca and London: Cornell University Press.

Richie, D. (1971) *Japanese Cinema*. New York: Doubleday.

Ritter, N. (1989) *Art as Spectacle: Images of the Entertainer since Romanticism*. Columbia and London: University of Missouri Press.

Roberts, D. (1994) 'Sublime Theories: Reason and Imagination in Modernity', in G. Robinson and J. Rundell (eds), *Rethinking Imagination: Culture and Creativity*. London and New York: Routledge.

Román Velázquez, P. (1999) *The Making of Latin London: Salsa Music, Place and Identity*. Aldershot: Ashgate.

Rorty, R. (1989) *Contingency, Irony and Solidarity*. Cambridge: Cambridge University Press.

Rose, J. (2001) *The Intellectual Life of the British Working Class*. New Haven and London: Yale University Press.

Rushdie, S. (1991) *Imaginary Homelands*. London: Granta.

Rushdie, S. (2003) 'Divided Selves', *The Guardian Review*, 23 November, pp. 5–7.

Ruskin, J. (1907) *Sesame and Lilies*. London: George Allen.

Ryan, M. (1998) *Knowledge Diplomacy: Global Competition and the Politics of Intellectual Property*. Washington DC: Brookings Institute.

Ryan, L. (2002) *Gender, Identity and the Irish Press, 1922–1937*. Lewiston, Queenston, Lampeter: The Edwin Mellen Press.

Sahlins, M. (1985) *Islands of History*. Chicago: Chicago University Press.

Sahlins, M. (2002) *Waiting for Foucault, Still*. Chicago: Prickly Paradigm Press.

Said, E. (1983) *The World, the Text, and the Critic*. Cambridge, MA: Harvard University Press.

Said, E. (1984) 'Reflections on Exile', *Granta*, 13, Autumn, pp. 157–72.

Said, E. (1991) *Musical Elaborations*. London: Chatto and Windus.

Said, E. (1994) *Culture and Imperialism*. London: Vintage.

Saunders, D. (1992) *Authorship and Copyright*. London: Routledge.

Scruton, R. (1983) *The Aesthetic Understanding*. Manchester: Carcanet Press.

Scruton, R. (2002) 'The Decline of Musical Culture', in A. Neill and A. Ridley (eds), *Arguing about Art*. London and New York: Routledge.

Scruton, R. (ed.) (1991) *Conservative Texts*. Basingstoke and New York: Macmillan.

Seed, J. (1988) '"Commerce and the Liberal Arts": The Political Economy of Art in Manchester, 1775–1860', in J. Wolff and J. Seed (eds) *The Culture of Capital: Art, Power and the Nineteenth Century Middle Class*. Manchester: Manchester University Press.

Sell, R. (2000) *Literature as Communication*. Amsterdam and Philadelphia: John Benjamins Publishing Company.

Sereny, G. (1999) *Cries Unheard: The Story of Mary Bell*. Basingstoke and London: Macmillan.

Sharp, C. (1907) *English Folk Song: Some Conclusions*. London: Simpkin.

Shils, E. (1981) *Tradition*. London and Boston: Faber & Faber.

Sinfield, A. (1989) *Literature, Politics and Culture in Postwar Britain*. Oxford: Blackwell.

Steiner, G. (2001) *Grammars of Creation*. London: Faber and Faber.

Taylor, C. (1985) *Human Agency and Language: Philosophical Papers I*. Cambridge, London and New York: Cambridge University Press.

Taylor, C. (1989) *Sources of the Self: The Making of Modern Identity*. Cambridge and New York: Cambridge University Press.

Taylor, C. (1991) *The Ethics of Authenticity*. Cambridge, MA and London: Harvard University Press.

Taylor, C. (1995) *Philosophical Arguments*. Cambridge, MA: Harvard University Press.

Thomas, N. (1997) *In Oceania*. Durham and London: Duke University Press.

Thompson, E.P. (1977) *William Morris: Romantic to Revolutionary*. London: Merlin Press.

Tirro, F. (1993) *Jazz: A History*. New York and London: W.W. Norton.

Todorov, T. (1990) *Genres in Discourse*. Cambridge: Cambridge University Press.

Tolson, A. (1996) *Mediations*. London and New York: Arnold.

Tremlett, G. (1990) *Rock Gold: The Music Millionaires*. Unwin Hyman.

Troutt Powell, E.M. (2003) *A Different Shade of Colonialism*. Berkeley, Los Angeles, London: University of California Press.

Ulanov, B. (1952) *A History of Jazz in America*. New York: Viking Press.

UNESCO (1982) *Culture Industries: A Challenge for the Future of Culture*. Paris: UNESCO.

Viereck, S. (1929) 'What Life Means to Einstein: An Interview with Sylvester Viereck', *The Saturday Evening Post*, 26 October.

Vladislav, J. (1990) 'Exile, Responsibility, Destiny', in J. Glad (ed.), *Literature in Exile*. Durham and London: Duke University Press, pp. 14–27.

Wainwright, H. (1994) *Arguments for a New Left*. Oxford UK and Cambridge USA: Blackwell.

Walcott, D. (1998) *What the Twilight Says*. London: Faber and Faber.

Walmsley, A. (1992) *The Caribbean Artists Movement 1966–1972*. London: New Beacon Books.

Ward, A. (1875) *A History of English Dramatic Literature*, 3 volumes. London: Macmillan.

Warner, K.Q. (1992) 'Film, Literature and Identity in the Caribbean', in M.B. Cham (ed.), *Ex-Iles: Essays on Caribbean Cinema*. Trenton, New Jersey: Africa World Press Inc.

Warnke, G. (1995) 'Communicative Rationality and Cultural Values', in S.K. White (ed.), *The Cambridge Companion to Habermas*. Cambridge and New York: Cambridge University Press.

Waters, J. (1988) 'Deus ex Machina: The Band Who Grew to Earth', in E. Dunphy (ed.) *The Unforgettable Fire: The Story of U2*. Harmondsworth: Penguin.

Whitman, W. (1982) 'Slang in America', in his *Complete Poetry and Collected Prose*. Edited by J. Kaplan. New York: Library of America.

Williams, P. (1993) *The Alchemy of Race and Rights*. London: Virago.

Williams, R. (1961) *The Long Revolution*. Harmondsworth: Penguin.

Williams, R. (1976) *Keywords*. Glasgow: Fontana.

Williams, R. (1977) *Marxism and Literature*. Oxford: Oxford University Press.

Williams, R. (1979) *Politics and Letters*. London: New Left Books.

Williams, R. (1989) *Resources of Hope*. London and New York: Verso.

Willis, P. (1990) *Common Culture*. Milton Keynes: Open University Press.

Wilson, E. (2000) *Bohemians: The Glamorous Outcasts*. London and New York: I.B. Tauris.

Wolff, J. (1981) *The Social Production of Art*. London and Basingstoke: Macmillan.

Wolff, J. (1990) *Feminine Sentences*. Cambridge: Polity.

Wolff, J. (1995) *Resident Alien*. Cambridge: Polity.

Wordsworth, W. (1969) *The Prelude*. London, New York, Toronto: Oxford University Press.

Zipes, J. (1995) *Creative Storytelling*. London: Routledge.

Zolberg, V. and Cherbo, J. (eds) (1997) *Outsider Art: Contesting Boundaries in Contemporary Culture*. Cambridge: Cambridge University Press.

Index